Provinces & Regions

MOON
ATLANTIC CANADA
Nova Scotia, New Brunswick, Prince Edward Island, Newfoundland & Labrador
ANDREW HEMPSTEAD

MOON
BANFF NATIONAL PARK
ANDREW HEMPSTEAD

MOON
BRITISH COLUMBIA
Including the Alaska Highway
ANDREW HEMPSTEAD

MOON
CANADIAN ROCKIES
Including Banff & Jasper National Parks
ANDREW HEMPSTEAD

MOON
NEWFOUNDLAND & LABRADOR
ANDREW HEMPSTEAD

MOON
NOVA SCOTIA
NEW BRUNSWICK & PRINCE EDWARD ISLAND
ANDREW HEMPSTEAD

MOON
ONTARIO
CAROLYN B. HELLER

MOON
VICTORIA & VANCOUVER ISLAND
ANDREW HEMPSTEAD

Road Trips

MOON
PACIFIC NORTHWEST Road Trip
SEATTLE, VANCOUVER, VICTORIA, THE OLYMPIC PENINSULA, PORTLAND, THE OREGON COAST & MOUNT RAINIER
ALLISON WILLIAMS

MOON
VANCOUVER & CANADIAN ROCKIES Road Trip

MOON.COM
@MOONGUIDES
f y P @

D0009961

MAP SYMBOLS

▦ Expressway	○ City/Town	✈ Airport	⚐ Golf Course
▬ Primary Road	◉ State Capital	✗ Airfield	P Parking Area
▦ Secondary Road	⊛ National Capital	▲ Mountain	◿ Archaeological Site
▫ Unpaved Road	★ Point of Interest	✛ Unique Natural Feature	⬥ Church
▬ Feature Trail	• Accommodation	⟿ Waterfall	⬛ Gas Station
▬ Other Trail	▼ Restaurant/Bar	▲ Park	Glacier
▬ Ferry	■ Other Location	⛺ Trailhead	Mangrove
▦ Pedestrian Walkway	⋀ Campground	🎿 Skiing Area	Reef
▦ Stairs			Swamp

CONVERSION TABLES

$^{\circ}C = (^{\circ}F - 32) / 1.8$
$^{\circ}F = (^{\circ}C \times 1.8) + 32$
1 inch = 2.54 centimeters (cm)
1 foot = 0.304 meters (m)
1 yard = 0.914 meters
1 mile = 1.6093 kilometers (km)
1 km = 0.6214 miles
1 fathom = 1.8288 m
1 chain = 20.1168 m
1 furlong = 201.168 m
1 acre = 0.4047 hectares
1 sq km = 100 hectares
1 sq mile = 2.59 square km
1 ounce = 28.35 grams
1 pound = 0.4536 kilograms
1 short ton = 0.90718 metric ton
1 short ton = 2,000 pounds
1 long ton = 1.016 metric tons
1 long ton = 2,240 pounds
1 metric ton = 1,000 kilograms
1 quart = 0.94635 liters
1 US gallon = 3.7854 liters
1 Imperial gallon = 4.5459 liters
1 nautical mile = 1.852 km

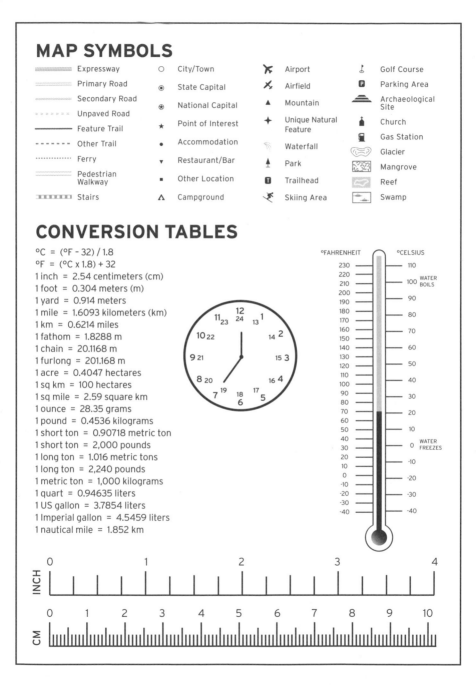

°FAHRENHEIT / °CELSIUS

WATER BOILS (100 / 210)
WATER FREEZES (0 / 30)

INCH: 0 1 2 3 4

CM: 0 1 2 3 4 5 6 7 8 9 10

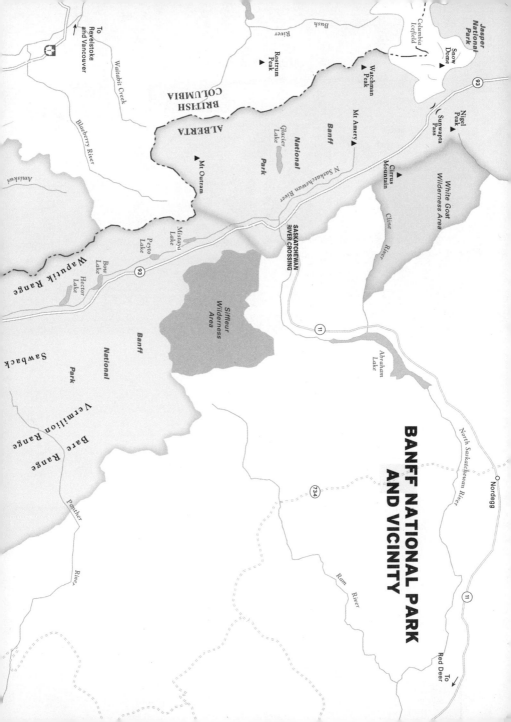

Contents

Discover
  Banff National Park **6**
    Planning Your Trip 8

Banff National Park **11**
    Town of Banff 25
    Lake Louise and Vicinity 68
    Icefields Parkway (Banff) 83
    Nearby Parks 91

Background **95**
    The Landscape 96
    Plants........................... 99
    Animals......................... 100
    History.......................... 107

Essentials **113**
    Getting There 114
    Getting Around.................. 119
    Recreation...................... 121
    Accommodations and Camping..... 128
    Travel Tips 132
    Health and Safety 134
    Information and Services 135

Resources **138**
    Suggested Reading............... 138
    Internet Resources 142

Index **145**

List of Maps **148**

DISCOVER

Banff National Park

Banff is the crown jewel in Canada's national park system and home to the world's most photographed lakes. Lake Louise, Moraine Lake, and the Icefields Parkway are just some of the park's awe-inspiring highlights. Biking along the shoreline of Lake Minnewanka, exploring Larch Valley when fall colors are at their height, canoeing across Bow Lake, and hiking in to backcountry Mount Assiniboine Provincial Park may not be as well known, but each activity allows a glimpse of the park you won't see inw the tourist brochures.

Clockwise from top left: Lake Agnes; the Fairmont Banff Springs; fall in Larch Valley; Bow Lake; canoeing on Lake Louise; the spectacular view across Lake Louise.

Planning Your Trip

When to Go

While the Canadian Rockies can be visited year-round, there are two influxes of visitors—one in the warmer months and the other in winter.

Summer

Summer (late June-mid-Sept.) is definitely **high season,** especially the school holiday period of July through August. Simply said, the **weather is unbeatable.** The season is dominated by long, warm—and sometimes hot—days, everything is open, and there's plenty to do and see. **Crowded parks, higher prices,** and difficulty securing **reservations** are the downside of summer travel.

Spring and Fall

Late spring and early fall are excellent times to visit the Canadian Rockies for two reasons: You'll **avoid the crowds,** and you'll **save money.**

Spring (mid-Apr.-late June) is notable for **long days** of sunlight (in late June it stays light until after 10pm) and a sense of optimism for the upcoming warm months.

Fall (mid-Sept.-Nov.) can be delightful, especially September, with lingering **warm temperatures** and a noticeable decrease in crowds immediately after the long weekend (at the beginning of the month). While **fall colors** in general lack the intensity of those in the eastern provinces and New England, larch turn a brilliant

Fall is prime elk-viewing season in Banff.

winter at Lake Louise

yellow throughout subalpine areas of Banff and Kananaskis in mid- to late September.

Winter

Local **ski resorts** begin opening for the **winter** **(Dec.-mid-Apr.)** in late November. The best **powder snow** conditions are **January-February,** although for enthusiasts looking for a combination of good snow and warmer weather, March is an excellent time of year to visit.

Before You Go

Passports and Visas

To enter Canada, a **passport** is required of citizens and permanent residents of the United States. For further information, see the website http://travel.state.gov. For current **entry requirements** to Canada, check the Citizenship and Immigration Canada website (www.cic.gc.ca).

All other foreign visitors must have a valid passport and may need a **visa** or **visitors permit** depending on their country of residence and the vagaries of international politics. At present, visas are not required for citizens of the United States, British Commonwealth, or Western Europe. The standard entry permit is for **six months,** and you may be asked to show onward tickets or proof of sufficient funds to last you through your intended stay.

No vaccinations are necessary for visiting Canada.

Transportation

Visitors to the Canadian Rockies have the option of arriving by **road, rail,** or **air.** The main gateway city for flights from North America and Europe is **Calgary,** while **Vancouver** is also a popular starting point. From these two cities, as well as points across Canada, scheduled train and bus services pass through the region year-round.

the Bow River near the town of Banff

Driving, whether it be your own vehicle or a rental car, is by far the best way to get around the Canadian Rockies, although most towns are served by bus.

Park Passes

Unless you're passing directly through, passes are required for entry into the five national parks of the Canadian Rockies. Monies collected from these passes go directly to Parks Canada for park maintenance and improvements.

A National Parks Day Pass for Banff is adult $9.80, senior $8.30, child $4.90, up to a maximum of $19.60 per vehicle. It is interchangeable among parks and is valid until 4pm the day following its purchase.

An annual Discovery Pass, good for entry into all of Canada's national parks and national historic sites for one year from purchase, is adult $67.70, senior $57.90, child $33.30, to a maximum of $136.40 per vehicle.

Both types of pass can be purchased at park gates at the tollbooths at either end of the Icefields Parkway, at all park information centers, and at campground fee stations. For more information on passes, check the Parks Canada website (www.pc.gc.ca).

Banff National Park

Town of Banff. 25

Lake Louise and Vicinity 68

Icefields Parkway (Banff). 83

Nearby Parks 91

Highlights

★ **Whyte Museum of the Canadian Rockies:** If you visit only one museum in Banff, make it this one for a snapshot of the park's human history (page 28).

★ **Fairmont Banff Springs:** You don't need to book a room here to enjoy the many wonders of one of the world's great mountain resorts—join a guided tour, enjoy a meal, or simply wander through the grandiose public areas (page 30).

★ **Bow Valley Parkway:** This scenic drive between Banff and Lake Louise provides views of abundant wildlife and many worthwhile stops (page 34).

★ **Lake Louise:** Famous Lake Louise has hypnotized visitors with her beauty for more than 100 years. Visitors can rent canoes from the boathouse (page 68).

★ **Moraine Lake:** If anywhere in the Canadian Rockies qualifies as a Double Must-See, it would be this deep-blue body of water surrounded by glaciated peaks (page 71).

★ **Lake Agnes Trail:** You won't completely escape the crowds by hiking this trail from Lake Louise, but you will leave many of them behind (page 73).

★ **Larch Valley Trail:** This walk is a good introduction to hiking in the Canadian Rockies, especially in fall when the larch trees have turned a brilliant gold (page 75).

★ **Peyto Lake:** Another one of Banff's famous lakes. The main difference is the perspective from which it is viewed—a lookout high above its shoreline (page 84).

★ **Helen Lake Trail:** A moderately steep hiking trail leads through glorious wildflower meadows to this beautiful lake, whose shores are populated by noisy marmots (page 87).

★ **Mount Assiniboine Provincial Park:** Accessible only on foot or by helicopter, this roadless park is filled with glacier-capped peaks and turquoise lakes (page 91).

This park encompasses some of the world's most magnificent scenery. The snowcapped peaks of the Rocky Mountains form a spectacular backdrop for glacial lakes, fast-flowing rivers, and endless forests.

Deer, moose, elk, mountain goats, bighorn sheep, black and grizzly bears, wolves, and cougars inhabit the park's vast wilderness, while the human species is concentrated in the picture-postcard towns of Banff and Lake Louise—two of North America's most famous resorts. Banff is near the park's southeast gate, 128 kilometers (80 miles) west of Calgary. Lake Louise, northwest of Banff along the Trans-Canada Highway, sits astride its namesake lake, which is regarded as one of the seven natural wonders of the world. The lake is rivaled for sheer beauty only by Moraine Lake, down the road. Just north of Lake Louise, the Icefields Parkway begins its spectacular course alongside the Continental Divide to Jasper National Park.

One of the greatest draws of this 6,641-square-kilometer (2,564-square-mile) park is the accessibility of its natural wonders. Most highlights are close to the road system, but adventurous visitors can follow an excellent network of hiking trails to alpine lakes, along glacial valleys, and to spectacular viewpoints where crowds are scarce and human impact has been minimal. Summer in the park is busy. In fact, the park receives nearly half of its four million annual visitors in just two months (July and August). The rest of the year, crowds outside the town of Banff are negligible. In winter, three world-class winter resorts—Ski Norquay, Sunshine Village, and Lake Louise (Canada's second-largest winter resort)—crank up their lifts. During this low season, hotel rates are reasonable. If you tire of downhill skiing and snowboarding, you can try cross-country skiing, ice-skating, or snowshoeing; take a sleigh ride; soak in a hot spring; or go heli-skiing nearby.

The park is open year-round, although occasional road closures occur on mountain passes along its western boundary in winter due to avalanche-control work and snowstorms.

Previous: Fairmont Chateau Lake Louise; Giant Steps in Paradise Valley. **Above:** enjoying a cruise on Lake Minnewanka.

PLANNING YOUR TIME

If you are planning to visit the Canadian Rockies, it is almost inevitable that your itinerary will include Banff National Park, both for its many and varied outdoor attractions and for its central location. The park can be anything you want it to be, depending on the time of year you visit and what your interests are. The main population center is Banff, which has all the services of a large town, as well as attractions such as the landmark **Fairmont Banff Springs** hotel and the **Whyte Museum of the Canadian Rockies.** The park holds three lakes that you won't want to miss for their scenic beauty: **Lake Louise, Moraine Lake,** and **Peyto Lake.** All three are easily accessible by road but also offer surrounding hiking, and the first two have canoe rentals. Hiking is the park's biggest attraction, and many visitors plan their itinerary around it. I'd suggest mixing it up—choosing from the hikes that reflect your fitness level and combining them with visits to the major natural attractions. For example, when in the vicinity of Lake Louise, walk the **Lake Agnes Trail,** and while at Moraine Lake, plan on visiting **Larch Valley.** For the more adventurous, **Helen Lake** is a stunning day-hike destination. Keen hikers with more time should also consider including **Mount Assiniboine Provincial Park,** which is renowned for its network of trails and backcountry lodging and camping.

You can book one accommodation for your entire stay or spend an equal number of nights in Banff and Lake Louise. If you have a family or like the convenience of staying put for your entire vacation, it is practical to book a room in either Banff or Lake Louise and use it as a base—spending your days in the park but also venturing farther afield.

Unless you're a die-hard skier or snowboarder, summer is definitely the best time of year to visit. The months of July and August are the busiest, with crowds decreasing exponentially in the weeks before and after these two months. June and September are

Park Entry

Permits are required for entry into Banff National Park. A **National Parks Day Pass** is adult $9.80, senior $8.30, child $4.90, to a maximum of $19.60 per vehicle. It is interchangeable between parks and is valid until 4pm the day following its purchase.

An annual **Discovery Pass,** good for entry into national parks and national historic sites across Canada (including two within Banff National Park), is adult $67.70, senior $57.90, child $33.30, to a maximum of $136.40 per vehicle.

All passes can be bought at the eastern park gate on the Trans-Canada Highway, the park information centers in Banff or Lake Louise, and at campground kiosks. For more information, check the Parks Canada website (www.pc.gc.ca).

wonderful times to visit the park. Aside from the crowd factor, in June, wildflowers start blooming and wildlife is abundant. September sees temperatures ideal for hiking, and the turning colors are at their peak. In either month, discounted accommodations are a welcome bonus. In May and October-November, the park is at its quietest. Temperatures in any of these three months are generally too cool for hiking (although welcome warm spells are common). The park's three alpine resorts begin opening in November and remain in operation until April or May. While skiing and boarding are the big wintertime draws, plan on expanding your experience by joining a sleigh ride, learning to snowshoe, or heading out for some ice fishing.

THE LANDSCAPE

The park lies within the main and front ranges of the Rocky Mountains, a mountain range that extends the length of the North American continent. Although the mountains are composed of bedrock laid down up to one billion years ago, it wasn't until 100 million years ago that forces below the earth's surface transformed the lowland plain of what is now western Canada into the varied, mountainous topography we see today.

The front ranges lie to the east, bordering the foothills. These geologically complex mountains are made up of younger bedrock that has been folded, faulted, and uplifted. The main ranges are older and higher, with the bedrock lying mainly horizontal and not as severely disturbed as the front ranges. Here the pressures have been most powerful; these mountains are characterized by castlelike buttresses and pinnacles and warped waves of stratified rock. Most glaciers are found among these lofty peaks. The spine of the main range is the **Continental Divide**. In Canadian longitudes to the east of the divide, all waters flow to the Atlantic Ocean; those to the west flow into the Pacific.

Since rising above the surrounding plains, these mountains have been eroding. At least four times in the last million years, sheets of ice have covered much of the land. Advancing and retreating back and forth like steel wool across the landscape, they rounded off lower peaks and carved formerly V-shaped valleys into broad U-shaped ones: **Bow Valley** is the most distinctive. Meanwhile, glacial meltwater continued carving ever-deeper channels into the valleys, and rivers changed course many times.

This long history of powerful and even violent natural events over the eons has left behind the dramatic landscape visitors marvel over today. Now forming the exposed sides of many a mountain peak, layers of drastically altered sediment are visible from miles away, especially when accentuated by a particular angle of sunlight or a light fall of snow. **Cirques,** gouged into the mountains by glacial action, fill with glacial meltwater each spring, creating trademark translucent green lakes that will take your breath away. The wide, sweeping U-shaped valleys scoured out by glaciers past now create magnificent panoramas that will draw you to pull off the road and gasp in awe; open views are easy to come by here, thanks to a climate that keeps the tree line low.

PLANTS

Nearly 700 species of plants have been recorded in the park. Each species falls into one of three distinct vegetation zones, based primarily on altitude. Lowest is the montane zone, which covers the valley floor. Above it, the subalpine zone comprises most of the forested area. Highest of all is the alpine zone, where the climate is severe and vegetation cover is limited.

Montane-zone vegetation is usually found at elevations below 1,350 meters (4,430 feet) but can grow at higher elevations on sun-drenched, south-facing slopes. Because fires frequently affect this zone, **lodgepole pine** is the dominant species; its tightly sealed cones only open with the heat of a forest fire, thereby regenerating the species quickly after a blaze. **Douglas fir** is the zone's climax species and is found in open stands, such as on Tunnel Mountain. **Aspen** is common in older burn areas, while **limber pine** thrives on rocky outcrops.

Dense forests of **white spruce** and **Engelmann spruce** typify the subalpine zone. White spruce dominates up to 2,100 meters (6,890 feet); above 2,100 meters (6,890 feet) to 2,400 meters (7,870 feet), Engelmann spruce is dominant. In areas affected by fire, such as west of Castle Junction, lodgepole pine occurs in dense stands. **Subalpine fir** grows above 2,200 meters (7,220 feet) and is often stunted by the high winds experienced at such lofty elevations.

The transition from subalpine to alpine is gradual and usually occurs around 2,300 meters (7,550 feet). The alpine zone has a severe climate, with temperatures averaging below zero. Low temperatures, strong winds, and a very short summer force alpine plants to adapt by growing low to the ground with long roots. Mosses, mountain avens, saxifrage, and alpine dandelion all thrive in this environment. The best place to view the brightly colored carpet of **alpine flowers** is at Sunshine Meadows or Parker's Ridge.

Banff National Park

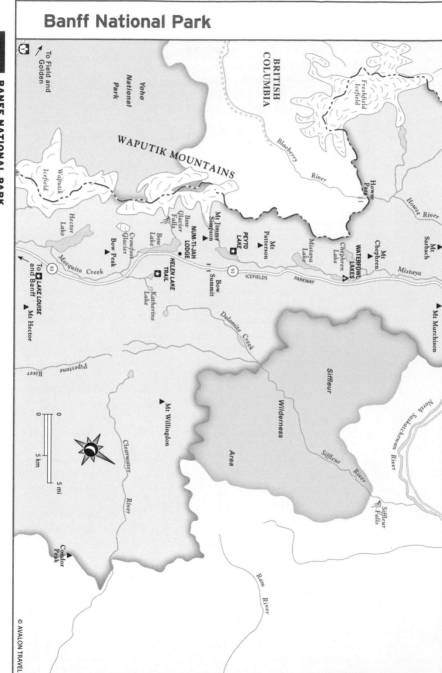

To Field and
Golden

Yoho
National
Park

BRITISH
COLUMBIA

Freshfield
Icefield

WAPUTIK MOUNTAINS

Blaeberry

River

Howse
Pass

Waputik
Icefield

Howse River

Hector
Lake

Bow
Glacier
Falls

Mt Jimmy
Simpson

Mt
Patterson

Mt
Sarbach

NUM-TI-JAH
LODGE

PEYTO
LAKE

Mistaya
Lake

Mt
Chephren

Crowfoot
Glacier

Bow
Lake

WATERFOWL
LAKES

Bow Peak

Chephren
Lake

Mosquito Creek

93

HELEN LAKE
TRAIL

93

Bow
Summit

ICEFIELDS

PARKWAY

Mistaya

To LAKE LOUISE
and Banff

Katherine
Lake

Mt Hector

Dolomite Creek

Mt Murchison

Pipestone

River

Siffleur

Mt Willingdon

Wilderness

0   0

Area

Clearwater

North Saskatchewan River

5 km   5 mi

Siffleur

River

River

Siffleur
Falls

Condor
Peak

Ram

River

© AVALON TRAVEL

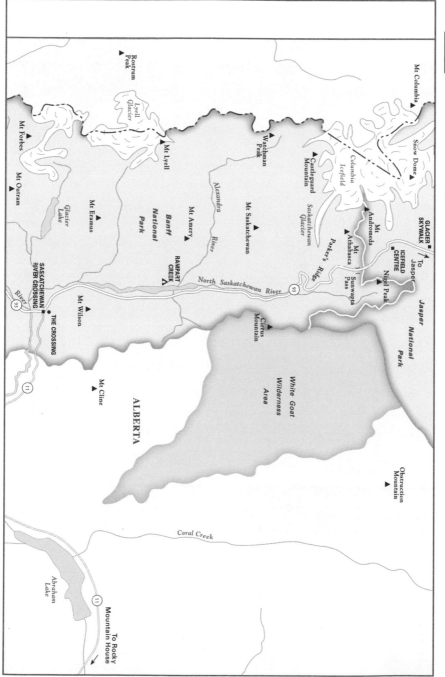

Banff National Park (continued)

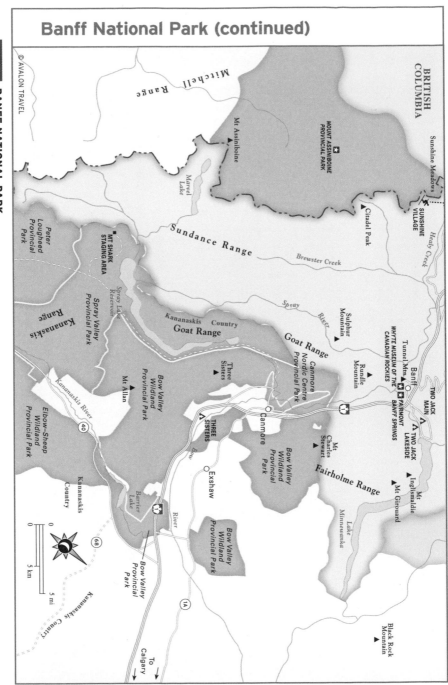

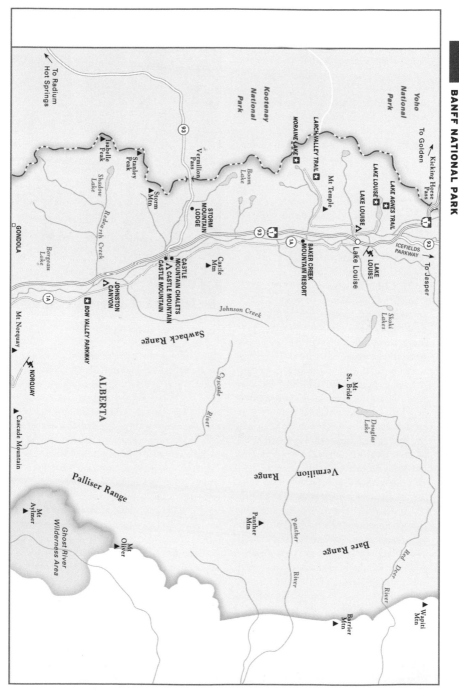

ANIMALS

Viewing the park's abundant and varied wildlife is one of the most popular visitor activities in Banff. In summer, with the onslaught of the tourist hordes, many of the larger mammals move away from the heavily traveled areas. It then becomes a case of knowing when and where to look for them. Spring and fall are the best times of year for wildlife viewing; the crowds are thinner than in summer, and big-game animals are more likely to be seen at lower elevations. Winter also has its advantages. Although **bears** are hibernating, a large herd of **elk** winters on the outskirts of the town of Banff, **coyotes** are often seen roaming around town, **bighorn sheep** have descended from the heights, and **wolf** packs can be seen along the Bow Valley Corridor.

aspen forest

Small Mammals

One of the first mammals you're likely to come in contact with is the **Columbian ground squirrel,** seen throughout the park's lower elevations. The **golden-mantled ground squirrel,** similar in size but with a striped back, is common at higher elevations or around rocky outcrops. The one collecting Engelmann spruce cones is the **red squirrel.** The **least chipmunk** is striped, but it's smaller than the golden-mantled squirrel. It lives in dry, rocky areas throughout the park.

    Short-tailed weasels are common, but **long-tailed weasels** are rare. Look for both in higher subalpine forests. **Pikas** (commonly called rock rabbits) and **hoary marmots** (well known for their shrill whistles) live among rockslides near high-country lakes; look for them around Moraine Lake and along the Bow Summit Loop. **Porcupines** are widespread in montane forests and are most active at night.

    The Fenland Trail is an excellent place to view the **beaver** at work; the best time is dawn or dusk. **Muskrats** are common in all wetlands within the park.

Hoofed Residents

The most common and widespread of the park's hoofed residents are **elk,** which number around 2,000. A concerted effort has been made to keep them out of Banff's downtown core, but they are still congregating around the outskirts of the town, including up near the Tunnel Mountain campgrounds. They can also be seen along the Bow Valley Parkway. **Moose** were once common around Vermilion Lakes, but competition from an artificially expanded elk population caused their numbers to decline, and now only around 100 live in the park. Look for them at Waterfowl Lakes and along the Icefields Parkway near Rampart Creek.

    Mule deer, named for their large ears, are most common in the southern part of the park. In addition to within town limits, watch for them along the Mount Norquay Road and Bow Valley Parkway. **White-tailed deer** are much less common but are seen occasionally at Saskatchewan River Crossing.

    It is estimated that the park is home to around 900 **mountain goats.** These nimble-footed creatures occupy all mountain peaks,

The Elk of Banff National Park

Few visitors leave Banff without having seen elk—a large member of the deer family easily distinguished by its white rump. Though the animals have been reported passing through the park for a century, they've never been indigenous. In 1917, 57 elk were moved to Banff from Yellowstone National Park. Two years later, 20 more were transplanted, and the new herd multiplied rapidly. At that time, coyotes, cougars, and wolves were being slaughtered under a predator-control program, leaving the elk unfettered by nature's population-control mechanisms. The elk proliferated and soon became a problem as they took to wintering in the range of bighorn sheep, deer, moose, and beaver. Between 1941 and 1969, controlled slaughters of elk were conducted in an attempt to reduce the population.

Today, with wolf packs returning to the park, the elk population has stabilized at about 2,000. In summer, look for them in open meadows along the Bow Valley Parkway, along the road to Two Jack Lake, or at Vermilion Lakes.

Each fall, traditionally, hundreds of elk moved into the town itself, but starting in recent years, Parks Canada has been making a concerted effort to keep them away from areas such as the golf course and recreation grounds. The main reason for this is that fall is rutting season, and the libidinal bull elk become dangerous as they gather their harems.

You may still see the odd elk feeding in downtown Central Park or walking proudly down a fairway at the Fairmont Banff Springs Golf Course, but it's more likely you'll spot one while driving along park highways.

living almost the entire year in the higher subalpine and alpine regions. The most accessible place to view these high-altitude hermits is along Parker's Ridge in the far northwestern corner of the park. The park's **bighorn sheep** have for the most part lost their fear of humans and often congregate at certain spots to lick salt from the road. Your best chance of seeing one of the park's 2,000-2,300 bighorn is at the south end of the Bow Valley Parkway, between switchbacks on Mount Norquay Road, and between Lake Minnewanka and Two Jack Lake.

Wild Dogs and Cats

Coyotes are widespread along the entire Bow River watershed. They are attracted to Vermilion Lakes by an abundance of small game, and many have permanent dens there. **Wolves** had been driven close to extinction by the early 1950s, but today at least two wolf packs are present within in the park. One pack winters along the Bow Valley Parkway and is occasionally seen at Vermilion Lakes during that period. The **lynx** population fluctuates greatly; look for them in the backcountry

during winter. **Cougars** are shy and number fewer than 20 in the park. They are occasionally seen along the front ranges behind Cascade Mountain.

Bears

The exhilaration of seeing one of these magnificent creatures in its natural habitat is unforgettable. From the road you're most likely to see **black bears,** which actually range in color from jet black to cinnamon brown and number around 50. Try the Bow Valley Parkway at dawn or late in the afternoon. Farther north they are occasionally seen near the Icefields Parkway as it passes Cirrus Mountain. Banff's 50-odd **grizzly bears** spend most of the year in remote valleys, often on south-facing slopes away from the Bow Valley Corridor. During late spring they are occasionally seen in residential areas, along the Lake Minnewanka loop road, on the golf course, and in the area of Bow Pass.

The chance of encountering a bear face-to-face in the backcountry is remote. To lessen the chances even further, you should take some simple precautions: Never hike alone or at dusk. Make lots of noise when passing through heavy vegetation. Keep a clean camp. Read the pamphlets available at all park visitors centers. At the Banff Visitor Centre (224 Banff Ave.), daily trail reports list all recent bear sightings. Report any bears you see to the Warden's Office (403/762-4506).

Reptiles and Amphibians

The **wandering garter snake** is rare and found only near the Cave and Basin, where warm water from the mineral spring flows down a shaded slope into Vermilion Lakes. Amphibians found in the park include the widespread **western toad;** the **wood frog,** commonly found along the Bow River; the rare **spotted frog;** and the **long-toed salamander,** which spawns in shallow ponds and spends the summer under logs or rocks in the vicinity of its spawning grounds.

Birds

Although more than 240 species of birds have been recorded in the park, most are shy and live in heavily wooded areas. One species that definitely isn't shy is the fearless **gray jay,** which haunts all campgrounds and picnic areas. Similar in color, but larger, is the **Clark's nutcracker,** which lives in higher subalpine forests. Another common bird is the black-and-white **magpie. Ravens** are frequently encountered, especially around campgrounds.

Several species of **woodpeckers** live in subalpine forests. A number of species of grouse are also in residence. Most common is the **ruffed grouse,** seen in montane forest. The **blue grouse** and **spruce grouse** are seen at higher elevations, as is the **white-tailed ptarmigan,** which lives above the tree line. (Watch for them in Sunshine Meadows or on the Bow Summit Loop.) A colony of **black swifts** in Johnston Canyon is one of only two in the Canadian Rockies.

Good spots to view **dippers** and migrating waterfowl are Hector Lake, Vermilion Lakes, and the wetland area near Muleshoe Picnic Area. A bird blind has been set up below the Cave and Basin but is only worth visiting at dawn and dusk when the hordes of human visitors aren't around. Part of the nearby marsh stays ice-free during winter, attracting **killdeer** and other birds.

Although raptors are not common in the park, **bald eagles** and **golden eagles** are present part of the year, and Alberta's provincial bird, the **great horned owl,** lives in the park year-round.

HISTORY

Although the valleys of the Canadian Rockies became ice-free nearly 8,000 years ago and humans periodically hunted in the area since that time, the story of Banff National Park really began with the arrival of the railroad to the area.

The Coming of the Railway

In 1871, Canadian prime minister John A. MacDonald promised to build a rail line linking British Columbia to the rest of the country as a condition of the new province joining the confederation. It wasn't until early 1883 that the line reached Calgary, pushing through to **Laggan,** now known as Lake Louise, that fall. The rail line was one of the largest and costliest engineering jobs ever undertaken in Canada.

Discovery of the Cave and Basin

On November 8, 1883, three young railway workers—Franklin McCabe and William and Thomas McCardell—went prospecting for gold on their day off. After crossing the Bow River by raft, they came across a warm stream and traced it to its source at a small, log-choked basin of warm water that had a distinct smell of sulfur. Nearby they detected the source of the foul smell coming from a hole in the ground. Nervously, one of the three men lowered himself into the hole and came across a subterranean pool of aqua-green warm water. The three men had found not gold, but something just as precious—a hot mineral spring that in time would attract

the Cave and Basin

Avenue. The general manager of the CPR (later to become its vice president), William Cornelius Van Horne, was instrumental in creating a hotel business along the rail line. His most recognized achievement was the Banff Springs Hotel, which opened in 1888. It was the world's largest hotel at the time. Enterprising locals soon realized the area's potential and began opening restaurants, offering guided hunting and boating trips, and developing manicured gardens. Banff soon became Canada's best-known tourist resort, attracting visitors from around the world. It was named after Banffshire, the Scottish birthplace of George Stephen, the CPR's first president.

In 1902, the park boundary was again expanded to include 11,440 square kilometers (4,417 square miles) of the Canadian Rockies. This dramatic expansion meant that the park became not just a tourist resort but also home to existing coal-mining and logging operations and hydroelectric dams. Government officials saw no conflict of interest, actually stating that the coal mine and township at Bankhead added to the park's many attractions. Many of the forests were logged, providing wood for construction, while other areas were burned to allow clear sightings for surveyors' instruments.

After a restriction on automobiles in the park was lifted in 1916, Canada's best-known tourist resort also became its busiest. More and more commercial facilities sprang up, offering luxury and opulence amid the wilderness of the Canadian Rockies. Calgarians built summer cottages, and the town began advertising itself as a year-round destination. As attitudes began to change, the government set up the Dominion Parks Branch, whose first commissioner, J. B. Harkin, believed that land set aside for parks should be used for recreation and education. Gradually, resource industries were phased out. Harkin's work culminated in the National Parks Act of 1930, which in turn led Rocky Mountains Park to be renamed Banff National Park. The park's present boundaries, encompassing

wealthy customers from around the world. Word of the discovery soon got out, and the government encouraged visitors to the Cave and Basin as an ongoing source of revenue to support the new railway.

A 2,500-hectare (6,177-acre) reserve was established around the springs on November 25, 1885, and two years later the reserve was expanded and renamed **Rocky Mountains Park.** It was primarily a business enterprise centered on the unique springs and catering to wealthy patrons of the railway. At the turn of the 20th century, Canada had an abundance of wilderness; it certainly didn't need a park to preserve it. The only goal of Rocky Mountains Park was to generate income for the government and the Canadian Pacific Railway (CPR).

A Town Grows

After the discovery of the Cave and Basin across the Bow River from the railway station (then known as Siding 29), many commercial facilities sprang up along what is now Banff

Wild Bill Peyto

These words from a friend sum up Bill Peyto, one of Banff's earliest characters and one of the Canadian Rockies' greatest guides: "rarely speaking—his forte was doing things, not talking about them." In 1886, at the tender age of 18, Ebenezer William Peyto left England for Canada. After traveling extensively, he settled in Banff and was hired as an apprentice guide for legendary outfitter Tom Wilson. Wearing a tilted sombrero, fringed buckskin coat, cartridge belt, hunting knife, and six-shooter, he looked more like a gunslinger than a mountain man.

As his reputation as a competent guide grew, so did the stories. While guiding clients on one occasion, he led them to his cabin. Before entering, Peyto threw stones in the front door until a loud snap was heard. It was a bear trap that he'd set up to catch a certain trapper who'd been stealing his food. One of the guests commented that if caught, the trapper would surely have died. "You're damned right he would have," Bill replied. "Then I'd have known for sure it was him."

In 1900, Peyto left Banff to fight in the Boer War and was promoted to corporal for bravery. This title was revoked before it became official after army officials learned he'd "borrowed" an officer's jacket and several bottles of booze for the celebration. Returning to a hero's welcome in Banff, Peyto established an outfitting business and continued prospecting for copper in Simpson Pass. Although his outfitting business thrived, the death of his wife left him despondent. He built a house on Banff Avenue; its name, "Ain't it Hell," summed up his view of life.

In his later years, he became a warden in the Healy Creek-Sunshine district, where his exploits during the 1920s added to his already legendary name. After 20 years of service he retired, and in 1943, at the age of 75, he passed away. One of the park's most beautiful lakes is named after him, as are a glacier and a popular Banff watering hole (Wild Bill's—a designation he would have appreciated).

6,641 square kilometers (2,564 square miles), were established in 1964.

Icefields Parkway

Indigenous peoples and early explorers found the swampy nature of the Bow Valley north of Lake Louise difficult for foot and horse travel. When heading north, they used instead the Pipestone River Valley to the east. In 1896, Banff guide Bill Peyto led American explorer Walter Wilcox up the Bow Valley to the high peaks along the Continental Divide northeast of Lake Louise. The first complete journey along this route was made by Jim Brewster in 1904. Soon after, A. P. Coleman made the arduous journey, becoming a strong supporter of the route aptly known as The Wonder Trail. During the Great Depression of the 1930s, as part of a relief-work project, construction began on what was to become the Icefields Parkway. The road was completed in 1939,

and the first car traveled the route in 1940. In tribute to the excellence of the road's early construction, the original roadbed, when upgraded to its present standard in 1961, was followed nearly the entire way.

Town of Banff

For most of its existence, the town of Banff was run as a service center for park visitors by the Canadian Parks Service in Ottawa, a government department with plenty of economic resources but little idea about how to handle the day-to-day running of a midsized town. Any inconvenience this arrangement caused park residents was offset by cheap rent and subsidized services. In June 1988, Banff's residents voted to sever this tie, and on January 1, 1990, Banff officially became an incorporated town, no different than any other in Alberta (except that Parks Canada controls environmental protection within the town of Banff).

Town of Banff

Many visitors planning a trip to the national park don't realize that the town of Banff is a bustling commercial center. The town's location is magnificent. It is spread out along the Bow River, extending to the lower slopes of Sulphur Mountain to the south and Tunnel Mountain to the east. In one direction is the towering face of Mount Rundle, and in the other, framed by the buildings along Banff Avenue, is Cascade Mountain. Hotels and motels line the north end of Banff Avenue, while a profusion of shops, boutiques, cafés, and restaurants hugs the south end. Also at the south end, just over the Bow River, is the Park Administration Building. Here the road forks—to the right is the historic Cave and Basin Hot Springs, to the left the Fairmont Banff Springs and Banff Gondola. Some people are happy walking along the crowded streets or shopping in a unique setting; those more interested in some peace and quiet can easily slip into pristine wilderness just a five-minute walk from town.

SIGHTS AND DRIVES

Banff Park Museum

Although displays of stuffed animals are not usually associated with national parks, the downtown **Banff Park Museum** (93 Banff Ave., 403/762-1558, 10am-5pm Wed.-Sun. mid-May-June, 10am-5pm daily July-Aug., 10am-5pm Wed.-Sun. Sept.-early Oct., closed the rest of the year, adult $4, senior $3.50, child $3) provides insight into the park's early history. Visitors during the Victorian era were eager to see the park's animals without actually having to venture into the bush. A lack of roads and the scarcity of large game (a result of hunting) meant that the best places to see animals, stuffed or otherwise, were the game paddock, the zoo, and this museum, which was built in 1903. In its early years, the Banff Zoo and Aviary occupied the grounds behind the museum. The zoo kept more than 60 species of animals, including a polar bear. The museum itself was built before the park had electricity, hence the railroad pagoda design using skylights on all levels.

Banff Park Museum

Town of Banff

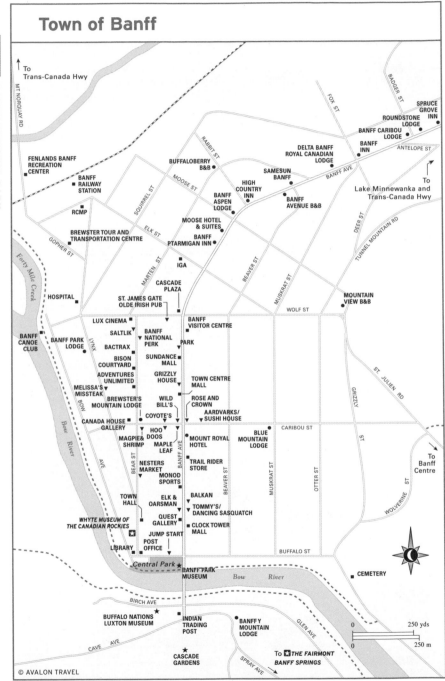

© AVALON TRAVEL

Vicinity of Banff

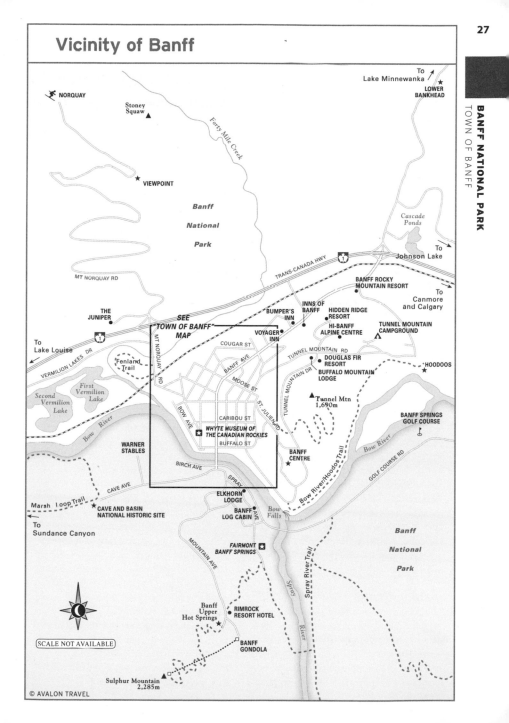

As times changed, the museum was considered outdated; plans for its demolition were put forward in the 1950s. Fortunately, the museum was spared and later restored for the park's 100th anniversary in 1985. While the exhibits still provide visitors with an insight into the intricate workings of various park ecosystems, they are also an interesting link to the park's past. The museum has a Discovery Room, too, where touching the displays is encouraged, and a reading room that is stocked with natural history books.

★ Whyte Museum of the Canadian Rockies

The Whyte Foundation was established in the mid-1950s by local artists Peter and Catharine Whyte to help preserve artistic and historical material relating to the Canadian Rockies. Their **Whyte Museum of the Canadian Rockies** (111 Bear St., 403/762-2291, 10am-5pm daily, adult $8, senior $4, child free) opened in 1968 and has continued to grow ever since. It now houses the world's largest collection of Canadian Rockies literature and art. Included in the archives are more than 4,000 volumes, oral tapes of early pioneers and outfitters, antique postcards, old cameras, manuscripts, and a large photography collection. The highlight is the photography of Byron Harmon, whose black-and-white studies of mountain geography have shown people around the world the beauty of the Canadian Rockies. The downstairs gallery features changing art exhibitions. The museum also houses the library and archives of the Alpine Club of Canada. On the grounds are several heritage homes and cabins formerly occupied by local pioneers.

MUSEUM TOURS

The Whyte Museum hosts interesting walking tours during the summer. The most popular of these is the **Heritage Homes Tour,** which allows an opportunity for visitors to take a closer look at the historic residences located among the trees behind the museum, including that of Peter and Catharine Whyte. This tour departs up to five times daily through the summer. The tour is $8 per person, or free with museum admission.

Cascade Gardens

Across the river from downtown, Cascade Gardens offers a commanding view of Banff Avenue and Cascade Mountain. The gardens are immaculately manicured, making for enjoyable strolling on a sunny day. The stone edifice in the center of the garden is the **Park Administration Building** (101 Mountain Ave.), which dates to 1936. It replaced a private spa and hospital operated by one of the park's earliest entrepreneurs, Dr. R. G. Brett. Known as Brett's Sanatorium, the original 1886 structure was built to accommodate guests drawn to Banff by the purported healing qualities of the hot springs' water.

Buffalo Nations Luxton Museum

Looking like a stockade, the **Buffalo Nations Luxton Museum** (1 Birch Ave., 403/762-2388, 10am-7pm daily in summer, 11am-5pm daily the rest of the year, adult $10, senior $9, child $5) overlooks the Bow River across from Central Park. It is dedicated to the heritage of the First Nations who once inhabited the Canadian Rockies and adjacent prairies. The museum was developed by prominent local resident Norman Luxton in the early 1900s. At that time it was within the Indian Trading Post, an adjacent gift shop that still stands. The museum contains memorabilia from Luxton's lifelong relationship with the Stoney people, including an elaborately decorated tepee, hunting equipment, arrowheads dating back 4,000 years, stuffed animals, original artwork, peace pipes, and traditional clothing. Various aspects of First Nations culture—such as ceremonial gatherings, living in a tepee, and weaving—are also displayed. The Indian Trading Post is one of Banff's more distinctive gift shops and is definitely worth a browse.

Cave and Basin National Historic Site

At the end of Cave Avenue, the **Cave and Basin National Historic Site** (403/762-1566, 10am-5pm daily in summer, noon-4pm Wed.-Sun. the rest of the year, adult $4, senior $3.50, child $2.50) is the birthplace of Banff National Park and of the Canadian National Parks system. Here, in 1883, three men employed by the Canadian Pacific Railway (CPR) stumbled on the hot springs now known as the Cave and Basin and were soon lounging in the hot water—a real luxury in the Wild West. They built a fence around the springs, constructed a crude cabin, and began the long process of establishing a claim to the site. But the government beat them to it, settling their claims for a few thousand dollars and acquiring the hot springs.

Bathhouses were installed in 1887, and bathers paid $0.10 for a swim. The pools were eventually lined with concrete, and additions were built onto the original structures. Ironically, the soothing minerals in the water that had attracted millions of people to bathe here eventually caused the pools' demise. The minerals, combined with chlorine, produced sediments that ate away at the concrete structure until the pools were deemed unsuitable for swimming in 1993.

Although the pools are now closed to swimming, the site is still one of Banff's most popular attractions. Interpretive displays describe the hows and whys of the springs. A narrow tunnel winds into the dimly lit cave, and short trails lead to the cave entrance and through a unique environment created by the hot water from the springs.

Banff Upper Hot Springs

The **Banff Upper Hot Springs** (Mountain Ave., 403/762-1515, 9am-11pm daily mid-May-mid-Oct., 10am-10pm Sun.-Thurs. and 10am-11pm Fri.-Sat. mid-Oct.-mid-May), toward the Banff Gondola, were first developed in 1901. The present building was completed in 1935, with extensive renovations made in 1996. Water flows out of the bedrock at 47°C (116.6°F) and is cooled to 40°C (104°F) in the main pool. Swimming is $7.50 adults, $6.50 seniors and children; lockers and towel rental are a couple dollars extra. Within the complex is **Pleiades Massage & Spa** (403/760-2500), offering a wide range of therapeutic treatments, including a two-hour body treatment and massage for $180, as well as body wraps, aromatherapy, and hydrotherapy.

Banff Upper Hot Springs

Banff Gondola

The easiest way to get high above town without breaking a sweat is on the **Banff Gondola** (403/762-2523, 8:30am-9pm daily in summer, shorter hours the rest of the year, closed for two weeks in January, adult $62, child $31). The modern four-person cars rise 700 meters (2,300 feet) in eight minutes to the summit of 2,285-meter (7,500-foot) **Sulphur Mountain.** From the observation deck at the upper terminal, the breathtaking 360-degree view includes the town, the Bow Valley, Cascade Mountain, Lake Minnewanka, and the Fairholme Range. Inside the upper terminal are interactive displays, a theater, and three eateries. Bighorn sheep often hang around below the upper terminal. The short **Sulphur Mountain Boardwalk** leads along a ridge to a restored weather observatory. Between 1903 and 1931, long before the gondola was built, Norman Sanson was the meteorological observer who collected data at the station. During this period he made more than 1,000 ascents of Sulphur Mountain, all in the line of duty.

From downtown, the gondola is three kilometers (1.9 miles) along Mountain Avenue. May-October, **Brewster** (403/762-6767) provides free shuttle service to the gondola from downtown hotels.

A 5.5-kilometer (3.4-mile) hiking trail to the summit begins from the Upper Hot Springs parking lot. Although it's a long slog, you have the option of a gondola ride down ($31 one-way).

★ Fairmont Banff Springs

On a terrace above a bend in the Bow River is one of the largest, grandest, and most opulent mountain-resort hotels in the world. What better way to spend a rainy afternoon than to explore the turreted 20th-century castle that is the **Fairmont Banff Springs** (405 Spray Ave., 403/762-2211, www.fairmont.com), seeking out a writing desk overlooking one of the world's most-photographed scenes and penning a long letter to the folks back home?

"The Springs" has grown with the town and is an integral part of local history. William Cornelius Van Horne, vice president of the CPR, decided that the best way to encourage customers to travel on his newly completed rail line across the Rockies was to build a series of luxurious mountain accommodations. The largest of these was begun in 1886, as close as possible to Banff's newly discovered hot springs. The location chosen had magnificent views and was only a short carriage ride from the train station. Money was

Fairmont Banff Springs

no object, and architect Bruce Price began designing a mountain resort the likes of which the world had never seen. At some stage of construction his plans were misinterpreted, and much to Van Horne's shock, the building was built back to front: The best guest rooms faced the forested slopes of Sulphur Mountain while the kitchen had panoramic views of the Bow Valley.

On June 1, 1888, it opened, the largest hotel in the world, with 250 rooms beginning at $3.50 per night including meals. Water from the nearby hot springs was piped into the hotel's steam baths. Rumor has it that when the pipes blocked, water from the Bow River was used, secretly supplemented by bags of sulfur-smelling chemicals. Overnight, the quiet community of Banff became a destination resort for wealthy guests from around the world, and the hotel soon became one of North America's most popular accommodations. Every room was booked every day during the short summer seasons. In 1903 a wing was added, doubling the hotel's capacity. The following year a tower was added to each wing. Guest numbers reached 22,000 in 1911, and construction of a new hotel, designed by Walter Painter, began that year. The original design—an 11-story tower joining two wings in a baronial style—was reminiscent of a Scottish castle mixed with a French country château. This concrete-and-rock-faced, green-roofed building stood as it did at its completion in 1928 until 1999, when an ambitious multiyear program of renovations commenced. The most obvious change was a new lobby, moved to a more accessible location; in addition, all rooms were refurbished and many of the restaurants changed or upgraded. The Canadian Pacific moniker remained part of the Banff Springs's official name until 2000, when the hotel, and all other Canadian Pacific hotels, became part of the Fairmont Hotels and Resorts chain.

Don't let the hotel's opulence keep you from spending time here. Wander through, admiring the 5,000 pieces of furniture and antiques (most of those in public areas are reproductions), paintings, prints, tapestries, and rugs. Take in the medieval atmosphere of Mount Stephen Hall, with its lime flagstone floor, enormous windows, and large oak beams; take advantage of the luxurious spa facility; or relax in one of 12 eateries or four lounges.

The hotel is a 15-minute walk southeast of town, either along Spray Avenue or via the trail along the south bank of the Bow River. **Roam** buses leave Banff Avenue for the Springs twice an hour; $2. Alternatively, horse-drawn buggies take passengers from the Trail Rider Store (132 Banff Ave., 403/762-4551) to the Springs for about $120 for two passengers.

Bow Falls

Small but spectacular Bow Falls is below the Fairmont Banff Springs, only a short walk from downtown. The waterfall is the result of a dramatic change in the course of the Bow River brought about by glaciation. At one time the river flowed north of Tunnel Mountain and out of the mountains via the valley of Lake Minnewanka. As the glaciers retreated, they left terminal moraines, forming natural dams and changing the course of the river. Eventually the backed-up water found an outlet here between Tunnel Mountain and the northwest ridge of Mount Rundle. The falls are most spectacular in late spring when runoff from the winter snows fills every river and stream in the Bow Valley watershed.

To get there from town, cross the bridge at the south end of Banff Avenue, scramble down the grassy embankment to the left, and follow a pleasant trail along the Bow River to a point above the falls. This easy walk is one kilometer (0.6 mile); 20 minutes each way. By car, cross the bridge and follow the Golf Course signs. From the falls, a paved road crosses the Spray River and passes through the golf course.

Banff Centre

On the lower slopes of Tunnel Mountain is Banff Centre, whose surroundings provide inspiration for one of Canada's leading centers for postgraduate students in a variety of disciplines, including Mountain Culture, Arts, and Leadership Development. The Banff Centre opened in the summer of 1933 as a theater school. Since then it has grown to become a prestigious institution attracting artists of many disciplines from throughout Canada. The Centre's **Walter Phillips Gallery** (St. Julien Rd., 403/762-6281, 12:30pm-5pm Wed.-Sun., free) presents changing exhibits of visual arts from throughout the world.

Activities are held on the grounds of the Banff Centre year-round. Highlights include a summer educational program, concerts, displays, live performances, the Playbill Series, the Banff Arts Festival, and Banff Mountain Festivals, to name a few. Call 403/762-6100 for a program or go to the website www.banff-centre.ca.

Vermilion Lakes

This series of three shallow lakes forms an expansive montane wetland supporting a variety of mammals and more than 200 species of birds. Vermilion Lakes Drive, paralleling the Trans-Canada Highway immediately west of Banff, provides the easiest access to the area. The level of **First Vermilion Lake** was once controlled by a dam. Since its removal, the level of the lake has dropped. This is the beginning of a long process that will eventually see the area evolve into a floodplain forest such as is found along the Fenland Trail. The entire area is excellent for wildlife viewing, especially in winter when it provides habitat for elk, coyotes, and the occasional wolf.

Mount Norquay Road

One of the best views of town accessible by vehicle is on this road, which switchbacks steeply to the base of Mount Norquay, the local winter hangout for skiers and boarders. On the way up are several lookouts, including one near the top where bighorn sheep often graze.

Want even better views? Where the road ends, the North American chairlift at the **Norquay** ski resort (2 Mt. Norquay Rd., 403/762-4421, 9am-6pm daily mid-June-mid-Oct., adult $20, child $10) lifts visitors even higher—to an elevation of 2,400 meters (8,000 feet) for unparalleled views across the town and Bow Valley. Also at the top is the Via Ferrata, a European-style climbing route in which even visitors without mountaineering experience can try their hand at climbing (from $139 for two hours), and the **Cliffhouse Bistro** (11am-5:50pm daily mid-June-mid-Oct., lunches $10-18), ensconced in a stone building clinging to the mountain slope.

Vermilion Lakes

To Lake Minnewanka

Lake Minnewanka Road begins where Banff Avenue ends at the northeast end of town. An alternative to driving along Banff Avenue is to take Buffalo Street, opposite the Banff Park Museum, and follow it around Tunnel Mountain, passing the campground and several viewpoints of the north face of Mount Rundle, rising vertically from the forested valley. This road eventually rejoins Banff Avenue at the Banff Rocky Mountain Resort.

After passing under the Trans-Canada Highway, **Cascade Falls** is obvious off to the left. The base of the falls can be reached in 15 minutes, although the trail is steep and has lots of loose rock (climbing higher without the proper equipment is dangerous). In winter, these falls freeze, and you'll often see ice climbers slowly making their way up the narrow thread of frozen water. Directly opposite is a turn to **Cascade Ponds,** a popular day-use area where families gather on warmer days to picnic and barbecue.

The next turnout along this road is at **Lower Bankhead.** During the early 1900s, Bankhead was a booming mining town producing 200,000 tons of coal a year. The poor quality of the coal and bitter labor disputes led to the mine's closure in 1922. Soon after, all the buildings were moved or demolished. From the parking lot at Lower Bankhead, a 1.1-kilometer (0.7-mile) interpretive trail leads down through the industrial section of the former town and past an old mine train. The town's 1,000 residents lived on the other side of the road at what is now known as **Upper Bankhead.** Just before the Upper Bankhead turnoff, the foundation of the Holy Trinity Church can be seen on the side of the hill to the right. Not much remains of Upper Bankhead. It is now a day-use area with picnic tables, a kitchen shelter, and firewood. Through the meadow to the west are some large slag heaps, concealed mine entrances, and various stone foundations.

Lake Minnewanka

Minnewanka (Lake of the Water Spirit) is the largest body of water in Banff National Park. Mount Inglismaldie (2,964 meters/9,720 feet) and the Fairholme Range form an imposing backdrop. The reservoir was first constructed in 1912, and additional dams were built in 1922 and 1941 to supply hydroelectric power to Banff. Even if you don't feel up to an energetic hike, it's worth parking at the facility area and going for a short walk along the lakeshore. You'll pass a concession selling

Cascade Ponds

snacks and drinks, then the tour boat dock, before entering an area of picnic tables and covered cooking shelters—the perfect place for a picnic. Children will love exploring the rocky shoreline and stony beaches in this area, but you should continue farther around the lake, if only to escape the crowds.

Banff Lake Cruise (403/762-3473) is a 90-minute cruise to the far reaches of the lake, passing the Devil's Gap formation. It departs from the dock from late May to early October 4-8 times daily (first sailing at 10am, adult $60, child $30). An easy walking trail leads past a number of picnic spots and rocky beaches to Stewart Canyon. The lake is great for fishing (lake trout to 15 kilograms/33 pounds) and is the only one in the park where motorboats are allowed. The same company operating the tour boats rents aluminum boats with small outboard engines.

From Lake Minnewanka, the road continues along the reservoir wall, passing a lookout point. You'll often have to slow down along this stretch of road for bighorn sheep. The road then descends to **Two Jack Lake** and a lakefront day-use area. Take the turnoff to **Johnson Lake** to access a lakeside trail, Banff's busiest swimming and sunbathing spot on the warmest days of summer, and picnic facilities with views across to Mount Rundle.

★ Bow Valley Parkway

Two roads link Banff to Lake Louise. The Trans-Canada Highway is the quicker route and more popular with through traffic. The other is the more scenic 51-kilometer (32-mile) Bow Valley Parkway, which branches off the Trans-Canada Highway five kilometers (3.1 miles) west of Banff. Cyclists will appreciate this road's two long, divided sections and low speed limit (60 kph/37 mph). Along this route are several impressive viewpoints, interpretive displays, picnic areas, good hiking, great opportunities for viewing wildlife, three lodges, campgrounds, and one of the park's best restaurants. Between March and late June, the southern end of the parkway (as

far north as Johnston Canyon) is closed 6pm-9am daily for the protection of wildlife.

As you enter the parkway, you pass a short side road to creekside **Fireside** picnic area. At **Backswamp Viewpoint,** you can look upstream to the site of a former dam, now a swampy wetland filled with aquatic vegetation. Farther along the road is another wetland at **Muleshoe.** This wetland consists of oxbow lakes that were formed when the Bow River changed its course and abandoned its meanders for a more direct path. Across the parkway is a one-kilometer (0.6-mile) trail that climbs to a viewpoint overlooking the valley. (The slope around this trail is infested with wood ticks during late spring and early summer, so be sure to check yourself carefully after hiking in this area.) To the east, **Hole-in-the-Wall** is visible. This large-mouthed cave was created by the Bow Glacier, which once filled the valley. As the glacier receded, its meltwater dissolved the soft limestone bedrock, creating what is known as a solution cave.

Beyond Muleshoe the road inexplicably divides for a few car lengths. A large white spruce stood on the island until it blew down in 1984. The story goes that while the road was being constructed, a surly foreman was asleep in the shade of the tree, and not daring to rouse him, workers cleared the roadway around him. The road then passes through particularly hilly terrain, part of a massive rockslide that occurred approximately 8,000 years ago.

Continuing down the parkway, you'll pass the following sights.

JOHNSTON CANYON

Johnston Creek drops over a series of spectacular waterfalls here, deep within the chasm it has carved into the limestone bedrock. The canyon is not nearly as deep as Maligne Canyon in Jasper National Park—30 meters (100 feet) at its deepest, compared to 50 meters (165 feet) at Maligne—but the catwalk that leads to the lower falls has been built through the depths of the canyon rather than along its

Bow Valley Parkway

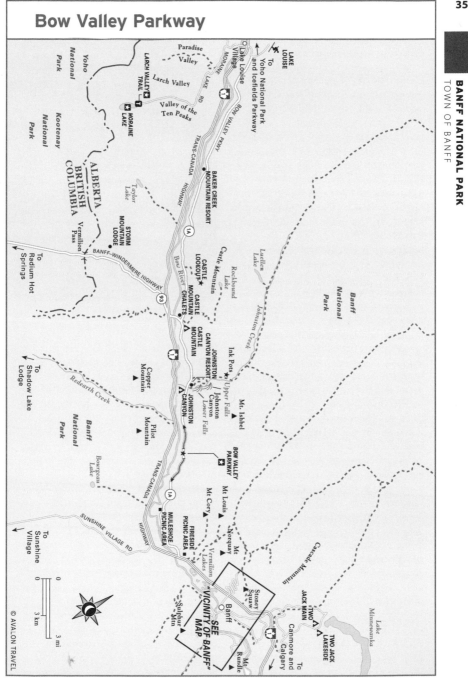

Yoho National Park

Kootenay National Park

Paradise Valley

Larch Valley

Valley of the Ten Peaks

LARCH VALLEY TRAIL

MORAINE LAKE

MORAINE LAKE RD

LAKE LOUISE

Lake Louise Village

To Yoho National Park and Icefields Parkway

BOW VALLEY PKWY

ALBERTA
BRITISH COLUMBIA

Taylor Lake

Vermilion Pass

STORM MOUNTAIN LODGE

BAKER CREEK
MOUNTAIN RESORT

TRANS-CANADA HIGHWAY

1A

BANFF–WINDERMERE HIGHWAY

To Radium Hot Springs

Bow River

CASTLE LOOKOUT

CASTLE MOUNTAIN CHALETS

CASTLE MOUNTAIN

93

Castle Mountain

Rockbound Lake

Luellen Lake

Johnston Creek

Ink Pots

JOHNSTON CANYON RESORT

JOHNSTON CANYON

Upper Falls

Johnston Canyon

Lower Falls

Copper Mountain

Pilot Mountain

Redearth Creek

Mt. Isabel

Banff National Park

BOW VALLEY PARKWAY

Bourgeau Lake

To Shadow Lake Lodge

TRANS-CANADA

1A

SUNSHINE VILLAGE RD

Banff National Park

To Sunshine Village

MULESHOE PICNIC AREA

FIRESIDE PICNIC AREA

HIGHWAY

Mt Cory

Mt Louis

Mt Norquay

Vermilion Lakes

Mt Rundle

Cascade Mountain

Stoney Squaw

Banff

Sulphur Mtn

"VICINITY OF BANFF" SEE MAP

To Canmore and Calgary

JACK MAIN

TWO JACK LAKESIDE

Lake Minnewanka

Two Jack

0   3 km
0   3 mi

© AVALON TRAVEL

lip, making it seem just as spectacular. The lower falls are one kilometer (0.6 mile) from the Bow Valley Parkway, while the equally spectacular upper falls are a further 1.6 kilometers (one mile) upstream. Beyond this point are the **Ink Pots,** shallow pools of spring-fed water. While in the canyon, look for fast-moving black swifts zipping through the air.

SILVER CITY

At the west end of **Moose Meadows,** a small plaque marks the site of Silver City. At its peak in the mid-1800s, this boomtown had a population of 2,000, making it bigger than Calgary at the time. The city was founded by John Healy, who also founded the notorious Fort Whoop-Up in Lethbridge. During its heady days, five mines were operating, extracting not silver but ore rich in copper and lead. The town had a half-dozen hotels, four or five stores, two real estate offices, and a station on the transcontinental rail line when its demise began. Two men, named Patton and Pettigrew, salted their mine with gold and silver ore to attract investors. After selling 2,000 shares at $5 each, they vanished, leaving investors with a useless mine. Investment in the town ceased, mines closed, and the people left. Only one man refused to leave. His name was James Smith, but he was known to everyone as Joe. In 1887, when Silver City came under the jurisdiction of the National Parks Service, Joe was allowed to remain. He did so and was friendly to everyone, including Stoney people, Father Albert Lacombe (who occasionally stopped by), well-known Banff guide Tom Wilson, and of course the animals who grazed around his cabin. By 1926, he was unable to trap or hunt due to failing eyesight, and many people tried to persuade him to leave. It wasn't until 1937 that he finally moved to a Calgary retirement home, where he died soon after.

CASTLE MOUNTAIN
TO LAKE LOUISE

After you leave the former site of Silver City, the aptly named Castle Mountain comes into

lower falls, Johnston Canyon

view. It's one of the park's most recognizable peaks and most interesting geographical features. The mountain consists of very old rock (approximately 500 million years old) sitting atop much younger rock (a mere 200 million years old). This unusual situation occurred as the mountains were forced upward by pressure below the earth's surface, thrusting the older rock up and over the younger rock in places.

The road skirts the base of the mountain, passes Castle Mountain Village (with gas, groceries, and accommodations), and climbs a small hill to Storm Mountain Viewpoint, which provides more stunning views and a picnic area. The next commercial facility is **Baker Creek Mountain Resort** (403/522-3761), where the mountain-style restaurant is an excellent spot for a meal, especially if you can snag an outdoor seat on a warm day. Then it's on to another viewpoint at Morant's Curve, from where rail line, river, and mountains combine for perfect symmetry. After passing another picnic area, the Bow Valley

Parkway rejoins the Trans-Canada Highway at Lake Louise.

HIKING

After experiencing the international thrills of Banff Avenue, most people will want to see the *real* park, which is, after all, the reason that millions of visitors flock here, thousands take low-paying jobs just to stay here, and others become so severely addicted that they start families and live happily ever after here.

Although many landmarks can be seen from the roadside, to really experience the park's personality you'll need to go for a hike. One of the best things about Banff's 80-odd hiking trails is the variety. From short interpretive walks originating in town to easy hikes rewarded by spectacular vistas to myriad overnight backcountry opportunities, Banff's trails offer something for everyone.

Before attempting any hikes, visit the **Banff Visitor Centre** (224 Banff Ave., 403/762-1550), where staff can advise you on the condition of trails and closures. The best book on hiking in the park is the *Canadian Rockies Trail Guide*, which covers each trail in exacting detail.

If you are planning an overnight trip into the backcountry, you *must* pick up a backcountry camping pass from either of the park information centers before heading out; $10 per person per night or $70 for an annual pass.

Fenland

Length: 2 kilometers/1.2 miles (30 minutes) round-trip
Elevation gain: none
Rating: easy
Trailhead: Forty Mile Creek Picnic Area, Mount Norquay Road, 300 meters (0.2 mile) north of the rail crossing

If you've just arrived in town, this short interpretive trail provides an excellent introduction to the Bow Valley ecosystem. A brochure, available at the trailhead, explains the various stages in the transition between wetland and floodplain spruce forest, visible as you progress around the loop. This fen environment is prime habitat for many species of birds. The work of beavers can be seen where the trail parallels the creek, and elk are here during winter. This trail is also a popular shortcut for joggers and cyclists heading out from town to Vermilion Lakes.

Tunnel Mountain

Length: 2.3 kilometers/1.4 miles (30-60 minutes) one-way
Elevation gain: 300 meters/990 feet
Rating: easy/moderate
Trailhead: St. Julien Road, 350 meters (0.2 mile) south of Wolf Street

Accessible from town, this short hike is an easy climb to one of the park's lower peaks. It ascends the western flank of Tunnel Mountain through a forest of lodgepole pine, switchbacking past some viewpoints before reaching a ridge just below the summit. Here the trail turns northward, climbing through a forest of Douglas fir to the summit (which is partially treed, preventing 360-degree views).

Bow River/Hoodoos

Length: 4.8 kilometers/3 miles (60-90 minutes) one-way
Elevation gain: minimal
Rating: easy
Trailhead: Bow River Viewpoint, Tunnel Mountain Drive

From a viewpoint famous for its Fairmont Banff Springs outlook, the trail descends to the Bow River, passing under the sheer east face of Tunnel Mountain. It then follows the river a short distance before climbing into a meadow where deer and elk often graze. From this perspective the north face of Mount Rundle is particularly imposing. As the trail climbs, you'll hear the traffic on Tunnel Mountain Road long before you see it. The trail ends at a viewpoint above the hoodoos, strange-looking limestone-and-gravel columns jutting mysteriously out of the forest. An alternative to returning the same way is to catch the Banff Transit bus from Tunnel Mountain Campground. It leaves every half hour; the trip costs $2.

Sundance Canyon

Length: 4.4 kilometers/2.7 miles (90 minutes) one-way
Elevation gain: 100 meters/330 feet
Rating: easy
Trailhead: Cave and Basin National Historic Site

Sundance Canyon is a rewarding destination across the river from downtown. Unfortunately, the first three kilometers (1.9 miles) are along a paved road that is closed to traffic (but not bikes) and hard on your soles. Occasional glimpses of the Sawback Range are afforded by breaks in the forest. Where the paved road ends, the 2.4-kilometer (1.5-mile) Sundance Loop begins. Sundance Creek was once a larger river whose upper drainage basin was diverted by glacial action. Its powerful waters have eroded into the soft bedrock, forming a spectacular overhanging canyon whose bed is strewn with large boulders that have tumbled in.

Spray River

Length: 12 kilometers/7.4 miles (4 hours) round-trip
Elevation gain: 70 meters/230 feet
Rating: easy/moderate
Trailhead: From the Bow Falls parking lot, cross the Spray River and walk along Golf Course Road to behind the green of the first golf hole on the right-hand side of the road.

This trail follows one of the many fire roads in the park. It is not particularly interesting, but it's accessible from downtown Banff and makes a pleasant way to escape the crowds. From behind the green of the 15th hole, the trail heads uphill into the forest. It follows the Spray River closely—even when not in sight, the river can always be heard. For those so inclined, a river crossing one kilometer (0.6 mile) from the golf course allows for a shorter loop. Continuing south, the trail climbs a bluff for a good view of the Fairmont Banff Springs and Bow Valley. The return journey is straightforward with occasional views, ending at a locked gate behind the Fairmont Banff Springs, a short walk to Bow Falls.

For serious hikers, this trail provides access to the park's rugged and remote southern reaches, but there's another interesting option involving this trail for eager day hikers. It requires arranging a lift to the trailhead of the Goat Creek hike in Spray Valley Provincial Park in Kananaskis Country. From this trailhead, it's 19 kilometers/11.8 miles (six hours) one-way back to Banff down the Spray River watershed on a trail that drops 370 meters (1,210 feet) in elevation. The trail is most popular with mountain bikers and cross-country skiers.

pedestrian bridge across the Bow River

Sunshine Meadows

Rock Isle Lake

Sunshine Meadows, straddling the Continental Divide, is a unique and beautiful region of the Canadian Rockies. It's best known as home to Sunshine Village, a self-contained alpine resort accessible only by gondola from the valley floor. But for a few short months each summer, the area is clear of snow and becomes a wonderland for hiking. Large amounts of precipitation create a lush cover of vegetation—over 300 species of wildflowers alone have been recorded here.

From Sunshine Village, trails radiate across the alpine meadow, which is covered in a colorful carpet of fireweed, glacier lilies, mountain avens, white mountain heather, and forget-me-nots (the meadows are in full bloom mid-July-early August). The most popular destination is **Rock Isle Lake,** an easy 2.5-kilometer (1.6-mile) jaunt from the upper village that crosses the Continental Divide while only gaining 100 meters (330 feet) of elevation. Mount Assiniboine (3,618 meters/11,870 feet), known as the "Matterhorn of the Rockies," is easily distinguished to the southeast. Various viewpoints punctuate the descent to an observation point overlooking the lake. From here, options include a loop around Larix and Grizzly Lakes and a traverse along Standish Ridge. If the weather is cooperating, it won't matter which direction you head (so long as it's along a formed trail); you'll experience the Canadian Rockies in all their glory.

It's possible to walk the six-kilometer (3.7-mile) restricted-access road up to the meadows, but a more practical alternative is to take the Sunshine Meadows Gondola (8am-6pm Fri.-Mon. July-Aug.) or the shuttle bus (8am-6pm Fri.-Mon. July-Aug., Tues.-Thurs. and 8am-6pm daily in Sept.). For information, call 403/705-4000 or visit www.skibanff.com. Advance reservations are recommended for the bus in midsummer. To get to the base of the gondola from Banff, follow the Trans-Canada Highway nine kilometers (5.6 miles) west to Sunshine Village Road, which continues a similar distance along Healy Creek to the Sunshine Village parking lot.

Western Slope of Mount Rundle

Length: 5.4 kilometers/3.3 miles (2 hours) one-way
Elevation gain: 480 meters/1,755 feet
Rating: moderate
Trailhead: From the Bow Falls parking lot, cross the

Spray River and walk along Golf Course Road to behind the green of the first golf hole on the right-hand side of the road.

At 2,950 meters (9,680 feet), Mount Rundle is one of the park's dominant peaks. Climbing to its summit is possible without ropes, but previous scrambling experience is necessary. An alternative is to ascend the mountain's western slope along an easy-to-follow trail that ends just over 1,000 vertical meters (3,280 vertical feet) before the summit. The trail follows the Spray River Trail from Golf Course Road, branching off left after 700 meters (0.4 mile). Climbing steadily, it breaks out of the enclosed forest after 2.5 kilometers (1.6 miles). The trail ends in a gully from which the undefined route to the summit begins.

Stoney Squaw

Length: 2.4-kilometer/1.5-mile loop (1 hour round-trip)
Elevation gain: 180 meters/590 feet
Rating: easy
Trailhead: day lodge, top of Mount Norquay Road, 6 kilometers (3.7 miles) from town

As you look north along Banff Avenue, Stoney Squaw's 1,884-meter (6,180-foot) summit is dwarfed by Cascade Mountain, directly behind it. To get to the trailhead of a route that leads to its easily reached summit, follow Mount Norquay Road to a parking lot in front of the resort's day lodge. Immediately to the right of the entrance, a small sign marks the trail. The narrow, slightly overgrown trail passes through a thick forest of lodgepole pine and spruce before breaking out into the open near the summit. The sweeping panorama includes Vermilion Lakes, the Bow Valley, Banff, Spray River Valley, Mount Rundle, Lake Minnewanka, and the imposing face of Cascade Mountain (2,998 meters/9,840 feet). The return trail follows the northwest slope of Stoney Squaw to an old ski run at the opposite end of the parking lot.

Cascade Amphitheatre

Length: 6.6 kilometers/4.1 miles (2-3 hours) one-way
Elevation gain: 610 meters/2,000 feet
Rating: moderate/difficult
Trailhead: day lodge, top of Mount Norquay Road, 6 kilometers (3.7 miles) from town

This enormous cirque and the subalpine meadows directly behind Cascade Mountain are one of the most rewarding destinations for hiking in the Banff area. The demanding trail begins by passing the day lodge, then skirting the base of several lifts and following an old road to the floor of Forty Mile Valley. Keep right at all trail junctions. One kilometer (0.6 mile) after crossing Forty Mile Creek, the trail begins switchbacking up the western flank of Cascade Mountain through a forest of lodgepole pine. Along the way are breathtaking views of Mount Louis's sheer east face. After the trail levels off, it enters a magnificent U-shaped valley, and the amphitheater begins to define itself. The trail becomes indistinct in the subalpine meadow, which is carpeted in colorful wildflowers during summer. Farther up the valley, vegetation thins out as boulder-strewn talus slopes cover the ground. If you sit still long enough on these rocks, marmots and pikas will slowly appear, emitting shrill whistles before disappearing again.

The most popular route to the summit of 2,998-meter (9,840-foot) Cascade Mountain is along the southern ridge of the amphitheater wall. It is a long scramble up scree slopes and is made more difficult by a false summit; it should be attempted only by experienced scramblers.

C Level Cirque

Length: 4 kilometers/2.5 miles (90 minutes) one-way
Elevation gain: 455 meters/1,500 feet
Rating: moderate
Trailhead: Upper Bankhead Picnic Area, Lake Minnewanka Road, 3.5 kilometers (2.2 miles) beyond the Trans-Canada Highway underpass

From a picnic area on the site of an abandoned mining town, the trail climbs steadily through a forest of lodgepole pine, aspen, and spruce to a pile of tailings and broken-down concrete walls. Soon after, there is a panoramic view of Lake Minnewanka, and then the trail reenters the forest before ending in a small cirque with views down the Bow Valley to Canmore and beyond. The cirque is carved into the eastern face of Cascade Mountain, where snow often lingers until July. When the snow melts, the lush soil is covered in a carpet of colorful wildflowers.

Aylmer Lookout

Length: 12 kilometers/7.5 miles (4 hours) one-way
Elevation gain: 810 meters/2,660 feet
Rating: moderate/difficult
Trailhead: Lake Minnewanka, Lake Minnewanka Road, 5.5 kilometers (3.4 miles) beyond the Trans-Canada Highway underpass

The first eight kilometers (five miles) of this trail follow the northern shore of Lake Minnewanka from the day-use area to a junction. The right fork leads to a campground, while the left climbs steeply to the site of an old fire tower on top of an exposed ridge. The deep-blue waters of Lake Minnewanka are visible, backed by the imposing peaks of Mount Girouard (2,995 meters/9,830 feet) and Mount Inglismaldie (2,964 meters/9,725 feet). Bighorn sheep often graze in this area. From here a trail forks left and continues climbing to the alpine tundra of Aylmer Pass. (Access along this trail is often restricted in summer due to bear activity—check at the visitor center before heading out.)

Cory Pass

Length: 5.8 kilometers/3.6 miles (2.5 hours) one-way
Elevation gain: 920 meters/3,020 feet
Rating: moderate/difficult
Trailhead: Fireside Picnic Area, Banff end of the Bow Valley Parkway

This strenuous hike has a rewarding objective—a magnificent view of dog-toothed Mount Louis. The towering slab of limestone rises more than 500 meters (1,640 feet) from the valley below. Just over one kilometer (0.6 mile) from the trailhead, the trail divides. The left fork climbs steeply across an open slope to an uneven ridge that it follows before ascending yet another steep slope to Cory Pass—a wild, windy, desolate area surrounded by jagged peaks dominated by Mount Louis. An alternative to returning along the same trail is continuing down into Gargoyle Valley, following the base of Mount Edith before ascending to Edith Pass and returning to the junction one kilometer (0.6 mile) from the picnic area. Total distance for this trip is 13 kilometers (eight miles), a long day considering the steep climbs and descents involved.

Bourgeau Lake

Length: 7.6 kilometers/4.7 miles (2.5 hours) one-way
Elevation gain: 730 meters/2,400 feet
Rating: moderate
Trailhead: signposted parking lot, Trans-Canada Highway, 3 kilometers (1.9 miles) west of Sunshine Village Junction

This trail follows Wolverine Creek to a small subalpine lake nestled at the base of an impressive limestone amphitheater. Although the trail is moderately steep, plenty of distractions along the way are worthy of a stop (and rest). Back across the Bow Valley, the Sawback Range is easy to distinguish. As the forest of lodgepole pine turns to spruce, the trail passes under the cliffs of Mount Bourgeau and crosses Wolverine Creek (below a spot where it tumbles photogenically over exposed bedrock). After strenuous switchbacks, the trail climbs into the cirque containing Bourgeau Lake. As you explore the lake's rocky shore, you'll hear the colonies of noisy pikas, even if you don't see them.

Shadow Lake

Length: 14.3 kilometers/8.9 miles (4 hours) one-way
Elevation gain: 440 meters/1,445 feet
Rating: moderate
Trailhead: Redearth Creek Parking Area, Trans-Canada Highway, 11 kilometers (6.8 miles) west of Sunshine Village Junction

Shadow is one of the many impressive subalpine lakes along the Continental Divide and, for those staying at **Shadow Lake Lodge** or the backcountry campground, a popular base for day trips. The trail follows an abandoned fire road for 11 kilometers (6.8 miles) before forking right and climbing into the forest. The campground is two kilometers (1.2 miles) beyond this junction, and just 300 meters (0.2 mile) farther is Shadow Lake Lodge. The lake is nearly two kilometers (1.2 miles) long, and from its eastern shore trails lead to Ball Pass, Gibbon Pass, and Haiduk Lake.

Castle Lookout

Length: 3.7 kilometers/2.3 miles (90 minutes) one-way
Elevation gain: 520 meters/1,700 feet
Rating: moderate
Trailhead: Bow Valley Parkway, 5 kilometers (3.1 miles) northwest of Castle Junction

However you travel through the Bow Valley, you can't help but be impressed by Castle Mountain rising proudly from the forest floor. This trail takes you above the tree line on the mountain's west face to the site of the Mount Eisenhower fire lookout, abandoned in the 1970s and burned in the 1980s. From the Bow Valley Parkway, the trail follows a wide pathway for 1.5 kilometers (0.9 mile) to an abandoned cabin in a forest of lodgepole pine and spruce. It then becomes narrower and steeper, switchbacking through a meadow before climbing through a narrow band of rock and leveling off near the lookout site. Magnificent panoramas of the Bow Valley spread out before you in both directions. Storm Mountain can be seen directly across the valley.

Rockbound Lake

Length: 8.4 kilometers/5.2 miles (2.5-3 hours) one-way
Elevation gain: 760 meters/2,500 feet
Rating: moderate/difficult
Trailhead: Castle Junction, Bow Valley Parkway, 30 kilometers (18.6 miles) west of Banff

This strenuous hike leads to a delightful body of water tucked behind Castle Mountain. For the first five kilometers (3.1 miles), the trail follows an old fire road along the southern flanks of Castle Mountain. Early in the season or after heavy rain, this section can be boggy. Glimpses of surrounding peaks ease the pain of the steady climb as the trail narrows. After eight kilometers (five miles) you'll come to Tower Lake, which the trail skirts to the right before climbing a steep slope. From the top of the ridge, Rockbound Lake comes into view, and the reason for its name immediately becomes apparent. A scramble up

Shadow Lake

any of the nearby slopes will reward you with good views.

MOUNTAIN BIKING

Whether you have your own bike or you rent one from the many bicycle shops in Banff or Lake Louise, cycling in the park is for everyone. The roads to Lake Minnewanka, Mount Norquay, through the golf course, and along the Bow Valley Parkway are all popular routes. Several trails radiating from Banff and ending deep in the backcountry have been designated as bicycle trails. These include Sundance (3.7 km/2.3 mi one-way), Rundle Riverside to Canmore (15 km/9.3 mi one-way), and the Spray River Loop (via Goat Creek; 48 km/30 mi round-trip). Farther afield, other trails are at Redearth Creek, Lake Louise, and in the northeastern reaches of the park near Saskatchewan River Crossing. Before heading into the backcountry, pick up the free *Mountain Biking and Cycling Guide* from the Banff or Lake Louise Visitor Centres. Riders are particularly susceptible to sudden bear encounters. Be alert and make loud noises when passing through heavy vegetation.

Bactrax (225 Bear St., 403/762-8177) and **Banff Adventures Unlimited** (211 Bear St., 403/762-4554) rent front- and full-suspension mountain bikes for $12-16 per hour and $40-70 per day. Rates include a helmet, lock, and biking map.

HORSEBACK RIDING

Jim and Bill Brewster led Banff's first paying guests into the backcountry on horseback more than 100 years ago. Today visitors are still able to enjoy the park on this traditional form of transportation.

Banff Trail Riders (403/762-4551 or 800/661-8352, www.horseback.com) offers a great variety of trips. Their main office is downtown in the **Trail Rider Store** (132 Banff Ave., 403/762-4551), although trips depart from either **Warner Stables** (Sundance Rd., 403/762-2832), behind the recreation grounds off Cave Avenue, or **Spray River Corrals** (Spray Ave., 403/762-2848), below the Fairmont Banff Springs. From Warner Stables, a two-hour trip around the Sundance Loop ($109) departs four times daily. Other longer trips include the three-hour Bow Valley Loop (departs twice daily; $159); Cowboy for a Day, a seven-hour ride up the Spray Valley (departs 9am; $259); and the Cowboy Cookout, a three-hour ride with a suitably Western steak and baked bean dinner along the trail (departs 5pm; $139).

In addition to day trips, Banff Trail Riders runs a variety of overnight rides that include lodgings in backcountry lodges or tent camps. The main accommodation is Sundance Lodge, an easy 18-kilometer (10-mile) ride, which has 10 guest rooms, a large living area, and even hot showers. The shortest option is an overnight trip departing twice weekly through the summer for $649 per person. A three-day trip is $989. Six-day ($1,949) trips split their time between Sundance Lodge and Halfway Lodge, which is farther up the Spray Valley. Rates include horse rental, all meals, and accommodation.

WATER SPORTS
White-Water Rafting

Anyone looking for white-water-rafting action will want to run the **Kicking Horse River,** which flows down the western slopes of the Canadian Rockies into British Columbia. Many operators provide transportation from Banff and Lake Louise. The rafting season

rafting on the Bow River

runs mid-May-mid-September, with river levels at their highest in late June. The Lower Canyon, immediately upstream of Golden, offers the biggest thrills, including a three-kilometer (1.9-mile) stretch of continuous rapids. Upstream of here, the river is tamer but still makes for an exciting trip, while even farther upstream, near the western boundary of Yoho National Park, it's more of a float—a good adventure for the more cautious visitor. The river is run by several companies, most of which offer the option of half-day ($70-90) or full-day ($110-160) trips. The cost varies with inclusions such as transportation from Banff and lunch.

From Lake Louise, **Wild Water Adventures** (403/522-2211 or 888/647-6444, www.wildwater.com) leads half-day trips down the river for $105, including a narrated bus trip to their purpose-built RiverBase put-in point 27 kilometers (17 miles) east of Golden. Departures are from Lake Louise at 8:15am and 1:30pm. The full-day ($139) trip is broken up by a riverside lunch. **Canadian Rockies Rafting** (403/678-6535 or 877/226-7625, www.rafting.ca) operates on the river from Banff, as does the similarly Banff-based **Hydra River Guides** (403/762-4554 or 800/644-8888, www.raftbanff.com).

Rocky Mountain Raft Tours (403/762-3632, www.banffrafttours.com) offers a one-hour (adult $55, child $25) float trip down the **Bow River,** beginning just below Bow Falls and ending along the golf course loop road. The three-hour Bow River Safari continues downriver to the park boundary (adult $95, child $45). No rapids are involved, so you'll stay dry.

Canoeing

On a quiet stretch of the Bow River at the north end of Wolf Street, **Banff Canoe Club** (403/762-5005, www.banffcanoeclub.com, 10am-6pm daily May-mid-June, 9am-9pm daily mid-June-Sept., $40 one hour, $20 each additional hour) rents canoes and paddleboards. From here you can paddle upstream,

or along Echo Creek to First Vermilion Lake. It's an extremely peaceful way to leave the bustle of Banff behind, especially the Forty Mile Creek option, where beavers are often spotted at dusk.

Fishing and Boating

The finest fishing in the park is in Lake Minnewanka, where lake trout as large as 15 kilograms (33 pounds) have been caught. One way to ensure a good catch is through **Banff Lake Cruise** (403/762-3473), which offers fishing trips in a heated cabin cruiser; trolling and downrigging are preferred methods of fishing the lake. A half-day's fishing (3.5 hours) is $455 for one or two persons. The company also rents small aluminum fishing boats with outboard motors for $65 for the first hour, then $35 for every extra hour.

Before fishing anywhere in the park, you need a national park fishing license ($10 per day, $35 per year), available from the Banff and Lake Louise Visitor Centres, Home Hardware in Banff, and sport shops throughout the park.

GOLFING

One of the world's most scenic golf courses, the **Banff Springs Golf Course** spreads out along the Bow River between Mount Rundle and Tunnel Mountain. The first course was laid out here in 1911, but in 1928 Stanley Thompson was brought in by the CPR to build what was at the time North America's most expensive course. In 1989, the Tunnel Nine opened (along with a new clubhouse), creating today's 27-hole course.

The course is typical Thompson, taking advantage of natural contours and featuring elevated tees, wide fairways, treacherous fescue grass rough, and holes aligned to distant mountains. From the back markers it is 7,087 yards and plays to a par of 71. The course is not only breathtakingly beautiful, but it's also challenging for every level of golfer. Pick up a copy of the book *The World's Greatest Golf Holes,* and you'll see a picture of the

TOURS

Brewster (403/762-6700 or 866/606-6700, www.brewster.ca) is the dominant tour company in the area. The 4.5-hour Explore Banff bus tour takes in downtown Banff, Tunnel Mountain Drive, the hoodoos, the Cave and Basin, and Banff Gondola (gondola fare included). This tour runs in summer only and departs from the bus depot at 8:30am daily; call for hotel pickup times. Adult fare is $110, children half price. Brewster also runs several other tours. A six-hour tour to Lake Louise departs select Banff hotels daily; $135. In winter this tour departs Tuesday and Friday mornings, runs five hours, and includes Banff sights; $95. During summer, the company also offers tours from Banff to Lake Minnewanka ($118; includes boat cruise) and the Columbia Icefield ($215).

Discover Banff Tours (Sundance Mall, 215 Banff Ave., 403/760-5007 or 877/565-9372, www.banfftours.com) is a smaller company, with smaller buses and more personalized service. Its tour routes are similar to Brewster's: A three-hour Discover Banff tour visits Lake Minnewanka, the Cave and Basin, the Fairmont Banff Springs, and the hoodoos for adult $65, child $35; and a two-hour Evening Wildlife Safari is adult $49, child $28. This company offers a good selection of other tours throughout the year, including a wintertime ice walk in frozen Johnston Canyon (adult $72, child $46).

WINTER RECREATION

From November to May, the entire park transforms itself into a winter playground covered in a blanket of snow. Of Alberta's six world-class winter resorts, three are in Banff National Park. Ski Norquay is a small but steep hill overlooking the town of Banff; Sunshine Village perches high in the mountains on the Continental Divide, catching more than its share of fluffy white powder; and Lake Louise, Canada's second-largest winter resort, spreads over four distinct mountain faces. Apart from an abundance

Banff Springs Golf Course

fourth hole on the Rundle 9. It's a par three, over Devil's Cauldron 70 meters (230 feet) below, to a small green backed by the sheer face of Mount Rundle rising vertically more than 1,000 meters (3,280 feet) above the putting surface. Another unique feature of the course is the abundance of wildlife: There's always the chance of seeing elk feeding on the fairways, or coyotes, deer, or bears scurrying across.

Greens fees (including cart and driving range privileges) are $240, discounted to $165 in May and late September-early October. The Tunnel 9 offers the same spectacular challenges as Thompson's original layout but lacks the history; nine holes cost $80. Free shuttle buses run from the Fairmont Banff Springs to the clubhouse. There you'll find club rentals ($55-75), putting greens, a driving range, a pro shop, two chipping greens, and a restaurant with a stunning wraparound deck. Booking tee times well in advance is essential; call 403/762-2211.

of snow, the resorts have something else in common—spectacular views, which alone are worth the price of a lift ticket. Although the resorts operate independently, the **Ski Hub** (119 Banff Ave., 403/762-4754, www.skibig3.com, 7am-10pm daily) represents all three and is the place to get information on multi-day ticketing and transportation.

Other winter activities in the park include cross-country skiing, ice-skating, snowshoeing, dogsledding, and just relaxing. Crowds are nonexistent, and hotels reduce rates by up to 70 percent (except Christmas holidays)—reason enough to venture into the mountains. Lift-and-lodging packages begin at $110 per person.

Ski Norquay

Norquay (403/762-4421, www.banffnorquay.com) has two distinct faces—literally and figuratively. There are some great cruising runs and a well-respected ski school, but also the experts-only North American Chair (the one you can see from town), which opens up the famous double-black-diamond Lone Pine run. A magnificent post-and-beam day lodge nestled below the main runs is flanked on one side by a wide deck that catches the afternoon sun, while holding a cafeteria, restaurant, and bar inside. Lift tickets are adult $80, youth and senior $66, child $36; lift, lesson, and rental packages cost about the same. One run is lit for night skiing and boarding on Friday and Saturday evenings January-March; adult $30, senior $25, child $20. A shuttle bus makes pickups from Banff hotels for the short six-kilometer (3.7-mile) ride up to the resort. The season at Norquay usually runs early December-early April.

Sunshine Village

Sunshine Village (403/762-6500 or 877/542-2633, www.skibanff.com) has lots going for it—more than six meters (20 feet) of snow annually (no need for snowmaking up here), wide-open bowls, a season stretching for nearly 200 days (late Nov.-late May), skiing and boarding in two provinces, North

The Brewster Boys

Few guides in Banff were as well known as Jim and Bill Brewster. In 1892, at ages 10 and 12, respectively, they were hired by the Banff Springs Hotel to take guests to local landmarks. As their reputation as guides grew, they built a thriving business. By 1900, they had their own livery and outfitting company, and soon thereafter they expanded operations to Lake Louise. Their other early business interests included a trading post, the original Mt. Royal Hotel, the first ski lodge in the Sunshine Meadows, and the hotel at the Columbia Icefield.

Today, a legacy of the boys' savvy, Brewster, a transportation and tour company, has grown to become an integral part of many visitors' stays (although it is no longer owned by the Brewster family). The company operates some of the world's most advanced sightseeing vehicles, including a fleet of Ice Explorers on the Columbia Icefield.

America's only heated chairlift, and the only slopeside accommodations in the park. For experts only, one of Canada's most infamous runs, Delirium Dive, drops off the northeast-facing slope of Lookout Mountain; to ski or board this up-to-50-degree run, you must be equipped with a transceiver, shovel, probe, and partner, but you'll have bragging rights that night at the bar (especially if you've descended the Bre-X line). Aside from Delirium Dive, the area is best known for its excellent beginner and intermediate terrain, which covers 60 percent of the mountain. The total vertical rise is 1,070 meters (3,510 feet), and the longest run (down to the lower parking lot) is eight kilometers (five miles). Day passes are adult $100, senior $85, youth $76, child $44, and those younger than six ride free. Two days of lift access and one night's lodging at slopeside Sunshine Inn cost $425 per person in high season—an excellent deal. The inn has a restaurant, lounge, game room, and large outdoor hot tub. Transportation from Banff, Canmore, or Lake Louise to the resort

Ski Banff!

Banff National Park is busiest during summer, but for many visitors from outside North America—especially Europeans and Australians—it is the winter season that they know Banff for. Regardless of its repute, and although winter (Dec.-Apr.) is considered low season, the park remains busy as powder enthusiasts from around the world gather for world-class skiing and boarding. It hasn't always been this way. As recently as the 1960s, many lodgings—including the famous Fairmont Banff Springs—were open only for the summer season.

With winter tourism nonexistent, the first skiers were Banff locals, who would climb the surrounding peaks under their own steam. Due mostly to its handy location close to town, a popular spot was **Mount Norquay,** which was skied as early as the 1920s. In 1948, Canada's first chairlift was installed on the mountain's eastern slopes. In the ensuing years, newer and faster lifts have created a convenient getaway that fulfills the needs of locals and visitors alike, who can buzz up for an afternoon of skiing or boarding on slopes that suit all levels of proficiency.

The first people to ski the **Sunshine Meadows** were two local men, Cliff White and Cyril Paris, who became lost in the spring of 1929 and returned to Banff with stories of deep snow and ideal slopes for skiing. In the following years, a primitive cabin was used as a base for overnight ski trips in the area. In 1938 the Canadian National Ski Championships were held here, and in 1942 a portable lift was constructed. The White family was synonymous with the Sunshine area for many years, running the lodge and ski area while Brewster buses negotiated the steep, narrow road that led to the meadows. In 1980, a gondola was installed to whisk skiers and snowboarders six kilometers (3.7 miles) from the valley floor to the alpine village.

The best known of Banff's three resorts is **Lake Louise,** an hour's drive north of town but still within park boundaries. This part of the park also attracted early interest from local skiers, beginning in 1930 when Cliff White and Cyril Paris built a small ski chalet in the Skoki Valley (now operating as Skoki Lodge). The remoteness of this hut turned out to be impractical, so another was built, closer to the road. In 1954, a crude lift was constructed up Larch Mountain from the chalet. The lift had only just begun operation when a young Englishman, Norman Watson (known as the "Barmy Baronet"), who had inherited a fortune, saw the potential for a world-class alpine resort and made the completion of his dream a lifelong obsession. Over the years more lifts were constructed, and two runs—Olympic Men's Downhill and Olympic Ladies' Downhill—were cut in anticipation of a successful bid for the 1968 Winter Olympics (the bid failed).

is $20 round-trip; check the website or inquire at local hotels for the timetable.

Rentals and Sales

Each resort has ski and snowboard rental and sales facilities, but getting your gear down in town is often easier. **Abominable Ski & Sportswear** (229 Banff Ave., 403/762-2905) and **Monod Sports** (129 Banff Ave., 403/762-4571) have been synonymous with Banff and the ski industry for decades, and while the **Rude Boys Snowboard Shop** (downstairs in the Sundance Mall, 215 Banff Ave., 403/762-8211) has only been around since the 1980s, it is *the* snowboarder hangout. Other shops with sales and rentals include **Chateau Mountain Sports** (Fairmont Banff Springs,

405 Spray Ave., 403/762-2500), **Ski Hub** (119 Banff Ave., 403/762-4754), **Soul Ski and Bike** (203 Bear St., 403/760-1650), and **Snow Tips** (225 Bear St., 403/762-8177). Basic packages—skis, poles, and boots—are $40-50 per day, while high-performance packages range $55-70. Snowboards and boots rent for $40-60 per day.

Cross-Country Skiing

No better way of experiencing the park's winter delights exists than gliding through the landscape on cross-country skis. Many summer hiking trails are groomed for winter travel. The most popular areas near town are Johnson Lake, Golf Course Road, Spray River, Sundance Canyon, and upstream from the canoe docks. The booklet *Cross-country Skiing—Nordic Trails in Banff National Park* is available from the Banff Visitor Centre. Weather forecasts (403/762-2088) are posted at both visitors centers.

Rental packages are available from **Snow Tips** (225 Bear St., 403/762-8177). Expect to pay $25-35 per day. **White Mountain Adventures** (403/678-4099 or 800/408-0005) offers lessons for $70 per person.

Ice-Skating

Skating rinks are located on the **high school grounds** across from Cascade Plaza and on the golf course side of the **Fairmont Banff Springs.** The former rink is lit after dark, and a raging fire is built beside it—the perfect place to enjoy a hot chocolate. Early in the season (check conditions first), skating is often possible on **Vermilion Lakes** and **Johnson Lake.** Rent skates from **Snow Tips** (225 Bear St., 403/762-8177) or **Chateau Mountain Sports** (Fairmont Banff Springs, 405 Spray Ave., 403/762-2500) for $8 per hour.

Sleigh Rides

Banff Trail Riders offers sleigh rides ($52 per person) on the frozen Bow River throughout winter. For reservations, call 403/762-4551 or stop by the Trail Rider Store (132 Banff Ave.).

Ice Walks

Between December and late March, Johnston Canyon, a 20-minute drive from Banff along the Bow Valley Parkway, is a wonderland of frozen waterfalls. Two local companies, **Discover Banff Tours** (403/760-5007 or 877/565-9372) and **White Mountain Adventures** (403/678-4099 or 800/408-0005), offer ice walks through the canyon. Both tours reach as far as the Upper Falls and provide guests with ice cleats for their shoes and hot drinks to take the chill off this outdoor activity. Transportation from Banff is included in the rates of $70-80 per person.

Other Winter Activities

Beyond the skating rink below the Fairmont Banff Springs is an unofficial **toboggan** run; ask at your hotel for sleds or rent them from the sports store at the Fairmont Banff Springs ($8 per hour).

Anyone interested in **ice climbing** must register at the national park desk in the Banff Visitor Centre or call 403/762-1550. The world-famous (if you're an ice climber) Terminator is just outside the park boundary.

INDOOR RECREATION

Swimming and Fitness Facilities

Many of Banff's bigger hotels have fitness rooms, and some have indoor pools. A popular place to swim and work out is in the **Sally Borden Fitness & Recreation Facility** (Banff Centre, St. Julien Rd., 403/762-6450, 6am-11pm daily), which holds a wide range of fitness facilities, a climbing gym, squash courts, a 25-meter-long heated pool, a wading pool, and a hot tub. General admission is $11, or pay $5 to swim only most evenings. Go to www.banffcentre.ca for a schedule.

Willow Stream Spa

The luxurious **Willow Stream Spa** in the Fairmont Banff Springs (405 Spray Ave., 403/762-2211, 6am-10pm daily) is the place to pamper yourself. It sprawls over two levels and 3,000 square meters (0.7 acre) of a private corner of the hotel. The epicenter of the facility is a circular mineral pool capped by a high glass-topped ceiling and ringed by floor-to-ceiling windows on one side and on the other by hot tubs fed by cascading waterfalls of varying temperatures. Other features include outdoor saltwater hot tubs, private solariums, steam rooms, luxurious bathrooms, and separate male and female lounges complete with fireplaces and complimentary drinks and snacks. Numerous other services are offered, including facials, body wraps, massage therapy, salon services, and hydrotherapy. Entry to Willow Stream is included in some package rates for guests at the hotel. Admission is $80 per day, which includes the use of a locker and spa attire, with almost 100 services available at additional cost (most of these include general admission, so, for example, you can spend the day at Willow Stream and receive a one-hour massage for $245).

Other Indoor Recreation

Fairmont Banff Springs Bowling & Entertainment Centre (405 Spray Ave., 403/762-2211, 4pm-10pm Sun.-Thurs., noon-11pm Fri.-Sat.) has a four-lane, five-pin bowling center; games are $7.25 per person. Also here is a golf simulator and pool table. The **Lux Cinema Centre** (229 Bear St., 403/762-8595) screens new releases for $14 ($10 on Tuesday).

Banff's only waterslide is in the **Douglas Fir Resort** (Tunnel Mountain Dr., 403/762-5591, 4pm-10pm Mon.-Fri., 9am-10pm Sat.-Sun.). The two slides are indoors, and the admission price of $20 (free for kids aged five or under) includes use of a hot tub and exercise room.

NIGHTLIFE

Like resort towns around the world, Banff has a deserved reputation as a party town, especially among seasonal workers, the après-ski crowd, and young Calgarians. Crowds seem to spread out, with no particular bar being more popular than another or being a place where you can mingle with fellow travelers. Given the location and vacation vibe, drink prices are as high as you may expect, with attitude thrown in for free.

Banff is a nonsmoking town. Also note that the Royal Canadian Mounted Police (RCMP) patrol Banff all night, promptly arresting anyone who even looks like trouble, including anyone drunk or drinking on the streets.

Bars and Lounges

One of Banff's most distinctive bars is **Park Distillery** (219 Banff Ave., 403/762-5114, 11am-2am daily), a beautifully designed two-story space that reflects the history of the park through the use of wood and stone and features such as a huge canvas tent that rolls over one section of the upstairs seating area. Beer choices represent many local breweries, while spirits such as gin are distilled in-house using glacial water and local Alberta grains.

Wild Bill's (upstairs at 201 Banff Ave., 403/762-0333, 11am-2am daily) is named for Banff guide Bill Peyto and is truly legendary. This frontier-style locale attracts the biggest and best bands of any Banff venue, with bookings that vary from local faves to washed-up rockers such as Nazareth. As a general rule, expect alternative music or underground country early in the week and better-known rock or pop Thursday-Sunday. Across the road, the **Maple Leaf** (137 Banff Ave., 403/760-7680, 10am-10pm daily) has a stylish space at street level set aside as a bar. A few doors down from the Maple Leaf, at the **Magpie & Stump** (203 Caribou St., 403/762-4067, 11:30am-2am daily), a casual, family-friendly vibe fills a room stuffed with eclectic furnishings. Choose from margaritas and Mexican beer, washed down with free peanuts or well-priced Mexican dishes. If the weather is warm, make your way upstairs to the fashionable rooftop patio.

The **Elk & Oarsman** (119 Banff Ave., 403/762-4616, 11am-1am daily) serves up beer and more in a clean, casual atmosphere that is as friendly as it gets in Banff. Across the road from Wild Bill's is the **Rose and Crown** (202 Banff Ave., 403/762-2121, 11am-2am daily), serving British beers and hearty pub fare. It also features a rooftop patio and rock-and-roll bands a few nights a week, but there's not much room for dancing. Also down the main drag is **Tommy's** (120 Banff Ave., 403/762-8888, 11am-2am daily), a perennial favorite for young seasonal workers and those who once were and now consider themselves locals.

Around the corner from Banff Avenue, the **St. James Gate Olde Irish Pub** (207 Wolf St., 403/762-9355, 11am-1am daily) is a large Irish-style bar with a reputation for excellent British-style meals and occasional appearances by Celtic bands.

One block back from Banff Avenue are two excellent choices for a quiet drink. Relative to other town drinking spots, prices at the **Bear**

Street Tavern (Bison Courtyard, 211 Bear St., 403/762-2021, 11:30am-10pm daily) are excellent. Add funky surroundings and a sunny courtyard to the mix, and you have an excellent choice for a drink and meal. Saltlik (221 Bear St., 403/762-2467, 11am-midnight Sun.-Wed., 11am-2am Thurs.-Sat.) is best known as an upscale (and upstairs) steakhouse. At street level, the stylish lounge opens to a streetside patio.

Around the corner from these two choices is Melissa's (218 Lynx St., 403/762-5776, 11am-1am daily), which is a longtime favorite drinking hole for locals. It has a small outdoor patio, a long evening happy hour, a pool table, and multiple TVs.

Hotel Hangouts

Many Banff hotels have lounges open to guests and nonguests alike. They are generally quieter than the bars in town and often offer abbreviated menus from adjacent restaurants. For old-world atmosphere, nothing in town comes close to matching the Grapes, in the Fairmont Banff Springs (405 Spray Ave., 403/762-2211, 5pm-9:30pm daily). Another place to enjoy a drink in the park's landmark hotel is the mezzanine-level Rundle Lounge (Fairmont Banff Springs, 403/762-2211, 11am-1am daily), an open space with

views extending down the Bow Valley, or the adjacent outdoor patio. Below the hotel is the Waldhaus Pub (Fairmont Banff Springs, 403/762-2211, 11am-11pm daily in summer). It has the best deck in town for sweeping mountain views, but it's mainly the haunt of locals coming off the golf course or savvy visitors (such as those who've read this book).

Downtown, the Mount Royal Hotel has a small lounge off the lobby, affiliated with the hotel's restaurant, Tony Roma's (corner of Banff Ave. and Caribou St., 403/762-3331, noon-10pm daily). Also in the hotel, but accessed from a different entrance farther up Banff Avenue, is the modern Toque Canadian Pub (138 Banff Ave., 403/760-8543, 4pm-10pm Mon.-Wed., 11:30am-10pm Thurs., 11:30am-11pm Fri.-Sat., 11:30am-10pm Sun.), which, as the name suggests, is Canadian in every respect—from the river rock fireplace to the toque-wearing waitstaff and the wide selection of local beers.

At the opposite end of the style scale is the lounge in the Voyager Inn (555 Banff Ave., 403/762-3301, noon-2am daily), which is worth listing for the fact that it has the cheapest beer in town and drink specials every night (and a liquor store with cheaper prices than downtown).

outdoor dining at the Rundle Lounge

Canada Day parade on Banff Avenue

skim across an almost-frozen pit of water. While winter enthusiasts are at higher elevations, swooshing down the slopes of some of North America's latest-closing resorts, early May sees the Banff Springs Golf Course open for the season.

During the second week of June, the **Banff World Media Festival** (403/678-1216, www. banffmediafestival.com) attracts the world's best television directors, producers, writers, and even actors for meetings, workshops, and awards, with many select screenings open to the public. For many delegates, pitching their ideas is what draws them to this event. The main venue is the Fairmont Banff Springs.

Summer

Summer is a time of hiking and camping, so festivals are few and far between. The main event is the **Banff Summer Arts Festival** (403/762-6301 or 800/413-8368, www.banff-centre.ca), a three-week (mid-July-early Aug.) extravaganza presented by professional artists studying at the Banff Centre. They perform dance, drama, opera, and jazz for the public at locations around town. Look for details in the *Crag and Canyon* newspaper.

On July 1, Banff kicks off **Canada Day** with a pancake breakfast on Lynx Street. Then there's a full day of fun and frivolity including Sidewalk Art in front of the Whyte Museum on Bear Street and musical performances in Central Park. An impressive parade along Banff Avenue begins at 5pm, followed by a concert in Central Park and fireworks.

Each summer the national park staff presents an extensive **Park Interpretive Program** at locations in town and throughout the park, including downstairs in the visitors center at 8:30pm daily. All programs are free and include guided hikes, nature tours, slide shows, campfire talks, and lectures. For details, drop by the Banff Visitor Centre (403/762-1550) or look for postings on campground bulletin boards.

Fall

Fall is the park's quietest season, but it's

Nightclubs

Banff has two nightclubs: **Sasquatch** (120 Banff Ave., 403/762-4002, 9pm-2am Fri.-Wed., cover charge varies) is a modern, intimate space but gets very loud, especially when a celebrity DJ is in town spinning discs. The other option is **Hoo Doos** (at 137 Banff Ave., but enter from Caribou St., 403/760-8636, 9pm-2am daily), a much larger space but with similar citylike surroundings.

FESTIVALS AND EVENTS
Spring

Most of the major spring events take place at local winter resorts, including a variety of snowboard competitions that make for great spectator viewing. At Lake Louise, a half-pipe and jump are constructed right in front of the day lodge for this specific purpose. One long-running spring event is the **Slush Cup,** which takes place at Sunshine Village (www. skibanff.com) in late May. Events include kamikaze skiers and boarders who attempt to busiest in terms of festivals and events. First of the fall events, on the last Saturday in September, **Melissa's Road Race** (www.melissasroadrace.ca) attracts more than 2,000 runners (the race sells out months in advance) in 10- and 22-kilometer (6- and 14-mile) races.

One of the year's biggest events is the **Banff Mountain Film Festival,** held on the first weekend of November. Mountain-adventure filmmakers from around the world submit films to be judged by a select committee. Films are then shown throughout the weekend to an enthusiastic crowd of thousands. Exhibits and seminars are also presented, and top climbers and mountaineers from around the world are invited as guest speakers.

Tickets to the Banff Mountain Film Festival go on sale one year in advance and sell out quickly. Tickets for daytime shows start at $50 (for up to 10 films). Night shows are priced from $45, and all-weekend passes cost around $200 (weekend passes with two nights' accommodations and breakfasts start at a reasonable $380). Films are shown in the two theaters of the Banff Centre (St. Julien Rd.). For more information, contact the festival office (403/762-6675); for tickets, contact the Banff Centre box office (403/762-6301 or 800/413-8368, www.banffcentre.ca). If you miss the actual festival, it hits the road on the Best of the Festival World Tour. Look for it in your town, or check out www.banffcentre.ca for venues and dates.

Starting in the days leading up to the film festival, then running in conjunction with it, is the **Banff Mountain Book Festival,** which showcases publishers, writers, and photographers whose work revolves around the world's great mountain ranges. Tickets can be bought to individual events ($16-30), or there's a Book Festival Pass ($130) and a pass combining both festivals ($320).

Winter

By mid-December, lifts at all local winter resorts are open. **Santa Claus** makes an appearance on Banff Avenue at noon on the last Saturday in November; if you miss him there,

he usually goes skiing at each of the local resorts on Christmas Day. Events at the resorts continue throughout the long winter season, among them **World Cup Downhill** skiing at Lake Louise in late November. **Snow Days** is a monthlong celebration starting mid-January that features ice sculpting on the frozen lake in front of the Chateau Lake Louise, the Lake Louise Loppet cross-country skiing race, live theater, a photography competition, and a spelling bee.

SHOPPING

Banff Avenue is renowned for its shops, but in reality has evolved into a continuous stretch of tacky tourist shops and international chains. An exception is **About Canada** (105 Banff Ave., 403/760-2996, 9am-10pm daily in summer, 10am-8pm daily the rest of the year), which does an excellent job of sourcing Canadian-made gifts.

Canadiana and Clothing

Few companies in the world were as responsible for the development of a country as was the **Hudson's Bay Company** (HBC) in Canada. Founded in 1670, the HBC established trading posts throughout western Canada, many of which attracted settlers, forming the nucleus for towns and cities that survive today, including Alberta's capital, Edmonton. HBC stores continue their traditional role of providing a wide range of goods, in towns big and small across the country. In Banff, the HBC store is at 125 Banff Avenue (403/762-5525, 9:30am-9pm Mon.-Sat., 9:30am-7pm Sun.).

Another Canadian store, this one famous for its fleeces, sweaters, and leather goods and for its role as supplier to the Canadian Olympic teams, is **Roots** (227 Banff Ave., 403/762-9434, 10am-9pm Mon.-Sat., 10am-8pm Sun.). For belts, buckles, and boots, check out the **Trail Rider Store** (132 Banff Ave., 403/762-4551, 9am-5pm daily). Also check out **Rude Boys Snowboard Shop** (205 Caribou St., 403/762-8211, 10am-9pm daily), but don't expect to find anything suitable for your grandparents.

Camping and Outdoor Gear

Inexpensive camping equipment and supplies can be found in **Home Hardware** (223 Bear St., 403/762-2080, 8:30am-6pm Mon.-Sat.). More specialized needs are catered to at **Monod Sports** (129 Banff Ave., 403/762-4571, 10am-9pm daily). Locally owned **Abominable Sports** (229 Banff Ave., 403/762-2905, 9am-9pm daily, until 10pm daily in summer) has a good selection of hiking boots and outdoor clothing.

Gifts and Galleries

Banff's numerous galleries display the work of mostly Canadian artists. **Canada House Gallery** (201 Bear St., 403/762-3757, 9:30am-6pm Sun.-Thurs., 9:30am-7pm Fri.-Sat.) features a wide selection of Canadian landscape and wildlife works and First Nations art. Up in the Fairmont Banff Springs, the **Quest Gallery** (405 Spray Ave., 403/762-4422, noon-5pm daily) offers a diverse range of affordable Canadian paintings and crafts, as well as more exotic pieces such as mammoth tusks from prehistoric times and Inuit carvings from Nunavut. Browse through First Nations arts and crafts at the **Indian Trading Post** (1 Birch Ave., 403/762-2456, 9am-9pm daily in summer, 10am-7pm daily the rest of the year), across the Bow River from downtown.

FOOD

Whether you're in search of an inexpensive snack for the family or silver service, you can find it in the town of Banff, which has more than 80 restaurants (more per capita than any other town or city across Canada). The quality of food varies greatly. Some restaurants revolve solely around the tourist trade, while others have reputations that attract diners from Calgary who have been known to stay overnight just to eat at their favorite haunt. While the quality of food is most people's number-one priority when dining out, the level of service (or lack of it) also comes into play in Banff, especially if you are paying big bucks for a fine-dining meal. Getting it all right—good food, top-notch service, and a

memorable ambience—in a tourism-oriented town is rare. Which leads to the restaurants I've recommended below, the best of a very varied bunch.

Groceries

Banff has two major grocery stores. In addition to a wide selection of basic groceries, **Nesters Market** (122 Bear St., 403/762-3663, 8am-11pm daily in summer, shorter hours the rest of the year) has a good deli with pre-made salads and sandwiches, as well as meats, cheeses, and rotisserie chickens. At the other end of downtown is **IGA** (318 Marten St., 403/762-5329, 8am-11pm daily). In summer, try to avoid both places between 5pm and 7pm as they get very crowded.

Cafés and Coffee Shops

My favorite Banff coffee joint is **Whitebark** (Banff Aspen Lodge, 401 Banff Ave., 403/760-7298, 6:30am-7pm daily), a few blocks north of the main shopping strip but well worth searching out for the best coffee in town, including one of the only places in Banff to pour Americanos. Seating is limited to a few window-facing stools, but the outside patio is a great place to soak up summer sun.

Banff's lone bakery is **Wild Flour** (Bison Courtyard, 211 Bear St., 403/760-5074, 7am-4pm Mon.-Thurs., 7am-5pm Fri.-Sun., $7-10), and it's a good one (albeit a little pricey). Organic ingredients are used whenever possible, and everything is freshly baked daily. The result is an array of healthy breads, gluten-free choices, mouthwatering cakes and pastries, and delicious meat pies. Eat inside or out in the courtyard.

Modern **Evelyn's Coffee World** (Sundance Mall, 215 Banff Ave., 403/762-0352, 7am-9pm daily, sandwiches $8) has a very central location pouring good coffee sourced from around the world and serving huge sandwiches. The few outside tables—on the busiest stretch of the busiest street in town—are perfect for people-watching. The **Banff National Perk** (220 Bear St., 403/762-8642, 7am-5pm daily, cakes from

$5) is another local place serving great coffee and delicious pastries, muffins, and cakes baked daily on the premises. **Jump Start** (206 Buffalo St., 403/762-0332, 7am-6pm daily, $5.50-7), opposite Central Park, has inexpensive coffee as well as homemade savories and sandwiches.

Cheap Eats

A good place to begin looking for cheap eats is the food court in the lower level of Cascade Plaza (317 Banff Ave.). Here you'll find a juice bar, a place selling pizza by the slice, and **Banff Edo,** which sells simple Japanese dishes for around $10, including a drink. Also downtown is **Barpa Bill's** (223 Bear St., 403/762-0377, 11am-midnight daily, $10-15), a hole-in-the-wall eatery with a couple of indoor tables and a menu of inexpensive Greek dishes. It's cash only.

The main reasons for visiting the Banff Centre include attending the many events, exercising at the fitness facility, or wandering through the grounds. Add to this list having a casual meal at **Le Cafe** (Banff Centre, Tunnel Mountain Dr., 403/762-6100, 10am-10pm daily, $8-14), overlooking the swimming pool within the Sally Borden Building. The coffee is roasted locally, sandwiches are made to order, or try a mini-pizza or bowl of steaming soup. In the adjacent Kinnear Centre, **Maclab Bistro** (Banff Centre, Tunnel Mountain Dr., 403/762-6100, 7am-2am daily, $14-18) is a much larger space with tables spilling outside onto a patio. The menu features flatbread pizzas, healthy sandwiches, and gourmet burgers.

Cougar Pete's Restaurant in the Banff Alpine Centre (810 Hidden Ridge Way, off Tunnel Mountain Rd., 403/762-4122, 7am-1pm and 5pm-10pm daily, $11-18) offers free wireless Internet and a great outdoor patio. The menu features all the usual café-style dishes, such as a pile of nachos for $11.

Aardvarks (304 Caribou St., 403/762-5500, noon-4am daily) is a late-night pizza hangout.

Family-Style Dining

Children will love the food and parents will love the prices at **Old Spaghetti Factory** (2nd Fl., Cascade Plaza on Banff Ave., 403/760-2779, 11:30am-10pm daily, $11-25). The large room is casual-rustic, with a few tables spread along a covered balcony. Sort through a maze of combinations and specials (kids get their own color-in menu), and the most you'll pay for a meal is $25, which includes soup or salad, a side of bread, dessert, and coffee.

A town favorite that has faithfully served locals and visitors alike for many years is **Melissa's Missteak** (218 Lynx St., 403/762-5511, 7am-9:30pm daily, $17-34), housed in a log building that dates from 1928. It's the best place in town for classic North American cooked breakfasts in the $14-16 range. Lunch and dinner are old-fashioned, casual affairs. Choose from a wide variety of generously sized burgers, freshly prepared salads, Alberta beef, and even live lobster.

Steak

Alberta beef is mostly raised on ranchland east of Banff National Park and features prominently on menus throughout town. Finely marbled AAA beef is used in most better restaurants and is unequaled in its tender, juicy qualities.

★ **Saltlik** (221 Bear St., 403/762-2467, 11am-midnight daily, $25-48) is the perfect choice for serious carnivores with cash to spare. At one of Banff's most fashionable restaurants, the dining room is big and bold, and the concrete-and-steel split-level interior is complemented by modish wood furnishings. Facing the street, glass doors in the street-level lounge fold back to a terrace for warm-weather dining. The specialty is AAA Alberta beef, finished with grain feeding to enhance the flavor, then flash-seared at 650°C (1,200°F) to seal in the juices, and served with a side platter of seasonal vegetables. Entrées are priced comparable to a city steakhouse, but the cost creeps up as you add side dishes.

Saltlik has a patio that catches the afternoon sun.

Classically Canadian

★ **Park** (219 Banff Ave., 403/762-5114, 11am-midnight daily, $16-31) does a wonderful job of combining classic campfire cooking with modern dining trends—all within a massive space in the heart of downtown that perfectly reflects the food and the history of the park, with a massive stone fireplace and seating choices that include a balcony overlooking Banff Avenue and communal tables beside the open kitchen. Many of the dishes are cooked over a wood-fired grill or on a rotisserie, creating deliciously smoky campfire-like flavors: You could start with rotisserie chicken chowder or corn bread smothered in maple-rum butter, and then choose from mains such as pork-and-beans or AAA T-bone. Craft beers and house-distilled spirits round out this excellent choice.

Sleeping Buffalo Dining Room (Buffalo Mountain Lodge, 700 Tunnel Mountain Dr., 403/762-4484, 7am-10pm daily, $26-46) offers the perfect setting for a moderate splurge. It features a distinctive interior of hand-hewn cedar beams and old-world elegance—complete with stone fireplace and a chandelier made entirely from elk antlers—along with large windows that frame the surrounding forest. The featured cuisine is referred to as Rocky Mountain, reflecting an abundance of Canadian game and seafood combined with native berries and fruits. The least-expensive way to dine on this uniquely Canadian fare is by visiting at lunch and ordering the Charcuterie Board, $32 for two people. Dinner entrées include fare such as caribou that's given a sweet touch with accompanying raspberry jus.

The food at ★ **Storm Mountain Lodge** (Hwy. 93, 403/762-4155, 8am-10:30am, 11:30am-3pm, and 5pm-9pm daily May-mid-Oct., 5pm-9pm Fri.-Sun. early Dec.-Apr., $29-45) is excellent, but it's the ambience you'll remember long after leaving—an intoxicating blend of historic appeal and rustic mountain charm. The chef uses mostly organic produce with seasonally available game and seafood—bison, venison, wild salmon, and the like—to create tasty and interesting dishes well suited to the I-must-be-in-the-Canadian-wilderness surroundings. Storm Mountain Lodge is a 25-minute drive northwest from Banff; take the Trans-Canada Highway toward Lake Louise and head west at the Castle Mountain interchange.

Canadian Contemporary

Occupying the prime position on one of Banff's busiest corners is the **Maple Leaf** (137 Banff Ave., 403/760-7680, 10am-10pm daily, $28-47). Take in the dramatic Canadian-themed decor—exposed river stone, polished log work, a two-story interior rock wall, and a moose head (tucked around the corner from the street-level lounge). Some tables surround a busy area by the bar, so try to talk your way into the upstairs back corner. The cooking uses modern styles with an abundance of Canadian game and produce. The lunch menu has a bison burger, along with lighter salads and gourmet sandwiches. Some of Canada's finest ingredients appear on the dinner menu: Stuffed halibut and the bacon-wrapped bison tenderloin are standouts. Treat yourself to a glass of Canadian ice wine to accompany dessert.

Bison Restaurant and Terrace (Bison Courtyard, Bear St., 403/762-5550, from 5pm daily, $25-38) is an upstairs eatery featuring the very best Canadian ingredients. The interesting decor sees chic-industrial blending with mountain rustic. Tables are inside or out at this upstairs dining room, and almost all have a view of the open kitchen. The food is solidly Canadian, with a menu that takes advantage of wild game, seafood, and Alberta beef.

Juniper Bistro (The Juniper, off Mt. Norquay Rd., 403/763-6219, 7am-11am and 3pm-9pm daily, $17-35) is well worth searching out for both Canadian cuisine and unparalleled views across town to Mount Rundle and the Spray Valley. The stylish interior may be inviting, but in warmer weather you'll want to be outside on the patio, where the panorama is most spectacular. The menu blends traditional tastes with Canadian produce. If your taste runs toward the adventurous, there's duck wings as a starter. For those looking for something a little more local, the AAA ribeye is a good choice. Most breakfasts are under $15, while at lunch, the Caesar salad is one of the best in town.

Southwestern

Banff's original bistro-style restaurant, which opened in the early 1990s, is **Coyote's** (206 Caribou St., 403/762-3963, 7:30am-10pm daily, $16-31). Well-priced meals are prepared in full view of diners, and the menu emphasizes fresh, health-conscious cooking, with just a hint of Southwestern/Mediterranean style. To start, it's hard to go past the sweet potato and corn chowder; then choose from mains such as a flank steak marinated in Cajun spices and topped with a generous dab of corn and tomato salsa.

European

The **Balkan** (120 Banff Ave., 403/762-3454, 11am-10pm daily, $18-37) is run by a local Greek family, but the menu blends their heritage with the cuisines of Italy, China, and Canada. Select from Greek ribs (pork ribs with a lemon sauce), the Greek chow mein (stir-fried vegetables, fried rice, and your choice of meat), or Greek spaghetti. But the most popular dishes are souvlaki and an enormous Greek platter for two.

★ **Ticino** (High Country Inn, 415 Banff Ave., 403/762-3848, 5:30pm-10pm daily, $18.50-36) reflects the heritage of the park's early mountain guides, with solid timber furnishings, lots of peeled and polished log work, and old wooden skis, huge cowbells, and an alpenhorn decorating the walls. It's named for the southern province of Switzerland, where the cuisine has a distinctive Italian influence. The Swiss chef is best known for a creamy wild mushroom soup, unique to the region; his beef and cheese fondues; juicy cuts of Alberta beef; and veal dishes. Save room for one of Ticino's sinfully rich desserts. Also of note is the professional service.

Fondue

Even if you've tried exotic meats, you probably haven't had them in a restaurant like the ★ **Grizzly House** (207 Banff Ave., 403/762-4055, 11:30am-midnight daily, $46-80 per person for four courses), which provides Banff's most unusual dining experience. The decor is, to say the least, eclectic (many say eccentric). Think lots of twisted woods, a motorbike hanging from the ceiling, a melted telephone on the wall. Each table has a phone for across-table conversation, or you can put a call through to your server, the bar, a cab, diners in the private booth, or even those who spend too long in the bathroom. The food is equally unique, and the service is as professional as anywhere in town. The menu hasn't changed in decades, and this doesn't displease anyone. Most dining revolves around traditional Swiss fondues, but with nontraditional dipping meats such as rattlesnake, alligator, shark, ostrich, scallops, elk, and wild boar. Four-course table d'hôte fondue dinners are $46-80 per person, which includes soup or salad, a cheese fondue, a choice of one of six meat and seafood fondue (or hot rock) selections, and finally a fruity chocolate fondue. The Grizzly House is also open at lunch, when you can sample Canadian game at reduced prices; wild game meat loaf is $21, and an Alberta-farmed buffalo burger is $20.

Asian

At the back of the Clock Tower Mall, **Pad Thai** (110 Banff Ave., 403/762-4911, lunch and dinner daily, $12-18) is a real find for those looking for inexpensive Thai cuisine. The namesake pad Thai is $14, curries are all around the same price, and delicious spring rolls are $5. You can eat in or take out.

A couple of doors off Banff Avenue, **Sushi House Banff** (304 Caribou St., 403/762-2971, 11:30am-10pm daily, $16-22) is a tiny space with a dozen stools set around a moving miniature railway that has diners picking sushi and other delicacies from a train as it circles the chef, who is loading the carriages as quickly as they empty.

Fairmont Banff Springs

Whether guests or not, most visitors to Banff drop by to see one of the town's biggest tourist attractions, and a meal here might not be as expensive as you think. The hotel itself has more eateries than most small towns—from a deli serving slices of pizza to the finest of fine dining in the 1888 Chop House.

If you are in the mood for a snack such as chili and bread or sandwiches to go, head to the lobby level and the **Castle Pantry,** which is open 24 hours daily.

Impressive buffets are the main draw at the **Bow Valley Grill,** a pleasantly laid out dining room that seats 275. Each morning from 6:30am, an expansive buffet of hot and cold delicacies, including freshly baked bread and seasonal fruits, is laid out for the masses ($32 per person). Lunch offers a wide-ranging menu featuring everything from salads to seafood. Through the busiest months of summer, a lunch buffet (noon-1:30pm Mon.-Fri., $35) is offered. In summer, evening diners

(6pm-9pm) order from a menu that appeals to all tastes, while the rest of the year dinner is offered as a buffet, with a different theme each night. The weekend brunch (11am-2pm Sat.-Sun., $46) is legendary, with chefs working at numerous stations scattered around the dining area and an enormous spread not equaled for variety anywhere in the mountains. Reservations are required for Sunday brunch (as far in advance as possible) and dinner.

Ensconced in an octagonal room of the Manor Wing, **Castello Ristorante** (6pm-9:30pm Fri.-Wed., $21-36) is a seductive dining room with a modern, upscale ambience. The menu is dominated by Italian favorites, with traditional pastas and specialties such as veal tenderloin. The **Rundle Lounge** (11:30am-1am daily, $16-33) combines an area filled with comfortable sofas with summer outdoor dining and an upstairs piano bar, where most tables offer views down the Bow Valley. **Grapes** (6pm-9pm daily, $18-26) is an intimate yet casual wine bar noted for its fine cheeses and pâtés. More substantial meals such as fondues are also offered.

The hotel's most acclaimed restaurant is **1888 Chop House** (6pm-9:30pm daily, $36-80), which seats just 65 guests. This fine-dining restaurant is a bastion of elegance, apparent once you arrive through a gated entrance. Inside, extravagantly rich wood furnishings, perfectly presented table settings, muted lighting, and professional staff create an atmosphere as far removed from the surrounding wilderness as is imaginable. Reservations are required.

Two restaurants lie within the grounds surrounding the hotel, and both are worthy of consideration. Originally the golf course clubhouse, the **Waldhaus Restaurant** (6pm-9pm daily, $23-34) is nestled in a forested area directly below the hotel. The big room is dominated by dark woods and is warmed by an open fireplace. The menu features German specialties, such as fondues. Below the restaurant is a pub of the same name, with a pub-style dinner menu offered in a casual atmosphere. Wonderful views are the main draw at **Stanley's Smokehouse** (11:30am-6pm daily in summer, $17-24), a seasonal restaurant on the golf course proper that serves casual meals throughout the golf season. A shuttle bus runs every 30 minutes between the main hotel lobby and the clubhouse.

For all Fairmont Banff Springs dining reservations, call 403/762-6860.

ACCOMMODATIONS AND CAMPING

Finding a room in Banff National Park in summer is nearly as hard as trying to justify its price. By late afternoon, just about every room and campsite in the park will be occupied, and basic hotel rooms start at $200. It is also worth noting that prices vary according to demand. If hotels have rooms available, they may sell them off more cheaply at the last minute, but when demand is high, room prices at many hotels can start at $400. Fortunately, many alternatives are available. Rooms in private homes begin at around $100 s, $120 d. HI-Banff Alpine Centre has dormitory-style accommodations for under $60 per person per night. Bungalows or cabins can be rented, which can be cost-effective for families or small groups. Approximately 2,400 campsites in 13 campgrounds accommodate campers. Wherever you decide to stay, it is vital to book well ahead during summer and the Christmas holidays. The park's off-season is October-May, and hotels offer huge rate reductions during this period. Shop around, and you'll find many bargains.

All rates quoted are for a standard room in the high season (June-Sept.).

In and Around the Town of Banff

Banff has a few accommodations right downtown, but most are strung out along Banff Avenue, an easy walk from the shopping and dining precinct. Nearby Tunnel Mountain is also home to a cluster of accommodations.

UNDER $100

The only beds in town less than $100 are in dormitories, and therefore, rates given are per person.

HI-Banff Alpine Centre (801 Hidden Ridge Way, 403/762-4123 or 866/762-4122, www.hihostels.ca) is just off Tunnel Mountain Road, three kilometers (1.9 miles) from downtown. This large, modern hostel sleeps 216 in small two-, four-, and six-bed dormitory rooms as well as four-bed cabins. The large lounge area has a fireplace, and other facilities include a recreation room, public Internet access, a bike and ski/snowboard workshop, large kitchen, self-service café/bar, and laundry. In summer, members of Hostelling International pay $59 per person per night (nonmembers $64) for a dorm bed or from $144 s or d ($160 for nonmembers) for a private room. During July and August, reserve at least a couple of months in advance to be assured of a bed. The hostel is open all day, but check-in isn't until midday. To get there from town, ride the Banff Transit bus ($2), which passes the hostel twice an hour during summer. The rest of the year the only transportation is by cab, about $10 from the bus depot.

A one-time hospital, **Banff Y Mountain Lodge** (102 Spray Ave., 403/762-3560 or 800/813-4138, www.ymountainlodge.com, dorm $46, private $105 s, $120 d) is an excellent, centrally located choice for budget travelers. Facilities include the casual Sundance Bistro (7am-10pm daily), a laundry facility, wireless Internet, and the Great Room—a huge living area where the centerpiece is a massive stone fireplace, with writing desks and shelves stocked with books scattered throughout. Some private rooms have en-suite bathrooms, while family rooms are $135. Rates are reduced outside of summer.

Along the main strip of accommodations and a five-minute walk to downtown is **Samesun Banff** (433 Banff Ave., 403/762-4499 or 877/972-6378, www.samesun.com, dorm $52-60, private $165 s or d). As converted motel rooms, each small dormitory has its own bathroom. Guest amenities include a lounge, wireless Internet, free continental breakfast, and underground (but not heated) parking.

$100-150

Accommodations in this price range are limited. In addition to private rooms at the HI-Banff Alpine Centre, Banff Y Mountain Lodge, and Samesun Banff, the following will give you a little more privacy. **Mountain View B&B** (347 Grizzly St., 403/760-9353, www.mountainviewbanff.ca, May-Sept., $130-160 s or d) is on a quiet residential street three blocks from the heart of downtown. The two guest rooms are simply furnished, each with a double bed, TV, sink, and bar fridge. They share a bathroom and a common area that includes basic cooking facilities (microwave, toaster, kettle) and opens to a private deck. Off-street parking and a light breakfast round out this excellent choice.

The eight guest rooms at the **Elkhorn Lodge** (124 Spray Ave., 403/762-2299, www.elkhornbanff.ca, $140-280) are nothing special, but travelers on a budget who aren't fans of bed-and-breakfasts will find this older lodge suitable. The four small sleeping rooms, each with a bathroom, TV, and coffeemaker, are $140 s or d, while four larger rooms with fridges are $240-280. Rates include a light breakfast. It's halfway up the hill to the Fairmont Banff Springs.

$150-200

Blue Mountain Lodge (137 Muskrat St., 403/762-5134, www.bluemtnlodge.com, $135-145 s, $155-205 d) is a rambling, older-style lodge with 10 guest rooms, each with a private bath, TV, and telephone. The Trapper's Cabin room is the most expensive, but the gabled ceiling, walls decorated with snowshoes and bearskin, and an electric fireplace create a funky mountain feel. All guests have use of shared kitchen facilities, a lounge, and Internet access while enjoying an expansive cold buffet breakfast to fuel a day of hiking.

$200-250

The 99 guest rooms at the **Banff Inn** (501 Banff Ave., 403/762-8844, www.banffinn.com, $249-389 s or d) are no-frills modern in appearance. Pluses include underground heated parking, a large indoor whirlpool, a guest lounge with a fireplace and plasma TV, and free continental breakfast.

Spruce Grove Inn (545 Banff Ave., 403/762-3301 or 800/879-1991, www.banffsprucegroveinn.com, $245-385 s or d) is a modern mountain-style lodge where the 120 guest rooms are spacious and a relatively good value (upgrade to a king bed for $295 s or d or a Loft Suite that sleeps four for $385).

Toward downtown from the Spruce Grove is the **High Country Inn** (419 Banff Ave., 403/762-2236 or 800/293-5142, www.banffhighcountryinn.com, from $245 s or d), which has a heated indoor pool, spacious hot tubs, a cedar-lined sauna, and the ever-popular Ticino Swiss/Italian restaurant. All rooms are adequately furnished with comfortable beds and an earthy color scheme. The High Country's honeymoon suite ($285) is an excellent value; it features a king-size bed, fireplace, jetted tub, and a large balcony with views to Cascade Mountain.

$250-300

One of the nicer bed-and-breakfasts in town, **Banff Avenue B&B** (430 Banff Avenue, 403/762-5410, www.banffavenuebb.com, $260-270 s or d) offers three simple yet inviting guest rooms, each with a private bathroom. Guests enjoy a cooked breakfast, free wireless Internet, a lounge area, and a deck overlooking a flower-filled garden—all just three blocks from the heart of downtown.

The **Rundlestone Lodge** (537 Banff Ave., 403/762-2201 or 800/661-8630, www.rundlestone.com, $295-400 s or d) features mountain-style architecture with an abundance of raw stonework and exposed timber inside and out. At street level is a comfortable sitting area centered on a fireplace, as well as an indoor pool, a lounge-style bar, and a restaurant.

Furniture and fittings in the 96 rooms are elegant, and all rooms come with a TV/DVD combo. Many rooms have small balconies and gas fireplaces; some are wheelchair accessible.

$300-400

More than 100 years since Jim and Bill Brewster guided their first guests through the park, their descendants are still actively involved in the tourist industry, operating the central and very stylish ★ **Brewster's Mountain Lodge** (208 Caribou St., 403/762-2900 or 888/762-2900, www.brewstermountainlodge.com, $345-425 s or d). The building features an eye-catching log exterior with an equally impressive lobby. The Western theme is continued in the 77 upstairs rooms. Standard rooms feature two queen-size beds, deluxe rooms offer a jetted tub and sitting area, and loft suites are designed for families. Packages provide good value here, while off-season rates are slashed up to 30 percent.

The 134-room **Banff Ptarmigan Inn** (337 Banff Ave., 403/762-2207 or 800/661-8310, www.bestofbanff.com, $375 s or d) is a slick, full-service hotel with tastefully decorated rooms, down comforters on all beds, the Meatball Italian restaurant, heated underground parking, wireless Internet, and a variety of facilities to soothe sore muscles, including a spa, whirlpool, and sauna.

Although the ★ **Banff Aspen Lodge** (401 Banff Ave., 403/762-4401 or 877/886-8857, www.banffaspenlodge.com, $379-429 s or d) is priced a little higher than other properties along this section of the motel strip, value is excellent. Standard rates include a full cooked breakfast buffet, use of two outdoor hot pools, and a steam room/sauna. Rooms themselves are modern and well maintained. It's worth the extra $20-40 for a room with a balcony and mountain views.

Banff Log Cabin (226 Glen Cres., 403/762-3516, www.bannflogcabin.ca, $350 s or d) is exactly as the name suggests—a beautifully handcrafted log cabin that sleeps two comfortably. Dating to the 1970s and completely renovated since, it features a wrought-iron

queen-sized bed, a deer-antler chandelier, a full bathroom, and a wall-mounted TV. Rates include a light breakfast (including freshly baked muffins) delivered to your door.

Bed-and-breakfast connoisseurs will fall in love with **Buffaloberry B&B** (417 Marten St., 403/762-3750, www.buffaloberry.com, $395 s or d), a purpose-built lodging within walking distance of downtown. The home itself is a beautiful timber-and-stone structure, while inside, guests soak up mountain-style luxury in the vaulted living area, which comes complete with a stone fireplace, super-comfortable couches, and a library of local-interest books. The spacious rooms come with niceties such as pillow-top mattresses, TV/DVD combos, heated bathroom floors, and bathrobes. Breakfast is equally impressive. Buffaloberry is also the only Banff bed-and-breakfast with heated underground parking.

Since opening in 1908, the centrally located **Mount Royal Hotel** (138 Banff Ave., 403/762-3331 or 877/442-2623, www.mountroyalhotel.com, $375 s or d) has seen various expansions, as well as disastrous fires in 1967 and 2016. Today guests are offered more than 130 tastefully decorated rooms and the use of a large health club with hot tub. Also on the premises is a family-style chain restaurant and small lounge. For a splurge, you won't find better than the one-bedroom suites (from $520).

The following two accommodations are on Tunnel Mountain Road, a 15-minute downhill walk (or short bus ride) to town. Although falling in the same price range as many of those on Banff Avenue, all units are self-contained, making them good for families, small groups, or those who want to cook their own meals.

Opened as a bungalow camp in 1946, **Douglas Fir Resort** (525 Tunnel Mountain Rd., 403/762-5591 or 800/661-9267, www.douglasfir.com, from $385 s or d) is now a sprawling complex of 133 large condo-style units. Each has a fully equipped kitchen and a living area with fireplace. Other facilities include a hot tub, an exercise room, squash and as rain showers. The one- and two-bedroom suites all have balconies, gas fireplaces, and basic cooking facilities. Other features include outdoor and indoor hot pools; a day spa with a private outdoor hot pool; a central courtyard with lots of outdoor seating, a fire pit, and a restored 1908 home used for special events; and a classy yet well-priced family-style Italian restaurant.

The best rooms along the motel strip are at **Delta Banff Royal Canadian Lodge** (459 Banff Ave., 403/762-3307 or 888/778-5050, www.deltahotels.com, from $455 s or d), which features 99 luxuriously appointed rooms, heated underground parking, a lounge, a dining room where upscale Canadian specialties are the highlight, a spa/pool complex, and a landscaped courtyard

Moose Hotel & Suites

tennis courts, a grocery store, and a laundry. Infinitely more important if you have children are the indoor waterslides. Check online for packages year-round.

Hidden Ridge Resort (901 Hidden Ridge Way, 403/762-3544 or 800/661-1372, www.bestofbanff.com, $395-650 s or d) sits on a forested hillside away from the main buzz of traffic. Choose from modern condo-style units to much larger premier king Jacuzzi suites. All units have wood-burning fireplaces, wireless Internet, and balconies or patios, and the condos have washer/dryer combos. In the center of the complex is a barbecue area and 30-person outdoor hot tub overlooking the valley.

$400-500

Two blocks from downtown is the sparkling **Moose Hotel & Suites** (345 Banff Ave., 403/762-2638 or 800/563-8764, www.moosehotelandsuites.com, from $425 s or d), which opened in 2016. Even the standard rooms are air-conditioned and come with luxuries such

OVER $500

At **Buffalo Mountain Lodge,** a 15-minute walk from town on Tunnel Mountain Road (700 Tunnel Mountain Rd., 403/762-2400 or 800/661-1367, www.crmr.com, $505 s or d), you'll notice the impressive timber-frame construction, as well as the hand-hewn construction of the lobby, with its vaulted ceiling and eye-catching fieldstone fireplace. The 108 rooms, chalets, and bungalows all have fireplaces, balconies, large bathrooms, and comfortable beds topped by feather-filled duvets; many have kitchens. Although rack rates start at over $500, book online to pick up summer rates around $400 including breakfast. (The lodge takes its name from Tunnel Mountain, which early park visitors called Buffalo Mountain for its shape.)

The 770-room **Fairmont Banff Springs** (405 Spray Ave., 403/762-2211 or 800/257-7544, www.fairmont.com, from $699 s or d) is Banff's best-known accommodation. Earlier this century, the hotel came under the ownership of Fairmont Hotels and Resorts, losing its century-old tag as a Canadian Pacific hotel and in the process its ties to the historic railway company that constructed the original hotel back in 1888. Even though the rooms have been modernized, many date to the 1920s, and as is common in older establishments, these accommodations are small (Fairmont rooms are 14.4 square meters/155 square feet). But room size is only a minor consideration when staying in this historic gem. With 12 eateries, four lounges, a luxurious spa facility, a huge indoor pool, elegant public spaces, a 27-hole golf course, tennis courts, horseback riding, and enough twisting, turning hallways, towers, and shops to warrant a detailed map, you'll not want to spend much time in your room. (Unless, of course, you are in the eight-room presidential suite.) During summer, rack rates for a regular Fairmont room are $699 (s or d), discounted to around $400 or less the rest of the year. Many summer visitors stay as part of a package—the place to find these is on the website www.fairmont.com. Packages may simply include breakfast, while others will have you golfing, horseback riding, or relaxing in the spa.

On Mountain Avenue, a short walk from the Upper Hot Springs, is **Rimrock Resort Hotel** (403/762-3356 or 888/746-7625, www.rimrockresort.com, $575-675 s or d). The original hotel was constructed in 1903 but was fully rebuilt and opened as a full-service luxury resort in the mid-1990s. Guest amenities include two restaurants, two lounges, a health club, an outdoor patio, and a multistory heated parking garage. Each of the 345 well-appointed rooms is decorated with earthy tones offset by brightly colored fabrics. They also feature picture windows, a king-size bed, a comfortable armchair, a writing desk, two phones, a minibar, and a hair dryer. Since the hotel is set high above the Bow Valley, views for the most part are excellent.

Along the Bow Valley Parkway and Vicinity

The Bow Valley Parkway is the original route between Banff and Lake Louise. It is a beautiful drive in all seasons, and along its length are several accommodations, each a viable alternative to staying in Banff.

$200-300

Johnston Canyon Resort (403/762-2971 or 888/378-1720, www.johnstoncanyon.com, mid-May-early Oct., $240-430 s or d) is 26 kilometers (16 miles) west of Banff at the beginning of a short trail that leads to the famous canyon. The 42 cabins are older but have been thoroughly renovated on the inside, giving them a distinctive alpine charm. The larger cabins have multiple bedrooms and kitchens. On the grounds are tennis courts, a barbecue area, and a gift store. Resort dining options are vary from munching on a burger and fries at the counter of an old-time cafeteria to enjoying pan-fried rainbow trout in a dining room that oozes alpine charm. Basic two-person duplex cabins are $179, two-person cabins with a gas fireplace and sitting area are $240, and offerings go up in price to $430 for a classic bungalow complete with two bedrooms, cooking facilities, and heritage-style furnishings—still very reasonable when compared to downtown Banff prices.

$300-400

Constructed by the Canadian Pacific Railway in 1922, ★ **Storm Mountain Lodge** (Hwy. 93, 403/762-4155, www.stormmountainlodge.com, daily in summer, Thurs.-Mon. only the rest of the year, $335-470 s or d) features 14 historic cabins restored to their former rustic glory. Each has its original log walls, along with a log bed, covered deck, a wood-burning fireplace, and bathroom with claw-foot tub. They don't have phones, Internet, or TVs, so there's little to distract you from the past. Off-season deals include a breakfast and dinner package (mid-Apr.-mid-June) for $350 d. Outside, the wilderness beckons, with Storm Mountain as a backdrop. The lodge is at Vermilion Pass, a 25-minute drive from Banff or Lake Louise (head west from the Castle Mountain interchange). The lodge restaurant (7:30am-10:30am and 5pm-9pm daily) is one of my favorite places to eat in the park.

At Castle Junction, 32 kilometers (20 miles) northwest of Banff, is **Castle Mountain Chalets** (403/762-3868 or

877/762-2281, www.castlemountain.com, $325-455 s or d). Set on 1.5 hectares (four acres), this resort is home to a collection of magnificent log chalets. Each has high ceilings, beautifully handcrafted log interiors, at least two beds, a stone fireplace, a full kitchen with dishwasher, a bathroom with hot tub, and satellite TV. Part of the complex has a grocery store, barbecue area, and the only gas between Banff and Lake Louise.

BACKCOUNTRY ACCOMMODATIONS

Shadow Lake Lodge (403/762-0116 or 866/762-0114, www.shadowlakelodge.com, mid-June-Sept. and Feb.-March) is 13 kilometers (eight miles) from the nearest road. Access is on foot or, in winter, on skis. The lodge is near picturesque Shadow Lake, and many hiking trails are nearby. Dating to 1928, the oldest structure has been restored as a rustic yet welcoming lounge area, complete with wood-burning fireplace and library. Guests overnight in 12 newer, comfortable cabins, each with a queen or king bed. Guests share bathroom facilities, but these are modern and kept spotless. The daily rate, including three meals served buffet-style and afternoon tea, is $330 s, $650 d per day. The trailhead is along the Trans-Canada Highway, 19 kilometers (12 miles) west of Banff, at the Redearth Creek parking area. In February and March, when access is on cross-country skis, the lodge is open Thursday-Sunday and rates are $140 per person.

Campgrounds

Within Banff National Park, 13 campgrounds hold more than 2,400 sites. Although the town of Banff has five of these facilities with more than 1,500 sites in its immediate vicinity, most fill by early afternoon. The three largest campgrounds are strung out over 1.5 kilometers (0.9 mile) along Tunnel Mountain Road, with the nearest sites 2.5 kilometers (1.6 miles) from town. Sites at most campgrounds can be reserved through the **Parks Canada Campground Reservation Service** (877/737-3783, www.pccamping. ca) starting in mid-January, and it's strongly recommended that you do reserve if you require electrical hookups or want to stay at one of the more popular campgrounds, such as Two Jack Lakeside. Although some sites are available for those without reservations, they fill fast each day (especially in July and August). The official checkout time is 11am, so if you don't have a reservation, plan on arriving at your campground of choice earlier in

Shadow Lake Lodge

the day than this to ensure getting a site. On summer weekends, a line often forms, waiting for sites to become vacant. Open fires are permitted in designated areas throughout all campgrounds, but you must purchase a firewood permit ($8.80 per site per night) to burn wood, which is provided at no cost. For general camping information, stop at the **Banff Visitor Centre** (224 Banff Ave., 403/762-1550) or go to the Parks Canada website, www.pc.gc.ca, and follow the links to Banff National Park.

AROUND THE TOWN OF BANFF

Closest to town is **Tunnel Mountain Campground,** which is three campgrounds rolled into one. The location is a lightly treed ridge east of downtown, with views north to Cascade Mountain and south to Mount Rundle. From town, follow Tunnel Mountain Road east to beyond the Douglas Fir Resort (which is within walking distance for groceries, liquor, and laundry). If you're coming in off the Trans-Canada Highway from the east, bypass town completely by turning left onto Tunnel Mountain Road at the Banff Rocky Mountain Resort. Approaching from this direction, the first campground you pass is the park's largest, with 622 well-spaced, relatively private sites ($28 per site), each with a fire ring and picnic table. Other amenities include drinking water, hot showers, and kitchen shelters. This campground has no hookups. It is open mid-May-early September. Less than one kilometer (0.6 mile) farther along Tunnel Mountain Road toward town is a signed turnoff ("Hookups") that leads to a registration booth for two more campgrounds. Unless you have a reservation from Parks Canada Campground Reservation Service (877/737-3783, www.pccamping.ca), you'll be asked whether you require an electrical hookup ($32 per site) or a site with power, water, and sewer ($38 per site), and then sent off into the corresponding campground. The power-only section (closest to town) stays open year-round, the other mid-May-September. Both have hot showers but little privacy between sites.

Along Lake Minnewanka Road northeast of town are two campgrounds offering fewer services than the others, but with sites that offer more privacy. The pick of the two is **Two Jack Lakeside Campground** (June-mid-Sept., $32 per site), for which you will need advance reservations. It features 80 sites tucked into trees at the south end of Two Jack Lake, an extension of Lake Minnewanka. Facilities include hot showers, kitchen shelters, drinking water, and flush toilets. It's just over six kilometers (3.7 miles) from the Trans-Canada Highway underpass. The much larger **Two Jack Main Campground** (mid-June-mid-Sept., $22 per site; no reservations) is a short distance farther along the road, with 381 sites spread throughout a shallow valley. It offers the same facilities as Two Jack Lakeside, sans showers. The overflow camping area ($10) for these and the three Tunnel Mountain campgrounds is at the beginning of the Lake Minnewanka Road loop.

BOW VALLEY PARKWAY

Along Bow Valley Parkway between the town of Banff and Lake Louise are three campgrounds. Closest to Banff is **Johnston Canyon Campground** (early June-mid-Sept., $28 per site), between the road and the rail line, 26 kilometers (16 miles) west of Banff. It is the largest of the three campgrounds, with 140 sites, and has hot showers but no hookups. Almost directly opposite is Johnston Canyon Resort, with groceries and a restaurant, and the beginning of a trail to the park's best-known waterfalls.

Continuing eight kilometers (five miles) toward Lake Louise, **Castle Mountain Campground** (late June-Aug., $22 per site) is also within walking distance of a grocery store (no restaurant), but it has just 44 sites and no showers. Services are limited to flush toilets, drinking water, and kitchen shelters.

INFORMATION

Many sources of information are available on the park and its commercial facilities. Once you've arrived, the best place to make your first stop is the **Banff Visitor Centre** (224 Banff Ave., 8am-8pm daily mid-June-Aug., 8am-6pm daily mid-May-mid-June and Sept., 9am-5pm daily the rest of the year). This central complex houses information desks for **Parks Canada** (403/762-1550) and the **Banff/Lake Louise Tourism Bureau** (403/762-0270), as well as a small retail outlet that stocks a good variety of park-related literature.

National Park Information

On the right-hand side of the **Banff Visitor Centre** is a row of desks staffed by Parks Canada employees. They will answer all your queries regarding Banff's natural wonders and advise you of trail closures. Anyone planning an overnight backcountry trip should register here and obtain a camping pass ($10 per person per night). Also here, you can pick up park brochures or wander down the back to peruse park maps, view a free slide show, and watch videos about the park. All questions pertaining to the national park itself can be answered here, or check out the Parks Canada website (www.pc.gc.ca).

To report wildlife sightings, call **Banff Dispatch** (403/762-1470) in the industrial park at the north entrance to town. The **weather office** (403/762-2088) offers updated forecasts. If you want to *see* the weather in Banff, check out the Gondola webcam at www.brewster.com.

Tourism Information

In the **Banff Visitor Centre,** across the floor from Parks Canada, is a desk for the **Banff/Lake Louise Tourism Bureau.** This organization represents businesses and commercial establishments in the park. Here you can find out about accommodations and restaurants, and have any other questions answered. To answer the most frequently asked question, the restrooms are downstairs. For general tourism information before arriving, contact the Banff/Lake Louise Tourism Bureau office (403/762-8421, www. banfflakelouise.com).

Newspapers

Look for the free *Crag and Canyon* each Wednesday. It's been keeping residents and visitors informed about park issues and town gossip for more than a century. The *Rocky Mountain Outlook* is another free weekly newspaper (Thursday) that offers coverage of mountain life and upcoming events. Both are available on stands at businesses throughout town.

BOOKS AND MAPS

The Canadian Rockies are one of the most written about, and definitely the most photographed, regions in Canada. As a walk along Banff Avenue will confirm, there is definitely no lack of postcards, calendars, and coffee-table books about the area.

Ted (E. J.) Hart, a former director of the Whyte Museum, has authored over a dozen books on the history of the park. **Summerthought Publishing** (www.summerthought.com) is a local company that has been publishing the authoritative *Canadian Rockies Trail Guide* since 1971.

Look for **Gem Trek** (www.gemtrek.com) maps at outdoor retailers throughout Banff National Park.

Bookstores

On Banff's busiest thoroughfare, **Banff Visitor Centre** (224 Banff Ave., 8am-8pm daily mid-June-Aug., 8am-6pm daily mid-May-mid-June and Sept., 9am-5pm daily rest of the year) has a selection of the best hiking guides as well as maps and scenic books.

The **Whyte Museum Shop** (111 Bear St., 403/762-2291, 10am-5pm daily) specializes in regional natural and human history books, and also has a good selection of historic prints.

Library

The **Banff Public Library** (opposite Central Park at 101 Bear St., 403/762-2661, 10am-8pm Mon.-Thurs., 10am-6pm Fri., 11am-5pm Sat., 1pm-5pm Sun.) boasts an extensive collection of nonfiction books, many about the park and its environs, which makes it an excellent rainy-day hangout. It also has a large collection of magazines and newspapers. Internet access is free.

SERVICES

The **post office** (9am-5:30pm Mon.-Fri.) is on the corner of Buffalo and Bear Streets opposite Central Park. The general-delivery service here is probably among the busiest in the country, due to the thousands of seasonal workers in the area.

Major banks can be found along Banff Avenue and are generally open 9:30am-4pm Mon.-Thurs., 9am-5pm Friday. The **Bank of Montreal** (107 Banff Ave., 403/762-2275) allows cash advances with MasterCard, while the **CIBC** (98 Banff Ave., 403/762-3317) accepts Visa. **Freya's Currency Exchange** is in the Clock Tower Mall (108 Banff Ave., 403/762-4652, 9am-9pm daily).

The only downtown laundry is **Cascade Coin Laundry** (317 Banff Ave., 403/762-3444, 7:30am-10pm daily), on the lower level of the Cascade Plaza. **Chalet Coin Laundry** (8am-10pm daily) is on Tunnel Mountain Road at the Douglas Fir Resort, within walking distance of all Tunnel Mountain accommodations.

Along Banff Avenue you'll find **Banff Camera Shop** (101 Banff Ave., 403/762-3562, 9am-9pm daily), with digital imaging capabilities and a full range of equipment.

Mineral Springs Hospital (301 Lynx St., 403/762-2222) has 24-hour emergency service. **Rexall Drug Store,** on the lower level of the Cascade Plaza (317 Banff Ave., 403/762-2245), is open until 9pm daily.

Send and receive email and surf the Internet at most downtown cafés, or head to the **Banff Public Library** (101 Bear St., 403/762-2661, 10am-8pm Mon.-Thurs., 10am-6pm Fri., 11am-5pm Sat., 1pm-5pm Sun.).

GETTING THERE

The town of Banff is along the Trans-Canada Highway 128 kilometers (80 miles) west of Calgary and 836 kilometers (519 miles) east of Vancouver. Allow 90 minutes and 10 hours respectively. From Jasper in the north, the Icefields Parkway leads 230 kilometers (143 miles) south to Lake Louise, from where it's a further 56 kilometers (35 miles) southeast to Banff. As there are speed restrictions and often heavy traffic on this route, allow at least four hours to travel from Jasper to Banff. If you're driving to Banff from the United States, the best approach route depends on your starting point. Although it may not appear so from looking quickly at a map, the best way to reach Banff from Seattle is to take I-5 north to Vancouver and then the Trans-Canada Highway west (total distance is 965 km/600 miles). From Colorado or other Rocky Mountain states, head north on Highway 93, crossing into Canada north of Kalispell, Montana, from where it's 430 kilometers (267 miles) to Banff along Highway 93/95 via Cranbrook and Kootenay National Park.

From Calgary International Airport

Calgary International Airport, 128 kilometers (80 miles) east, is the closest airport to Banff National Park. **Banff Airporter** (403/762-3330 or 888/449-2901, www.banffairporter.com) offers door-to-door service between the airport and Banff for adult $64, child $32. The earliest service back to the airport departs Banff at 5:30am. **Brewster** (403/762-6767 or 800/661-1152, www.brewster.ca) shuttles between the airport and Banff National Park twice daily, stopping at Banff, then continuing to Lake Louise. Calgary to Banff is adult $64, child $32. This shuttle delivers guests to all major Banff hotels as well as the **Brewster Tour and Transportation Centre** (100 Gopher St.), a five-minute walk from downtown Banff. The Banff depot has a ticket office, lockers, and a Tim Hortons café. It's open 7:30am-10:45pm daily. Adjacent desks at the airport's Arrivals level take bookings for both companies, but it's best to reserve a seat by booking over the phone or online in advance.

Parking Tips

The downtown core of Banff is busy year-round, but especially so between late June and early September after 10am. If you're staying in a motel along Banff Avenue or on Tunnel Mountain, don't drive into town—walk or catch a **Banff Transit bus** (ask at your accommodation for a schedule).

If you do drive into downtown, don't let not finding a parking spot on Banff Avenue ruin your holiday. Head to the **parking garage** at the corner of Bear and Lynx Streets, cross the Bow River and park in the **recreation grounds,** or cruise for a space along **Lynx or Beaver Streets.**

For travelers with **RVs** or **trailers,** finding a downtown parking spot can be a challenge. If you're planning on staying at one of the campgrounds on Tunnel Mountain, check in first, then walk or catch the Banff Transit bus (it departs the campground every 30 minutes; $2) to downtown. If you must bring your rig into town and the few RV-only parking spots at the corner of Lynx and Wolf Streets are taken, there are no options other than the suggestions I give above for regular vehicles.

The website **www.banffparking.ca** is an excellent resource that includes real-time updates of various parking areas, including the number of empty stalls at the Bear Street Parkade.

Greyhound

Greyhound (403/762-1092 or 800/661-8747, www.greyhound.ca) offers scheduled service from the Calgary bus depot at 877 Greyhound Way SW, five times daily to the Banff Railway Station and Samson Mall, Lake Louise. Greyhound buses leave Vancouver from the depot at 1150 Station Street, three times daily for the scenic 14-hour ride to the park.

GETTING AROUND

Most of the sights and some hiking trailheads are within walking distance of town. **Banff Transit** (403/760-8294) operates bus service along two routes through the town of Banff: one from the Banff Gondola north along Banff Avenue, the other from the Fairmont Banff Springs to the Tunnel Mountain campgrounds. Mid-May-September, buses run twice an hour between 7am and midnight. October-December, the two routes are merged as one, with buses running hourly midday-midnight. Travel costs $2 per sector.

Cabs around Banff are reasonably priced: flag drop is $6, then it's $3 per kilometer. A ride from the Banff bus depot to accommodations on Tunnel Mountain will run around $12, same to the Fairmont Banff Springs, more after midnight. Call **Banff Taxi** (403/762-4444).

The days when a row of horse-drawn buggies eagerly awaited the arrival of wealthy visitors at the CPR Station have long since passed, but the **Trail Rider Store** (132 Banff Ave., 403/762-4551, 9am-5pm daily) offers visitors rides around town in a beautifully restored carriage. Expect to pay $100 per carriage for a short loop along the Bow River.

Car Rental

Plan on renting a vehicle before you reach the park. In addition to high pricing for walk-in customers, the main catch is that local companies don't always offer unlimited mileage, especially for larger and premium vehicles. Agencies and their local contact numbers are **Avis** (Cascade Plaza, 317 Banff Ave., 403/762-3222), **Budget** (Cascade Plaza, 317 Banff Ave., 403/762-4565), and **Hertz** (Fairmont Banff Springs, 405 Spray Ave., 403/762-2027). Reservations for vehicles in Banff should be made well in advance, especially in July and August.

Lake Louise and Vicinity

Lake Louise is 56 kilometers (35 miles) northwest of Banff along the Trans-Canada Highway, or a little bit longer if you take the quieter Bow Valley Parkway. The hamlet of Lake Louise, composed of a small mall, hotels, and restaurants, is in the Bow Valley, just west of the Trans-Canada Highway. The lake itself is 200 vertical meters (660 vertical feet) above the valley floor, along a winding, four-kilometer (2.5-mile) road. Across the valley is Canada's second-largest winter resort, also called Lake Louise. It's a world-class facility renowned for diverse terrain, abundant snow, and breathtaking views.

When you see the first flush of morning sun hit Victoria Glacier, and the impossibly steep northern face of Mount Victoria reflected in the sparkling, emerald-green waters of Lake Louise, you'll understand why this lake is regarded as one of the world's seven natural wonders. Overlooking the magnificent scene, Fairmont Chateau Lake Louise is without a doubt one of the world's most photographed hotels. Apart from staring, photographing, and videotaping, the area has plenty

to keep you busy. Nearby you'll find some of the park's best hiking, canoeing, and horseback riding. Only a short distance away is Moraine Lake, not as famous as Lake Louise but rivaling it in beauty.

From Lake Louise the Trans-Canada Highway continues west, exiting the park over Kicking Horse Pass (1,647 meters/5,400 feet) and passing through Yoho National Park to Golden. Highway 93, the famous Icefields Parkway, begins one kilometer (0.6 mile) north of the village and heads northwest through the park's northern reaches to Jasper National Park.

SIGHTS
★ Lake Louise

In summer, about 10,000 visitors per day make the journey from the Bow Valley floor up to Lake Louise, famous for its stunning turquoise coloring. By 9am the tiered parking lot is often full. (During summer, free shuttles operate from the overflow campground along the Trans-Canada Highway east of town. Electronic signage along the highway

Lake Louise

Lake Louise and Vicinity

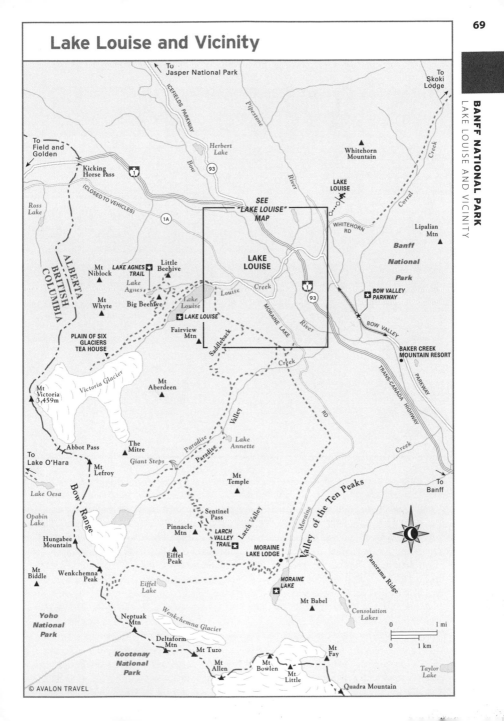

To Jasper National Park

To Skoki Lodge

ICEFIELDS PARKWAY

Pipestone

To Field and Golden

Herbert Lake

Whitehorn Mountain

Creek

Corral

Kicking Horse Pass

1

Bow

93

River

LAKE LOUISE

Ross Lake

(CLOSED TO VEHICLES)

1A

WHITEHORN RD

Lipalian Mtn

Banff

SEE "LAKE LOUISE" MAP

LAKE LOUISE

National

ALBERTA
BRITISH COLUMBIA

Mt Niblock

LAKE AGNES TRAIL

Little Beehive

Park

Lake Agnes

Louise

Creek

1

93

BOW VALLEY PARKWAY

Mt Whyte

Big Beehive

Lake Louise

River

BOW VALLEY

LAKE LOUISE

MORAINE LAKE

PLAIN OF SIX GLACIERS TEA HOUSE

Fairview Mtn

Saddleback

BAKER CREEK MOUNTAIN RESORT

Creek

TRANS-CANADA HIGHWAY

PARKWAY

Mt Victoria 3,459m

Victoria Glacier

Mt Aberdeen

RD

To Lake O'Hara

Abbot Pass

The Mitre

Paradise

Valley

Lake Annette

Creek

Giant Steps

Paradise

Mt Lefroy

Lake Oesa

Bow Range

Mt Temple

of the Ten Peaks

To Banff

Opabin Lake

Sentinel Pass

Pinnacle Mtn

LARCH VALLEY TRAIL

Larch Valley

Moraine

Valley

Hungabee Mountain

Eiffel Peak

MORAINE LAKE LODGE

Panorama Ridge

Mt Biddle

Wenkchemna Peak

Eiffel Lake

MORAINE LAKE

Mt Babel

Consolation Lakes

Yoho National Park

Neptuak Mtn

Wenkchemna Glacier

0   1 mi

0   1 km

Deltaform Mtn

Kootenay National Park

Mt Tuzo

Mt Allen

Mt Bowlen

Mt Fay

Taylor Lake

Mt Little

Quadra Mountain

© AVALON TRAVEL

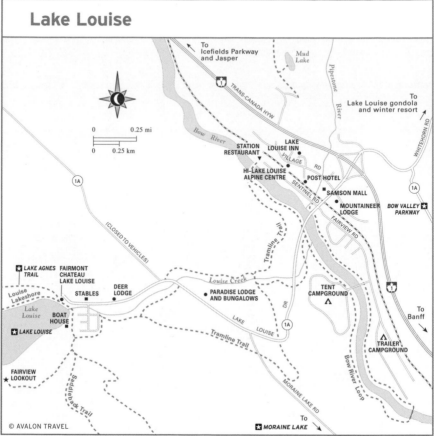

Lake Louise

To Icefields Parkway and Jasper

Mud Lake

Pipestone

To Lake Louise gondola and winter resort

TRANS-CANADA HYW

WHITEHORN RD

Bow River

0   0.25 mi
0   0.25 km

STATION RESTAURANT

LAKE LOUISE INN

LAKE LOUISE VILLAGE

RD

HI-LAKE LOUISE ALPINE CENTRE

POST HOTEL

SAMSON MALL

SENTINEL RD

MOUNTAINEER LODGE

BOW VALLEY PARKWAY

1A

FAIRVIEW RD

Tramline Trail

(CLOSED TO VEHICLES)

★ LAKE AGNES TRAIL

FAIRMONT CHATEAU LAKE LOUISE

STABLES

DEER LODGE

Louise Creek

PARADISE LODGE AND BUNGALOWS

TENT CAMPGROUND

To Banff

Louise Lakeshore

Lake Louise

BOAT HOUSE

★ LAKE LOUISE

DR

LAKE LOUISE

1A

Tramline Trail

TRAILER CAMPGROUND

★ FAIRVIEW LOOKOUT

Saddleback Trail

Bow River Loop

MORAINE LAKE RD

To
★ MORAINE LAKE

© AVALON TRAVEL

---

will direct you to this area when there is no parking at the lake). An alternative to the road is one of two hiking trails that begin in the village and end at the public parking lot. From here several paved trails lead to the lake's eastern shore. From these vantage points the dramatic setting can be fully appreciated. The lake is 2.4 kilometers (1.5 miles) long, 500 meters (1,640 feet) wide, and up to 90 meters (295 feet) deep. Its cold waters reach a maximum temperature of 4°C (39°F) in August.

Fairmont Chateau Lake Louise is a tourist attraction in itself. Built by the CPR to take the pressure off the popular Banff Springs Resort, the château has seen many changes over the years, yet it remains one of

the world's great mountain resorts. No one minds the hordes of camera- and phone-toting tourists who traipse through each day—and there's really no way to avoid them. The immaculately manicured gardens between the château and the lake make an interesting foreground for the millions of Lake Louise photographs taken each year. At the lakeshore boathouse, canoes are rented for $40 per hour.

The snow-covered peak at the back of the lake is **Mount Victoria** (3,459 meters/11,350 feet), which sits on the Continental Divide. Amazingly, its base is more than 10 kilometers (6.2 miles) from the eastern end of the lake. Mount Victoria, first climbed in 1897, remains one of the park's most popular peaks

Moraine Lake

for mountaineers. Although the difficult northeast face (facing the château) was first successfully ascended in 1922, the most popular and easiest route to the summit is along the southeast ridge, approached from Abbot Pass.

★ Moraine Lake

Although less than half the size of Lake Louise, Moraine Lake is just as spectacular and worthy of just as much time. It is up a winding road 13 kilometers (eight miles) off Lake Louise Drive. Its rugged setting, nestled in the Valley of the Ten Peaks among the towering mountains of the main ranges, has provided inspiration for millions of people from around the world since Walter Wilcox became the first white man to reach its shore in 1899. Wilcox's subsequent writings, such as "no scene has given me an equal impression of inspiring solitude and rugged grandeur," guaranteed the lake's future popularity. Although Wilcox was a knowledgeable man, he named the lake on the assumption that it was dammed by a glacial moraine deposited

by the retreating Wenkchemna Glacier. In fact, the large rock pile that blocks its waters was deposited by major rockfalls from the Tower of Babel to the south. The lake often remains frozen until June, and the access road is closed all winter. A trail leads along the lake's northern shore, and canoes are rented for $60 per hour from the concession below Moraine Lake Lodge.

Parking at Moraine Lake is even more limited than at Lake Louise. If you arrive at the beginning of the Moraine Lake Road after 9am, expect the road to be closed until vehicles begin leaving. I can't stress this enough—if you want to see Moraine Lake during July and August, arrive well before 9am.

Sightseeing Gondola

During summer, the main ski lift at the **Lake Louise resort** (403/522-3555 or 877/253-6888, www.skilouise.com) whisks visitors up the face of Mount Whitehorn to Whitehorn Lodge in either open chairs or enclosed gondola cars. At an altitude of more than two kilometers (1.2 miles) above sea level, the view from the top—across the Bow Valley, Lake Louise, and the Continental Divide—is among the most spectacular in the Canadian Rockies. Short trails lead through the forests, across open meadows, and, for the energetic, to the summit of Mount Whitehorn, more than 600 vertical meters (1,970 vertical feet) above. Visitors are free to walk these trails, but it pays to join a guided walk if you'd like to learn about the surrounding environment. After working up an appetite (and working off breakfast), head to the teahouse in the Whitehorn Lodge, try the outdoor barbecue, or, back at the base area, enjoy lunch at the **Lodge of the Ten Peaks,** the resort's impressive post-and-beam day lodge. The lift operates 9am-4pm daily May-September, with extended summer hours of 9am-5pm, adult $36, child $18. Ride-and-dine packages are an excellent deal. Pay an extra $6 per person and have a buffet breakfast (8am-11am) included with the gondola ride. Free

"Lake of Little Fishes"

During the summer of 1882, Tom Wilson, an outfitter, was camped near the confluence of the Bow and Pipestone Rivers when he heard the distant rumblings of an avalanche. He questioned Stoney Indian guides and was told the noises originated from the "Lake of Little Fishes." The following day, Wilson, led by a Stoney guide, hiked to the lake to investigate. He became the first white man to lay eyes on what he named Emerald Lake. Two years later, the name was changed to Lake Louise, honoring Princess Louise Caroline Alberta, daughter of Queen Victoria.

A railway station known as Laggan was built where the rail line passed closest to the lake, six kilometers (3.7 miles) away. Until a road was completed in 1926, everyone arrived by train. The station's name was changed to Lake Louise in 1913 to prevent confusion among visitors. In 1890, a modest two-bedroom wooden hotel replaced a crude cabin that had been built on the shore of the lake as word of its beauty spread. After many additions, a disastrous fire, and the addition of a concrete wing in 1925, the château of today took shape, minus a convention center that opened in 2004.

shuttles run from Lake Louise accommodations to the day lodge.

HIKING

The variety of hiking opportunities in the vicinity of Lake Louise and Moraine Lake is surely equal to those of any area on the face of the earth. The region's potential for outdoor recreation was first realized in the late 1800s, and it soon became the center of hiking activity in the Canadian Rockies. This popularity continues today; trails here are among the most heavily used in the park. Hiking is best early or late in the short summer season. Head out early in the morning to miss the strollers, high heels, dogs, and bear bells that you'll surely encounter during the busiest periods.

The two main trailheads are at Fairmont Chateau Lake Louise and Moraine Lake. Two trails lead from the village to the château (a pleasant alternative to driving the steep and busy Lake Louise Drive). Shortest is the 2.7-kilometer (1.7-mile) **Louise Creek Trail.** It begins on the downstream side of the point where Lake Louise Drive crosses the Bow River, crosses Louise Creek three times, and ends at the Lake Louise parking lot. The other trail, **Tramline,** is 4.5 kilometers (2.8 miles) longer but not as steep. It begins behind the railway station and follows the route of a narrow-gauge railway that

once transported guests from the CPR line to Chateau Lake Louise.

Bow River Loop

Length: 7 kilometers/4.3 miles (1.5-2 hours) round-trip
Elevation gain: minimal
Rating: easy
Trailheads: various points throughout Lake Louise village, including behind Samson Mall

This loop follows both banks of the Bow River southeast from the railway station. Used by joggers and cyclists to access various points in the village, the trail also links the railway station to the Lake Louise Alpine Centre, Post Hotel, Samson Mall, both campgrounds, and the Louise Creek and Tramline Trails to Lake Louise. Interpretive signs along its length provide information on the Bow River ecosystem.

Louise Lakeshore

Length: 2 kilometers/1.2 miles (30 minutes) one-way
Elevation gain: none
Rating: easy
Trailhead: Lake Louise, 4 kilometers (2.5 miles) from Trans-Canada Highway

Probably the busiest trail in all the Canadian Rockies, this one follows the north shore of Lake Louise from in front of the château to the west end of the lake. Here numerous braided glacial streams empty their silt-filled waters

Louise Lakeshore Trail

into Lake Louise. Along the trail's length are benches for sitting and pondering what English mountaineer James Outram once described as "a gem of composition and of coloring…perhaps unrivalled anywhere."

Plain of the Six Glaciers

Length: 5.3 kilometers/3.3 miles (90 minutes) one-way
Elevation gain: 370 meters/1,215 feet
Rating: moderate
Trailhead: Lake Louise

Hikers along this trail are rewarded not only with panoramic views of the glaciated peaks of the main range but also with a rustic trail's-end teahouse serving homemade goodies baked on a wooden stove. For the first two kilometers (1.2 miles), the trail follows the Louise Lakeshore Trail to the western end of the lake. From there it begins a steady climb through a forest of spruce and subalpine fir. It enters an open area where an avalanche has come tumbling down (now a colorful carpet of wildflowers), then passes through a forested

area into a vast wasteland of moraines produced by the advance and retreat of Victoria Glacier. Views of surrounding peaks continue to improve until the trail enters a stunted forest. After switchbacking up through this forest, the trail arrives at the teahouse.

Built by the CPR at the turn of the 20th century, the teahouse operates the same way now as it did then. Supplies are packed in by horse, and all cooking is done in a rustic kitchen. It's open July through early September.

After resting, continue one kilometer (0.6 mile) to the end of the trail on the narrow top of a lateral moraine. From here the trail's namesakes are visible. From left to right, the glaciers are Aberdeen, Upper Lefroy, Lower Lefroy, Upper Victoria, Lower Victoria, and Pope's. Between Mount Lefroy (3,441 meters/11,290 feet) and Mount Victoria (3,459 meters/11,350 feet) is Abbot Pass, where it's possible to make out Abbot Hut on the skyline. When constructed in 1922, this stone structure was the highest building in Canada. The pass and hut are named for Phillip Abbot, who died attempting to climb Mount Lefroy in 1896.

★ Lake Agnes

Length: 3.6 kilometers/2.2 miles (90 minutes) one-way
Elevation gain: 400 meters/1,312 feet
Rating: moderate
Trailhead: Lake Louise

This moderately strenuous hike is one of the park's most popular. It begins in front of the château, branching right near the beginning of the Louise Lakeshore Trail. For the first 2.5 kilometers (1.6 miles), the trail climbs steeply, switchbacking through a forest of subalpine fir and Engelmann spruce, crossing a horse trail, passing a lookout, and leveling out at tiny Mirror Lake. Here the old, traditional trail veers right (use it if the ground is wet or snowy), while a more direct route veers left to the Plain of the Six Glaciers. The final elevation gain along both trails is made easier by a flight of steps beside Bridal Veil Falls. The trail ends by a rustic teahouse overlooking

Lake Agnes, a subalpine lake nestled in a hanging valley. The teahouse (8am-5pm daily early June-early Oct.) offers homemade soups, healthy sandwiches, and a wide assortment of teas.

From the teahouse, a one-kilometer (0.6-mile) trail leads to Little Beehive and impressive views of the Bow Valley. Another trail leads around the northern shore of Lake Agnes, climbing to Big Beehive or joining the Plain of the Six Glaciers Trail, just 3.2 kilometers (two miles) from the château and 2.1 kilometers (1.3 miles) from the teahouse at the end of that trail.

Big Beehive

Length: 5 kilometers/3.1 miles (2 hours) one-way
Elevation gain: 520 meters/1,710 feet
Rating: moderate
Trailhead: Lake Louise

The lookout atop the larger of the two "beehives" is one of the best places to admire the uniquely colored waters of Lake Louise, more than 500 meters (1,640 feet) directly below. The various trails to the summit have one thing in common: All are steep. But the rewards are worth every drop of sweat along the way. The most popular route follows the Lake Agnes Trail for the first 3.6 kilometers (2.2 miles) to Lake Agnes. From the teahouse, a trail leads to the western end of the lake, then switchbacks steeply up an exposed north-facing ridge. At the crest of the ridge, the trail forks. To the right it descends to the Plain of the Six Glaciers Trail; to the left it continues 300 meters (0.2 mile) to a log gazebo. This trail is not well defined, but scrambling through the large boulders is easy. Across Lake Louise is Fairview Mountain (2,745 meters/9,000 feet), and behind this peak is the distinctive shape of Mount Temple (3,549 meters/11,645 feet). Views also extend up the lake to Mount Lefroy and northeast to the Lake Louise winter resort. Views from the edge of the cliff are spectacular, but be very careful—it's a long, long way down. By returning down the Lake Louise side of the Big Beehive, the loop is 11.5 kilometers (7.1 miles).

Saddleback

Length: 3.7 kilometers/2.3 miles (90 minutes) one-way
Elevation gain: 600 meters/1,970 feet
Rating: moderate/difficult
Trailhead: boathouse, Lake Louise

This trail climbs the lower slopes of Fairview Mountain from beside the boathouse on Lake Louise, ending in an alpine meadow with a view of Mount Temple from across Paradise Valley. Four hundred meters (0.2 mile) from the trailhead, the trail forks. Keep left and follow the steep switchbacks through a forest of Englemann spruce and subalpine fir until reaching the flower-filled meadow. The meadow is actually a pass between Fairview Mountain (to the northwest) and Saddle Mountain (to the southeast). Although most hikers are content with the awesome views from the pass and return along the same trail, it is possible to continue to the summit of Fairview (2,745 meters/9,000 feet), a further climb of 400 vertical meters (1,310 vertical feet). The barely discernible, switchbacking trail to the summit begins near a stand of larch trees above the crest of Saddleback. As you would expect, the view from the top is stupendous; Lake Louise is more than one kilometer (0.6 mile) directly below. This option is for strong, experienced hikers only. From the Saddleback, the trail descends into Sheol Valley, then into Paradise Valley. The entire loop would be 15 kilometers (9.3 miles).

Paradise Valley

Length: 18 kilometers/11.2 miles (6 hours) round-trip
Elevation gain: 380 meters/1,250 feet
Rating: moderate
Trailhead: Moraine Lake Road, 3.5 kilometers (2.2 miles) from Lake Louise Drive

This aptly named trail makes for a long day hike, but it can be broken up by overnighting at the backcountry campground at the far end of the loop. The trail climbs slowly for the first five kilometers (3.1 miles), crossing Paradise Creek numerous times and passing the junction of a trail that climbs the Sheol Valley to Saddleback. After five kilometers

(3.1 miles), the trail begins a steep ascent to **Lake Annette.** It's a typical subalpine lake in a unique setting, nestled against the near-vertical 1,200-meter (3,940-foot) north face of snow- and ice-capped **Mount Temple** (3,549 meters/11,645 feet), one of the 10 highest peaks in the Canadian Rockies. This difficult face was successfully climbed in 1966, relatively late for mountaineering firsts. The lake is a worthy destination in itself (allow yourself four hours round-trip from the trailhead). For those looking for a full day's outing, continue beyond the lake into an open avalanche area that affords views across Paradise Valley. Look and listen for pikas and marmots among the boulders. The trail eventually begins a steep descent to reach a series of waterfalls known as the Giant Steps.

★ Larch Valley

Length: 2.9 kilometers/1.8 miles (60 minutes) one-way
Elevation gain: 400 meters/1,310 feet
Rating: moderate
Trailhead: Moraine Lake, 13 kilometers (8 miles) from Lake Louise Drive

In mid- to late September, when the larch trees have turned a magnificent gold and the sun is shining, few spots in the Canadian Rockies can match the beauty of this valley, but don't expect to find much solitude. Although the most popular time for visiting the valley is fall, it is a worthy destination all summer, when the open meadows are filled with colorful wildflowers. The trail begins just past Moraine Lake Lodge and climbs fairly steeply, with occasional glimpses of Moraine Lake below. After reaching the junction of the Eiffel Lake Trail, keep right, passing through an open forest of larch and into the meadow beyond. The range of larch is restricted within the park, and this is one of the few areas where they are prolific. Mount Fay (3,235 meters/10,615 feet) is the dominant peak on the skyline, rising above the other mountains that make up the Valley of the Ten Peaks. Due to the risk of human-wildlife conflicts in Larch Valley, there is often a restriction on this trail requiring hikers to be in groups of four or more.

Sentinel Pass

Length: 5.8 kilometers/3.6 miles (2-3 hours) one-way
Elevation gain: 725 meters/2,380 feet
Rating: moderate/difficult
Trailhead: Moraine Lake

Keen hikers should consider continuing through the open meadows of Larch Valley to Sentinel Pass (2,608 meters/8,560 feet), one of the park's highest trail-accessible passes. The length and elevation gain listed are from Moraine Lake. Once in Larch Valley, you're halfway there and have made over half of the elevation gain. Upon reaching Larch Valley, take the formed trail that winds through the open meadow. After climbing steadily beyond Minnestimma Lakes, the trail switchbacks for 1.2 kilometers (0.7 mile) up a steep scree slope to the pass, sandwiched between Pinnacle Mountain (3,067 meters/10,060 feet) and Mount Temple (3,549 meters/11,645 feet). From the pass most hikers opt to return along the same trail, although with advance planning it is possible to continue into Paradise Valley and back to the Moraine Lake access road, a total of 17 kilometers (10.6 miles) one-way.

Eiffel Lake

Length: 5.6 kilometers/3.5 miles (2 hours) one-way
Elevation gain: 400 meters/1,310 feet
Rating: moderate/difficult
Trailhead: Moraine Lake

Eiffel Lake is small, and it looks even smaller in its rugged and desolate setting, surrounded by the famed Valley of the Ten Peaks. For the first 2.4 kilometers (1.5 miles), follow the Larch Valley Trail, then fork left. Most of the elevation gain has already been made, and the trail remains relatively level before emerging onto an open slope from where each of the 10 peaks can be seen, along with Moraine Lake far below. From left to right the peaks are Fay, Little, Bowlen, Perren, Septa, Allen, Tuzo, Deltaform, Neptuak, and Wenkchemna. The final two peaks are divided by Wenkchemna

Pass (2,605 meters/8,550 feet), a further four kilometers (2.5 miles) and 360 vertical meters (1,180 vertical feet) above Eiffel Lake. The lake itself soon comes into view. It lies in a depression formed by a rockslide from Neptuak Mountain. The lake is named for **Eiffel Peak** (3,085 meters/10,120 feet), a rock pinnacle behind it, which with a little imagination could be compared to the Eiffel Tower in Paris.

Consolation Lakes

Length: 3 kilometers/1.9 miles (1 hour) one-way
Elevation gain: 65 meters/213 feet
Rating: easy/moderate
Trailhead: beside the restrooms at Moraine Lake parking lot

This short trail begins with a crossing of Moraine Creek at the outlet of Moraine Lake and ends at a pleasant subalpine lake. The first section of the trail traverses a boulder-strewn rock pile—the result of rockslides on the imposing Tower of Babel (3,100 meters/10,170 feet)—before entering a dense forest of Engelmann spruce and subalpine fir and following Babel Creek to the lower lake. The wide valley affords 360-degree views of the surrounding jagged peaks, including Mount Temple back down the valley and Mounts Bident and Quadra at the far end of the lakes.

Skoki Valley

Length: 14.4 kilometers/8.9 miles (5 hours) one-way
Elevation gain: 775 meters/2,540 feet
Rating: moderate/difficult
Trailhead: end of Fish Creek Road, off Whitehorn Road 1.8 kilometers (1.1 miles) north of Lake Louise interchange

The trail into historic Skoki Lodge is only one of the endless hiking opportunities tucked behind the Lake Louise winter resort, across the valley from all hikes detailed previously. The first 3.4 kilometers (2.1 miles) of the trail are along a gravel access road leading to Temple Lodge, part of the Lake Louise winter resort. Guests of Skoki Lodge ride a shuttle for this first stretch, lessening the hiking distance to 11 kilometers (6.8 miles). From Temple Lodge, the trail climbs to Boulder Pass, passing a

campground and Halfway Hut, above Corral Creek. The pass harbors a large population of pikas and hoary marmots. The trail then follows the north shore of Ptarmigan Lake before climbing again to Deception Pass, named for its false summit. It then descends into Skoki Valley, passing the Skoki Lakes and eventually reaching Skoki Lodge. Just over one kilometer (0.6 mile) beyond the lodge is a campground, an excellent base for exploring the region.

OTHER SUMMER RECREATION

In Lake Louise, "summer fun" means hiking—and lots of it. You may see small fish swimming along the shore of Lake Louise, but the fishing in this lake and all others in the area is poor due to the super-cold glacial water. Talking of cold water, everyone is invited to take a swim in Lake Louise to celebrate the country's national holiday, **Canada Day** (July 1). You don't need to be Canadian to join in—just brave.

Through summer, **Brewster Adventures** (403/762-5454) offers two-hour horseback rides to the end of Lake Louise for $95, half-day rides to **Lake Agnes Teahouse** for $160, and all-day rides up **Paradise Valley,** including lunch, for $300.

WINTER RECREATION

Lake Louise is an immense winter playground, offering one of the world's premier alpine resorts, unlimited cross-country skiing, ice-skating, sleigh rides, and nearby heli-skiing. Between November and May, accommodation prices are reduced by up to 60 percent (except Christmas holidays). Lift-and-lodging packages begin at $180 per person, and you'll always be able to get a table at your favorite restaurant.

Lake Louise Resort

Canada's answer to U.S. megaresorts such as Vail and Killington is the **Lake Louise resort** (403/522-3555 or 877/253-6888, www. skilouise.com), which opens in November and operates until mid-May. The nation's second-largest winter resort (behind only Whistler/Blackcomb) comprises 1,700 hectares (4,200 acres) of gentle trails, mogul fields, long cruising runs, steep chutes, and vast bowls filled with famous Rocky Mountain powder.

The resort is made up of four distinct faces. The front side has a vertical drop of 1,000 meters (3,280 feet) and is served by eight lifts, including four high-speed quads and western Canada's only six-passenger chairlift. Resort statistics are impressive: a 990-meter (3,250-foot) vertical rise, 1,700 hectares (4,200 acres) of patrolled terrain, and more than 100 named runs. The four back bowls are each as big as many midsize resorts and are all well above the tree line. Larch and Ptarmigan faces have a variety of terrain, allowing you to follow the sun as it moves across the sky or escape into trees for protection on windy days. Each of the three day lodges has a restaurant and bar. Ski and snowboard rentals, clothing, and souvenirs are available in the Lodge of the Ten Peaks, a magnificent post-and-beam day lodge that overlooks the front face.

Lift tickets per day are adult $110, senior $92, youth $74, and child younger than 12 $46. Free guided tours of the mountain are available three times daily; inquire at customer service. Free shuttle buses run regularly from Lake Louise accommodations to the hill. From Banff you pay $20 round-trip for transportation to Lake Louise. For information on packages and multiday tickets that cover all three national park resorts, go to www.skibig3.com.

Cross-Country Skiing

The most popular cross-country skiing areas are on Lake Louise, along Moraine Lake Road, and in Skoki Valley at the back of the Lake Louise ski area. For details and helpful trail classifications, pick up a copy of *Cross-Country Skiing—Nordic Trails in Banff National Park* from the Lake Louise Visitor Centre. Before heading out, check the weather forecast at the visitors center or call 403/762-2088. For avalanche reports, call 403/762-1460.

Ice-Skating and Sleigh Rides

Of all the ice-skating rinks in Canada, the one on frozen Lake Louise, in front of the château, is surely the most spectacular. Spotlights allow skating after dark, and on special occasions hot chocolate is served. Skates are available in the château at **Chateau Mountain Sports** (403/522-3628); $12 for two hours.

Lake Agnes Teahouse

Brewster Lake Louise Sleigh Rides (403/522-3511) offers rides in traditional horse-drawn sleighs along the shores of Lake Louise beginning from in front of the château. Although blankets are supplied, you should still bundle up. The one-hour ride is $35 per person, $30 for children. Reservations are necessary. The rides are scheduled hourly from 11am on weekends and from 3pm on weekdays, with the last ride between 6pm and 8pm.

NIGHTLIFE

The **Sir Norman Lounge** in the Post Hotel (200 Pipestone Dr., 403/522-3989, 2pm-11pm daily) oozes mountain style and upscale charm. It's cozy, quiet, and the perfect place to relax in front of a fire with a cocktail before moving on to the adjacent fine-dining restaurant. Not your scene? Hang out with seasonal workers at the smoky **Lake Louise Village Grill & Bar** (upstairs in Samson Mall, 403/522-9011, 11am-2am daily), then move across the road with your newfound friends to **Explorer's Lounge** (Lake Louise Inn, 210 Village Rd., 403/522-3791, 11am-2am daily) for dancing to recorded music after 10pm. Up at the Fairmont Chateau Lake Louise is **The Glacier Saloon** (111 Lake Louise Dr., 403/522-3511, noon-midnight daily), where on most summer nights a DJ plays music ranging from pop to western.

FOOD

Other guidebooks encourage readers to "eat at your hotel." Not only is this not helpful, it's misleading. The village of Lake Louise may exist only to serve travelers, but there are good dining options serving all budgets.

Casual

If you don't feel like a cooked breakfast, start your day off at ★ **Laggan's Mountain Bakery** (Samson Mall, 403/552-2017, 6am-8pm daily, lunches $8-12), *the* place to hang out with a coffee and a freshly baked breakfast croissant, pastry, cake, or muffin. The chocolate brownie is delicious (order two slices to

save having to line up twice). If the tables are full, order takeout and enjoy your feast on the riverbank behind the mall.

For a casual meal, head to **Bill Peyto's Cafe** in the Lake Louise Alpine Centre (203 Village Rd., 403/522-2200, 7:30am-9:30pm daily, $12-18), where the food is consistent and well priced. A huge portion of nachos is $8, pasta is $12-14, and stir-fries range $12-15.

Across the Trans-Canada Highway, the **Lodge of the Ten Peaks,** at the base of the Lake Louise winter resort (403/522-3555, $12-20, 8am-4pm daily mid-May-early Oct., lunches $12-16), is open 8am-11am daily for a large and varied breakfast buffet, followed by cafeteria-style lunch service, with food best enjoyed out on the covered balcony. The lodge also has a café where you can grab coffee and muffins.

European

In 1987, the ★ **Post Hotel** (200 Pipestone Dr., 403/522-3989 or 800/661-1586, www.posthotel.com) was expanded to include a luxurious new wing. The original log building was renovated as a rustic, timbered dining room (6:30pm-10pm daily, $34-52) linked to the rest of the hotel by an intimate lounge. Although the dining room isn't cheap, it's a favorite of locals and visitors alike. The chef specializes in European cuisine, preparing several Swiss dishes (such as veal zurichois) to make owner George Schwarz feel less homesick. He's also renowned for his presentation of Alberta beef, Pacific salmon, and Peking duck. The 32,000-bottle cellar is one of the finest in Canada. Reservations are essential for dinner.

Canadian

Over one hundred years ago, visitors departing trains at Laggan Station were eager to get to the Chateau Lake Louise as quickly as possible to begin their adventure. Today guests from the château, other hotels, and even people from as far away as Banff are returning to dine in the ★ **The Station Restaurant** (200 Sentinel Rd., 403/522-2600, 11:30am-4pm and

5pm-9:30 daily, $21-40). Although the menu is not extensive, it puts an emphasis on creating imaginative dishes with a combination of Canadian produce and Asian ingredients. Lighter lunches include a Caesar salad topped with roasted garlic dressing—perfect for those planning an afternoon hike. In the evening, expect entrées like a memorable pan-seared salmon smothered in basil pesto.

Also well worth the drive is ★ **Baker Creek Bistro** (Baker Creek Mountain Resort, 10 km/6.2 mi from Lake Louise on the Bow Valley Parkway, 403/522-3761, 7am--10pm daily, $31-52). Dining is in a small room that characterizes the term "mountain hideaway," in an adjacent lounge bar, or out on a small deck decorated with pots of colorful flowers. The menu isn't large, but dishes feature lots of Canadian game and produce, with favorites such as beer-pork ribs, duck breast, and bison tenderloin.

Fairmont Chateau Lake Louise

Within this famous lakeside hotel is a choice of eateries and an ice-cream shop. For all château dining reservations, call 403/522-1818.

The **Poppy Brasserie** has obscured lake views and is the most casual place for a meal. Breakfasts (7am-10am daily), offered buffet-style ($32 per person), are a little expensive for light eaters. Lunch and dinner (11:30am-9pm daily, $24-38) are à la carte. The **Walliser Stube** (6pm-9pm daily, $31-46) is an elegant two-story wine bar decorated with rich wood paneling and solid oak furniture. It offers a simple menu of German dishes as well as a number of classic fondues. The **Lakeview Lounge** (11:30am-7pm daily, lunches $16-24) has floor-to-ceiling windows with magnificent lake views. Choose this dining area for lunch or afternoon tea (noon-3pm daily, reservations required, $43 per person, or $53 with a glass of champagne).

The **Fairview Dining Room** (6pm-9pm daily, $35-46) has a lot more than just a fair view. As the château's signature dining room, it enjoys the best views and offers the most elegant setting.

ACCOMMODATIONS AND CAMPING

In summer, accommodations at Lake Louise are even harder to come by than in Banff, so it's essential to make reservations well in advance. Any rooms not taken by early afternoon will be the expensive ones.

Under $100

With beds for $100 less than anyplace else in the village, the 164-bed **HI-Lake Louise Alpine Centre** (203 Village Rd., 403/522-2200 or 866/762-4122, www.hihostels.ca) is understandably popular. Of log construction, with large windows and high vaulted ceilings, the lodge is a joint venture between the Alpine Club of Canada and Hostelling International Canada. Beyond the reception area is Bill Peyto's Cafe, the least-expensive place to eat in Lake Louise. Upstairs is a large timber-frame lounge area and guide's room—a quiet place to plan your next hike or browse through the large collection of mountain literature. Other amenities include Wi-Fi, a laundry, a game room, and wintertime ski shuttle. Members of Hostelling International pay $60 per person per night (nonmembers $64) for a dorm bed or $180 s or d ($194 for nonmembers) in a private room. Rates are discounted to $38 for a dorm and $110 s or d for a private room ($42 and $114 respectively, for nonmembers) October-May, including throughout the extremely busy winter season. The hostel is open year-round, with check-in after 3pm. In summer and on weekends during the winter season, advance bookings (up to six months) are essential. The hostel is on Village Road, less than one kilometer (0.6 mile) from Samson Mall.

$200-300

Historic **Deer Lodge** (109 Lake Louise Dr., 403/410-7417 or 800/661-1595, www.crmr.com, $240-400 s or d) began life in 1921 as a teahouse, with rooms added in 1925. Facilities include a rooftop hot tub with glacier views, game room, restaurant (breakfast and dinner), and bar. The least-expensive rooms are older and don't have phones. Rooms in the $300 range are considerably larger, or pay $400 for a heritage-themed Tower Room. Deer Lodge is along Lake Louise Drive, up the hill from the village, and just a five-minute walk from the lake itself.

On the valley floor, **Mountaineer Lodge** (101 Village Rd., 403/522-3844, www.mountaineerlodge.com, $280-420 s or d) offers large, functional guest rooms, many with mountain views and all with wireless Internet access. On the downside, the rooms have no phones or air-conditioning, and there is no elevator.

Aside from the château, the **Lake Louise Inn** (210 Village Rd., 403/522-3791 or 800/661-9237, www.lakelouiseinn.com, from $285 s or d) is the village's largest lodging, with more than 200 units spread throughout five buildings. Across from the lobby, in the main lodge, is a gift shop and an activities desk, and beyond is a pizzeria, restaurant, bar, and indoor pool. Most rates booked online include breakfast.

$300-400

An excellent option for families and those looking for old-fashioned mountain charm is ★ **Paradise Lodge and Bungalows** (105 Lake Louise Dr., 403/522-3595, www.paradiselodge.com, mid-May-early Oct., from $300 s or d). This family-operated lodge provides outstanding value in a wonderfully tranquil setting. Spread out around well-manicured gardens are 21 attractive cabins in four configurations. Each has a rustic yet warm and inviting interior, with comfortable beds, a separate sitting area, and an en suite bathroom. Each cabin has a small fridge, microwave, and coffeemaker, while the larger ones have full kitchens and separate bedrooms. Instead of television, children are kept happy with a playground that includes a sandbox and jungle gym. The least-expensive cabins, complete with a classic cast-iron stove/fireplace combo, are $300 s or d, or pay $325 for a cabin with a big deck and sweeping valley views. Twenty-four luxury suites, each with a fireplace, TV, one or two bedrooms, and fabulous mountain

views, start at $330, or $365 with a kitchen. The Temple Suite, with all of the above as well as a large hot tub, is $400. To get there from the valley floor, follow Lake Louise Drive toward the Fairmont Chateau Lake Louise for three kilometers (1.9 miles); the lake itself is just one kilometer (0.6 mile) farther up the hill.

★ **Baker Creek Mountain Resort** (403/522-3761, www.bakercreek.com, $350-450 s or d) lies along the Bow Valley Parkway 10 kilometers (6.2 miles) from Lake Louise back toward Banff. Each of the log chalets has a kitchenette, separate bedroom, fireplace, and outside deck (complete with cute wood carvings of bears climbing over the railings). The Trapper's Cabin is a huge space with a log bed, antler chandelier, wood-burning fireplace, double-jetted tub, and cooking facilities. A lodge wing has eight luxurious suites, each with richly accented log work, a deck, a microwave and fridge, and a deluxe bathroom. (Check the website for great off-season deals.) The restaurant here is highly recommended.

Over $400

Originally called Lake Louise Ski Lodge, the ★ **Post Hotel** (200 Pipestone Dr., 403/522-3989 or 800/661-1586, www.posthotel.com, $465-800 s or d) is one of only a handful of Canadian accommodations that have been accepted into the prestigious Relais & Châteaux organization. Bordered to the east and south by the Pipestone River, it may lack views of Lake Louise, but it is as elegant—in a modern, woodsy way—as the château. Each bungalow-style room is furnished with Canadian pine and has a balcony. Many rooms have whirlpools and fireplaces, while some have kitchens. Other facilities include the upscale Temple Mountain Spa, an indoor pool, a steam room, and a library. The hotel has 17 different room types, with 26 different rates depending on the view. Between the main lodge and the Pipestone River are four sought-after cabins, each with a wood-burning fireplace.

At the lake for which it's named, four kilometers (2.5 miles) from the valley floor, is super-luxurious **Moraine Lake Lodge** (Moraine Lake Rd., 403/522-3733 or 877/522-2777, www.morainelake.com, June-Sept., $545-785 s or d). Designed by renowned architect Arthur Erickson, the lodge is a bastion of understated charm, partially obscured from the masses of day-trippers who visit the area and yet taking full advantage of its location beside one of the world's most-photographed lakes. The decor reflects the wilderness location, with an abundance of polished log work and solid, practical furnishings in heritage-themed rooms. The rooms have no TVs or phones; instead, guests take guided nature walks, have unlimited use of canoes, and are pampered with gourmet breakfast and afternoon tea.

The famously fabulous **Fairmont Chateau Lake Louise** (111 Lake Louise Dr., 403/522-3511 or 866/540-4413, www.fairmont.com, from $699), a historic 500-room hotel on the shore of Lake Louise, has views equal to any mountain resort in the world. But all this historic charm and mountain scenery comes at a price. Rooms on the Fairmont Gold Floor come with a private concierge and upgraded everything for a little over $1,000. Official rates drop as low as $350 s or d outside of summer, with accommodation and ski pass packages sometimes advertised for around $400 d. Children younger than 18 sharing with parents are free, but if you bring a pet, it'll be an extra $40.

Backcountry Accommodations

If you're prepared to lace up your hiking boots for a true mountain experience, consider spending time at ★ **Skoki Lodge** (403/256-8473 or 800/258-7669, www.skoki.com, late-June-early-Oct. and late Dec.-mid-Apr., $300 pp), north of the Lake Louise ski resort and far from the nearest road. Getting there requires an 11-kilometer (6.8-mile) hike or ski, depending on the season. The lodge is an excellent base for exploring nearby valleys and mountains. It dates to 1931, when it operated as a lodge for local Banff skiers, and is now a National Historic Site. Today it comprises a main lodge, sleeping cabins, and a wood-fired sauna. Accommodations are rustic (propane heat but no electricity) but comfortable, with mostly twin beds in the main lodge and cabins that sleep up to five. Rates include three meals daily, including a picnic lunch that guests build from a buffet-style layout before heading out hiking or skiing. The dining room and lounge center on a wood-burning fire, where guests come together each evening

Post Hotel

to swap tales from the trail and mingle with the convivial hosts.

Campgrounds

Exit the Trans-Canada Highway at the Lake Louise interchange, 56 kilometers (35 miles) northwest of Banff, and take the first left beyond Samson Mall and under the railway bridge to reach **Lake Louise Campground,** within easy walking distance of the village. The campground is divided into two sections by the Bow River but is linked by the Bow River Loop hiking trail that leads into the village along either side of the river. Individual sites throughout are close together, but some privacy and shade are provided by towering lodgepole pines. Just under 200 serviced (powered) sites are grouped together at the end of the road. In addition to hookups, this section has showers and flush toilets; $38. Across the river are 216 unserviced sites, each with a fire ring and picnic table. Other amenities include kitchen shelters and a modern bathroom complex complete with hot showers. These sites cost $34 per night. A dump station is near the entrance to the campground ($8 per use). An interpretive program runs throughout the summer, nightly at 9pm (except Tuesday) in the outdoor theater. Sites should be booked well in advance by contacting the **Parks Canada Campground Reservation Service** (877/737-3783, www.pccamping.ca). The serviced section of this campground is open year-round, the unserviced section mid-May–September.

INFORMATION AND SERVICES
Information

Lake Louise Visitor Centre (403/522-3833, 8am-8pm daily mid-June-Aug., 8am-6pm daily mid-May-mid-June and Sept., 9am-4pm daily the rest of the year) is beside Samson Mall on Village Road. This excellent Parks Canada facility has interpretive exhibits, slide and video displays, and staff on hand to answer questions, recommend hikes suited to

your ability, and issue camping passes to those heading out into the backcountry. Look for the stuffed (literally) female grizzly and read her fascinating but sad story.

Services

A small postal outlet in Samson Mall also serves as a bus depot and car rental agency. Although Lake Louise has no banks, there's a currency exchange in the Fairmont Chateau Lake Louise and a cash machine in the grocery store. The mall also holds a busy laundry (8am-8pm daily in summer, shorter hours the rest of the year). Camping supplies and bike rentals are available from **Wilson Mountain Sports** (Samson Mall, 403/522-3636, 8am-8pm daily).

The closest **hospital** is in Banff (403/762-2222). For the local **RCMP,** call 403/522-3811.

GETTING THERE

The village of Lake Louise is beside the Trans-Canada Highway 56 kilometers (35 miles) northwest of Banff and 184 kilometers (115 miles) west of Calgary. To access Lake Louise along the Icefields Parkway, allow around 3.5 hours from Jasper (230 km/143 miles) to the north. From Vancouver, it's a drive of approximately 784 kilometers (484 miles) east along the Trans-Canada Highway to Lake Louise.

Calgary International Airport is the closest airport to Lake Louise. **Brewster** (403/762-6767 or 800/760-6934, www.brewster.ca) and **Banff Airporter** (403/762-3330 or 888/449-2901, www.banffairporter.com) offer at least a couple of shuttles per day that continue beyond Banff to Lake Louise from the airport. All charge around the same: $80 each way, with a slight round-trip discount.

Greyhound (403/522-3870) leaves the Calgary bus depot (877 Greyhound Way SW) five times daily for Lake Louise. The fare is less than that charged by Brewster, and the Banff-Lake Louise portion only is around $24. From Vancouver, it's a 13-hour ride to Lake Louise aboard the Greyhound bus.

GETTING AROUND

Samson Mall is the commercial heart of Lake Louise village. If the parking lot out front is full, consider leaving your vehicle across the road behind the Esso gas station, where one area is set aside for large RVs. The campground, hostel, and some hotels are all within easy walking distance of Samson Mall. Fairmont Chateau Lake Louise is a 2.7-kilometer (1.7-mile) walk from the valley floor. The only car-rental agency in the village is **National** (403/522-3870). The agency doesn't have many vehicles; you'd be better off picking one up at Calgary International Airport. **Lake Louise Taxi & Tours** (Samson Mall, 403/522-2020) charges $6 for flag drop, then $3 per kilometer. From the mall to Fairmont Chateau Lake Louise runs around $34, to Moraine Lake $60, and to Banff $200. **Wilson Mountain Sports** (Samson Mall, 403/522-3636, 8am-8pm daily) has mountain bikes for rent from $18 per hour or $55 per day (includes a helmet, bike lock, and water bottle). They also rent camping, climbing, and fishing gear.

Icefields Parkway (Banff)

The 230-kilometer (143-mile) Icefields Parkway, between Lake Louise and Jasper, is one of the most scenic, exciting, and inspiring mountain roads ever built. From Lake Louise it parallels the Continental Divide, following in the shadow of the highest, most rugged mountains in the Canadian Rockies. The first 122 kilometers (76 miles) to Sunwapta Pass (the boundary between Banff and Jasper National Parks) can be driven in two hours, and the entire parkway in four hours. But it's likely you'll want to spend at least a day, probably more, stopping at each of the 13 viewpoints, hiking the trails, watching the abundant wildlife, and just generally enjoying one of the world's most magnificent landscapes. Along the section within Banff National Park are two lodges, three hostels, three campgrounds, and one gas station.

Although the road is steep and winding in places, it has a wide shoulder, making it ideal for an extended bike trip. Allow seven days to pedal north from Banff to Jasper, staying at hostels or camping along the route. This is the preferable direction to travel by bike because the elevation at the town of Jasper is more than 500 meters (1,640 feet) lower than either Banff or Lake Louise.

The parkway remains open year-round, although winter brings with it some special considerations. The road is often closed for short periods for avalanche control. Check road conditions in Banff or Lake Louise before setting out. And be sure to fill up with gas; no services are available between November and April.

SIGHTS AND DRIVES
Lake Louise to Crowfoot Glacier

The Icefields Parkway forks right from the Trans-Canada Highway just north of Lake Louise. The impressive scenery begins immediately. Just three kilometers (1.9 miles) from the junction is **Herbert Lake,** formed during the last ice age when retreating glaciers deposited a pile of rubble, known as a *moraine,* across a shallow valley and water filled in behind it. The lake is a perfect place for early-morning or early-evening photography, when the Waputik Range and distinctively shaped **Mount Temple** are reflected in its waters.

Traveling north, you'll notice numerous depressions in the steep, shaded slopes of the Waputik Range across the Bow Valley. The cooler climate on these north-facing slopes makes them prone to glaciation. Cirques were cut by small local glaciers. On the opposite side of the road, **Mount Hector** (3,394 meters/11,130 feet), easily recognized by its layered peak, soon comes into view.

Hector Lake Viewpoint is 16 kilometers

(10 miles) from the junction. Although the lake itself is a long way from the highway, the emerald-green waters nestled below a massive wall of limestone form a breathtaking scene. **Bow Peak,** seen looking northward along the highway, is only 2,868 meters (9,410 feet) high but is completely detached from the Waputik Range, making it a popular destination for climbers. As you leave this viewpoint, look across the northeast end of Hector Lake for glimpses of **Mount Balfour** (3,246 meters/10,650 feet) on the distant skyline.

Crowfoot Glacier

The aptly named Crowfoot Glacier can best be appreciated from a viewpoint 17 kilometers (10.6 miles) north of Hector Lake. The glacier sits on a wide ledge near the top of Crowfoot Mountain, from where its glacial claws cling to the mountain's steep slopes. The retreat of this glacier has been dramatic. In the 1960s, two of the claws extended to the base of the lower cliff. Today they are a shadow of their former selves, barely reaching over the cliff edge.

Bow Lake

The sparkling, translucent waters of Bow Lake are among the most beautiful that can be seen from the Icefields Parkway. The lake was created when moraines deposited by retreating glaciers dammed subsequent meltwater. On still days, the water reflects the snowy peaks, their sheer cliffs, and the scree slopes that run into the lake. You don't need photography experience to take good pictures here! At the southeast end of the lake, a day-use area offers waterfront picnic tables and a trail to a swampy area at the lake's outlet. At the upper end of the lake, you'll find the historic Numti-jah Lodge and the trailhead for a walk to Bow Glacier Falls.

The road leaves Bow Lake and climbs to **Bow Summit.** As you look back toward the lake, its true turquoise color becomes apparent, and the Crowfoot Glacier reveals its unique shape. At an elevation of 2,069 meters (6,790 feet), this pass is one of the highest points crossed by a public road in Canada. It is also the beginning of the Bow River, the one you camped beside at Lake Louise, photographed flowing through the town of Banff, and fished along downstream of Canmore.

★ Peyto Lake

From the parking lot at Bow Summit, a short paved trail leads to one of the most

Herbert Lake is the first worthwhile stop along the Icefields Parkway.

breathtaking views you could ever imagine. Far below the viewpoint is Peyto Lake, an impossibly intense green lake whose hues change according to season. Before heavy melting of nearby glaciers begins (in June or early July), the lake is dark blue. As summer progresses, meltwater flows across a delta and into the lake. This water is laden with finely ground particles of rock debris known as rock flour, which remains suspended in the water. It is not the mineral content of the rock flour that is responsible for the lake's unique color, but rather the particles reflecting the blue-green sector of the light spectrum. As the amount of suspended rock flour changes, so does the color of the lake.

The lake is one of many park landmarks named for early outfitter Bill Peyto. In 1898, Peyto was part of an expedition camped at Bow Lake. Seeking solitude (as he was wont to do), he slipped off during the night to sleep near this lake. Other members of the party coined the name Peyto's Lake, and it stuck.

A farther three kilometers (1.9 miles) along the parkway is a viewpoint from which **Peyto Glacier** is visible at the far end of Peyto Lake Valley. This glacier is part of the extensive **Wapta Icefield,** which straddles the Continental Divide and extends into the northern reaches of Yoho National Park in British Columbia.

Beside the Continental Divide

From Bow Summit, the parkway descends to a viewpoint directly across the Mistaya River from **Mount Patterson** (3,197 meters/10,490 feet). Snowbird Glacier clings precariously to the mountain's steep northeast face, and the mountain's lower, wooded slopes are heavily scarred where rock and ice slides have swept down the mountainside.

As the parkway continues to descend and crosses Silverhorn Creek, the jagged limestone peaks of the Continental Divide can be seen to the west. **Mistaya Lake** is a three-kilometer-long (1.9-mile-long) body of water that sits at the bottom of the valley between the road and the divide, but it can't be seen from the parkway. The best place to view it is from the Howse Peak Viewpoint at Upper Waterfowl Lake. From here the high ridge that forms the Continental Divide is easily distinguishable. Seven peaks can be seen from here, including **Howse Peak** (3,290 meters/10,790 feet). At no point along this ridge does the elevation drop below 2,750 meters (9,000 feet). From Howse Peak, the Continental Divide makes a 90-degree turn to the west. One dominant

The beauty of Bow Lake is unmistakable.

peak that can be seen from Bow Pass to north of Saskatchewan River Crossing is **Mount Chephren** (3,268 meters/10,720 feet). Its distinctive shape and position away from the main ridge of the Continental Divide make it easy to distinguish. (Look for it directly north of Howse Peak.)

To Saskatchewan River Crossing

A trail leads down to the swampy shore of **Upper Waterfowl Lake,** providing one of the park's best opportunities to view moose, which feed on the abundant aquatic vegetation. Rock and other debris that have been carried down nearby valley systems have built up, forming a wide alluvial fan, nearly blocking the Mistaya River and creating Upper Waterfowl Lake. **Lower Waterfowl Lake** gets all the attention for its beautiful turquoise hue. Continuing north is **Mount Murchison** (3,337 meters/10,950 feet), on the east side of the parkway. Although not one of the park's highest mountains, this gray and yellow massif of Cambrian rock comprises 10 individual peaks, covering an area of 3,000 hectares (7,400 acres).

From a parking lot 14 kilometers (8.9 miles) northeast of Waterfowl Lakes Campground, a short trail descends into the montane forest to **Mistaya Canyon.** Here the effects of erosion can be appreciated as the Mistaya River leaves the floor of Mistaya Valley, plunging through a narrow-walled canyon into the North Saskatchewan Valley. The area is scarred with potholes where boulders have been whirled around by the action of fast-flowing water, carving deep depressions into the softer limestone bedrock below.

The **North Saskatchewan River** posed a major problem for early travelers and later for the builders of the Icefields Parkway. This swift-running river eventually drains into Hudson Bay. In 1989 it was named a Canadian Heritage River. One kilometer (0.6 mile) past the bridge you'll come to a panoramic viewpoint of the entire valley. From here the Howse

and Mistaya Rivers can be seen converging with the North Saskatchewan at a silt-laden delta. This is also a junction with Highway 11 (also known as David Thompson Highway), which follows the North Saskatchewan River to Rocky Mountain House and Red Deer. From this viewpoint, numerous peaks can be seen to the west. Two sharp peaks are distinctive: **Mount Outram** (3,254 meters/10,680 feet) is the closer; the farther is **Mount Forbes** (3,630 meters/11,975 feet), the highest peak in Banff National Park (and the sixth highest in the Canadian Rockies).

To Sunwapta Pass

On the north side of the North Saskatchewan River is the towering hulk of **Mount Wilson** (3,261 meters/10,700 feet), named for Banff outfitter Tom Wilson. The Icefields Parkway passes this massif on its western flanks. A pullout just past Rampart Creek Campground offers good views of Mount Amery to the west and Mounts Sarbach, Chephren, and Murchison to the south. Beyond here is the **Weeping Wall,** a long cliff of gray limestone where a series of waterfalls tumbles more than 100 meters (330 feet) down the steep slopes of Cirrus Mountain. In winter this wall of water freezes, becoming a mecca for ice climbers.

After ascending quickly, the road drops again before beginning a long climb to Sunwapta Pass. Halfway up the 360-vertical-meter (1,180-vertical-foot) climb is a viewpoint well worth a stop (cyclists will definitely appreciate a rest). From here views extend down the valley to the slopes of Mount Saskatchewan and, on the other side of the parkway, Cirrus Mountain. Another viewpoint, farther up the road, has the added attraction of a view of Bridal Veil Falls across the valley.

A cairn at **Sunwapta Pass** (2,023 meters/6,640 feet) marks the boundary between Banff and Jasper National Parks. It also marks the divide between the North Saskatchewan and Sunwapta Rivers, whose waters drain into the Atlantic and Arctic Oceans, respectively.

HIKING
★ Helen Lake

Length: 6 kilometers/3.7 miles (2.5 hours) one-way
Elevation gain: 455 meters/1,500 feet
Rating: moderate
Trailhead: across the Icefields Parkway from Crowfoot Glacier Lookout, 33 kilometers (20 miles) northwest from the junction with the Trans-Canada Highway

The trail to Helen Lake is one of the easiest ways to access a true alpine environment from any highway within Banff National Park. The trail climbs steadily through a forest of Engelmann spruce and subalpine fir for the first 2.5 kilometers (1.6 miles) to an avalanche slope, reaching the tree line and the first good viewpoint after three kilometers (1.9 miles). The view across the valley is spectacular, with Crowfoot Glacier visible to the southwest. As the trail reaches a ridge, it turns sharply and passes through extensive meadows of wildflowers that are at their peak in late July and early August. The trail then crosses a photogenic stream and climbs to the glacial cirque where Helen Lake lies. Listen and look for hoary marmots along the last section of trail and around the lakeshore.

For those with the time and energy, it's possible to continue an additional three kilometers (1.9 miles) to Dolomite Pass; the trail switchbacks steeply up a further 100 vertical meters (330 vertical feet) in less than one kilometer (0.6 mile), then descends for a further one kilometer (0.6 mile) to Katherine Lake and beyond to the pass.

Bow Glacier Falls

Length: 3.4 kilometers/2.1 miles (1 hour) one-way
Elevation gain: 130 meters/430 feet
Rating: easy
Trailhead: Num-ti-jah Lodge, Bow Lake, 36 kilometers (22.3 miles) northwest from the Trans-Canada Highway

This hike skirts one of the most beautiful lakes in the Canadian Rockies before ending at a narrow but spectacular waterfall. From the public parking lot in front of Num-ti-jah Lodge, follow the shore through to a gravel outwash area at the northwest end of the lake. Across the lake are reflected views of Crowfoot Mountain. The trail then begins a short but steep climb up the rim of a canyon before leveling out at the edge of a vast moraine of gravel, scree, and boulders. Pick your way through the 800 meters (0.5 mile) of rough ground that remains to reach the base of Bow Glacier Falls. (The namesake glacier

The hike to Helen Lake is one of the most enjoyable in Banff National Park.

can be seen above the falls from the trailhead, but not from the falls themselves.)

Peyto Lake

Length: 1.4 kilometers/0.9 mile (30 minutes) one-way
Elevation loss: 100 meters/330 feet
Rating: easy
Trailhead: unmarked pullout, Icefields Parkway, 2.4 kilometers (1.5 miles) north of Bow Summit

Without a doubt, the best place to view Peyto Lake is from a popular viewpoint accessible via a short trail from Bow Summit, 41 kilometers (25.5 miles) along the Icefields Parkway from the Trans-Canada Highway. The easiest way to access the actual shoreline, though, is along this short trail farther along the highway. A pebbled beach, strewn with driftwood, is the perfect setting for picnicking, painting, or just admiring the lake's quieter side. Back at the lake lookout, a rough trail drops nearly 300 meters (980 feet) in 2.4 kilometers (1.5 miles) to the lake.

Chephren Lake

Length: 4 kilometers/2.5 miles (60-90 minutes) one-way
Elevation gain: 100 meters/330 feet
Rating: easy
Trailhead: Waterfowl Lakes Campground, Icefields Parkway, 57 kilometers (35 miles) northwest from the Trans-Canada Highway

This pale-green body of water (pronounced kef-ren) is hidden from the Icefields Parkway but easily reached. The official trailhead is a bridge across the Mistaya River at the back of Waterfowl Lakes Campground (behind site 86). If you're not registered at the campground, park at the end of the unpaved road running along the front of the campground and walk 300 meters (0.2 mile) down the well-worn path to the river crossing. From across the river, the trail dives headlong into a subalpine forest, reaching a crudely signposted junction after 1.6 kilometers (one mile). Take the right fork. This leads 2.4 kilometers (1.5 miles) to Chephren Lake, descending steeply at the end (this stretch of trail is often muddy). The lake is nestled under the buttresses of Mount Chephren. To the left, farther up the lake, is Howse Peak.

The trail to smaller **Cirque Lake** (4.5 km/2.8 mi from the trailhead) branches left 1.6 kilometers (one mile) along this trail. It is less heavily used, but this lake is popular with anglers for its healthy population of rainbow trout.

the shoreline of Peyto Lake

Glacier Lake

Length: 9 kilometers/5.6 miles (2.5-3 hours) one-way
Elevation gain: 220 meters/770 feet
Rating: moderate
Trailhead: an old gravel pit on the west side of the highway, 1 kilometer (0.6 mile) west of Saskatchewan River Crossing

This three-kilometer-long (1.9-mile-long) lake is one of the park's largest lakes not accessible by road. Although not as scenic as the more accessible lakes along the parkway, it's a pleasant destination for a full-day or overnight trip. For the first one kilometer (0.6 mile), the trail passes through an open forest of lodgepole pine to a fancy footbridge across the rushing North Saskatchewan River. From there it climbs gradually to a viewpoint overlooking the Howse River and the valley beyond, then turns away from the river for a long slog through dense forest to Glacier Lake. A primitive campground lies just over 300 meters (0.2 mile) from where the trail emerges at the lake.

Nigel Pass

Length: 7.4 kilometers/4.6 miles (2.5 hours) one-way
Elevation gain: 365 meters/1,200 feet
Rating: moderate
Trailhead: Icefields Parkway, 2.5 kilometers (1.6 miles) north of the switchback on the "Big Bend"

Park on the east side of the highway and follow the gravel road for two kilometers (1.2 miles) to the warden cabin. Descend to two creek crossings and you quickly reach the site of Camp Parker, an old campsite used first by indigenous hunting parties and then by mountaineers exploring the area around the Columbia Icefield. Look for carvings on trees recording these early visitors. From here the trail continues to climb steadily, only increasing in gradient for the last one kilometer (0.6 mile) to the pass. The pass (2,195 meters/7,200 feet) marks the boundary between Banff and Jasper National Parks. For the best view, scramble over the rocks to the left. To the north, the view extends down the Brazeau River Valley, surrounded by a mass of peaks. To the west (left) is Nigel Peak (3,211

meters/10,535 feet), and to the southwest are views of Parker's Ridge and the glaciated peaks of Mount Athabasca.

Parker's Ridge

Length: 2.4 kilometers/1.5 miles (1 hour) one-way
Elevation gain: 210 meters/690 feet
Rating: easy/moderate
Trailhead: Icefields Parkway, 4 kilometers (2.5 miles) south of Sunwapta Pass

From the trailhead on the west side of the highway, this wide path gains elevation quickly through open meadows and scattered stands of subalpine fir. This fragile environment is easily destroyed, so it's important that you stay on the trail. During the short alpine summer, these meadows are carpeted with red heather, white mountain avens, and blue alpine forget-me-nots. From the summit of the ridge, you look down on the two-kilometer-wide (1.2-mile-wide) Saskatchewan Glacier spreading out below. Beyond is Castleguard Mountain, renowned for its extensive cave system.

ACCOMMODATIONS AND CAMPING
Under $100

North of Lake Louise, four hostels are spread along the Icefields Parkway, two in Banff National Park and two in Jasper National Park. Facilities at all four are limited, and beds should be reserved as far in advance as possible. For reservations, call 778/328-2220 or 866/762-4122, or book online (www.hihostels.ca). The first, 24 kilometers (15 miles) from Lake Louise, is **HI-Mosquito Creek,** which is near good hiking and offers accommodations for 32 in four- and six-bed cabins. Facilities include a kitchen, wood-heated sauna, and a large common room with fireplace. Although the hostel has no showers, guests are permitted to use those at the nearby Lake Louise Alpine Centre. Rates are $26 per night for members of Hostelling International (nonmembers $30). Check-in is 5pm-10pm, and it's open June-March.

HI-Rampart Creek, a further 64 kilometers (40 miles) along the parkway, is nestled below the snowcapped peak of Mount Wilson, with views across the North Saskatchewan River to even higher peaks along the Continental Divide. Like Mosquito Creek, it's near good hiking and has a kitchen and sauna. Its four cabins have a total of 24 bunk beds. Members pay $26 per night (nonmembers $30). It's open nightly May-March. Check-in is 5pm-10pm.

$200-300

The Crossing Resort (403/761-7000, www. thecrossingresort.com, mid-Apr.-mid-Oct., $210-260 s or d) is a large complex 87 kilometers (54 miles) north of Lake Louise and 45 kilometers (28 miles) south of the Columbia Icefield. It's also at the junction of Highway 11, which spurs east along Abraham Lake to Rocky Mountain House and Red Deer. The rooms offer a good combination of size and value but lack the historic charm of those at Num-ti-jah Lodge to the south and the views enjoyed by those at the Columbia Icefield Centre to the north. Each of 66 units has a phone and TV. All rates are heavily discounted outside of June-September. In addition to overnight rooms, The Crossing has the only gas between Lake Louise and Jasper, a self-serve cafeteria, a restaurant, a pub, and a supersized gift shop.

Over $300

Pioneer guide and outfitter Jimmy Simpson built ★ **Simpson's Num-ti-jah Lodge** (403/522-2167, www.sntj.ca, mid-June-mid-Oct., from $365 s or d,) on the north shore of Bow Lake, 40 kilometers (25 miles) north of Lake Louise, as a base for his outfitting operation in 1920. In those days, the route north from Lake Louise was nothing more than a horse trail. The desire to build a large structure when only short timbers were available led to the unusual octagonal shape of the main lodge. Simpson remained at Bow Lake, a living legend, until his death in 1972 at the age of 95. With a rustic mountain ambience that has changed little since Simpson's passing,

Mosquito Creek Campground

Num-ti-jah provides a memorable overnight stay. Just don't expect the conveniences of a regular motel. Under the distinctively red, steep-pitched roof of the main lodge are 25 rooms, some that share bathrooms, and there's not a TV or phone in sight. Downstairs, guests soak up the warmth of a roaring log fire while mingling in a comfortable library filled with historical mountain literature. A dining room lined with memorabilia is open for breakfast and dinner daily ($24-44).

Campgrounds

Beyond Lake Louise, the first available camping along the Icefields Parkway is at **Mosquito Creek Campground** (late June-late Sept., $22 per site), 24 kilometers (15 miles) from the Trans-Canada Highway. Don't be scared by the name, though; the bugs here are no worse than anywhere else. The 32 sites are nestled in the forest, with a tumbling creek separating the campground from a hostel of the same name. Each site has a picnic table and fire ring, while other amenities include drinking water, pit toilets, and a kitchen shelter with an old-fashioned woodstove. If you're camping at Mosquito Creek and want a break from the usual camp fare, consider traveling 17 kilometers (10.6 miles) up the highway to the convivial, historic dining room at Num-ti-jah Lodge (403/522-2167, www.sntj.ca) to feast on Canadian-inspired cuisine.

Waterfowl Lakes Campground (late June-mid-Sept., $27 per site) is 33 kilometers (20 miles) north along the Icefields Parkway from Mosquito Creek. It features 116 sites between Upper and Lower Waterfowl Lakes, with a few sites in view of the lower lake. Facilities include drinking water, flush toilets, and kitchen shelters with wood-burning stoves. Rise early to watch the first rays of sun hit Mount Chephren from the shoreline of the lower lake, then plan on hiking the four-kilometer (2.5-mile) trail to Chephren Lake—you'll be the first on the trail and back in time for a late breakfast.

Continuing toward Jasper, the Icefields Parkway passes The Crossing, a good place to gas up and buy last-minute groceries before reaching **Rampart Creek Campground** (July-Aug., $22 per site), 31 kilometers (19 miles) beyond Waterfowl Lake and 88 kilometers (55 miles) from Lake Louise. With just 50 sites, this campground fills early each afternoon. Facilities include kitchen shelters, pit toilets, and drinking water.

Nearby Parks

★ MOUNT ASSINIBOINE PROVINCIAL PARK

Named for one of the Canadian Rockies' most spectacular peaks, this 39,050-hectare (96,500-acre), roughly triangular park lies northeast of Radium Hot Springs, sandwiched between Kootenay National Park to the west and Banff National Park to the east. It's inaccessible by road; access is on foot or by helicopter. A haven for experienced hikers, the park offers alpine meadows, lakes, glaciers, and many peaks higher than 3,050 meters (10,000 feet) to explore. The park's highest peak, 3,618-meter (11,870-foot) Mount Assiniboine (seventh highest in the Canadian Rockies), is known as the "Matterhorn of the Rockies" for its resemblance to that famous Swiss landmark. The striking peak can be seen from many points well outside the boundaries of the park, including the Sunshine Village winter resort in Banff National Park.

The peak is named for the Assiniboine people, who ventured into this section of the Canadian Rockies many thousands of years before European exploration. The name Assiniboine means "stone boilers," a reference to their preferred cooking method. The mountain was sighted and named by a geological survey team in 1885, but the first ascent wasn't made until 1901.

Lake Magog is the destination of most park visitors. Here you'll find the park's only facilities and the trailheads for several interesting and varied day hikes. One of the most popular walks is along the Sunburst Valley/ Nub Ridge Trail. From Lake Magog, small Sunburst Lake is reached in about 20 minutes, then the trail continues northwest a short distance to Cerulean Lake. From this lake's outlet, the trail descends slowly along the Mitchell River to a junction four kilometers (2.5 miles) from Lake Magog. Take the right fork, which climbs through a dense subalpine forest to Elizabeth Lake, nestled in the southern shadow of Nub Peak. From this point, instead of descending back to Cerulean Lake, plan on taking the Nub Ridge Trail, which climbs steadily for one kilometer (0.6 mile) to a magnificent viewpoint high above Lake Magog. From the viewpoint, it's just less than four kilometers (2.5 miles), downhill all the way, to the valley floor. The total length of this outing is 11 kilometers (6.8 miles), and as elevation gained is only just over 400 meters

(1,310 feet), the trail can comfortably be completed in four hours.

Accommodations

Getting to and staying at ★ **Mount Assiniboine Lodge** isn't cheap, but the number of repeat guests is testament to an experience that you will never forget. The mountain scenery may take most of the kudos, but the lodge's congenial atmosphere makes the stay equally memorable. Built in 1928 by the CPR, the delightfully rustic lodge is set in a lakeside meadow below its distinctive namesake peak. The main building holds six double rooms that share bathroom facilities and a dining area where hearty meals (included in the rates) are served up communal-style. Scattered in the surrounding trees are six one-room cabins that sleep 2-5 people. Each has running water and uses propane to heat and light the space. Outhouses and showers are shared. The rate for lodge rooms is $325 per person, while cabin accommodations range $325-400. Children 12 and under are $165.

You can reach the lodge on foot or fly in with Alpine Helicopters from a heliport in Spray Valley Provincial Park. The departure days are the same as for campers (Wednesday, Friday, and Sunday); the only difference is that helicopter departures begin at 11:30am for lodge guests. Lodge guests flying in may bring 18 kilograms (40 pounds) of gear, plus one pair of skis. If you decide to hike in (or out), the charge for luggage transfers is $3 per pound (0.45 kilogram).

The operating season is late June to the first weekend of October, and then mid-February to late March, for cross-country skiing. There is a minimum stay of two nights. The lodge has no landline phone; for reservations or information, call 403/678-2883 (8:30am-2:30pm Mon.-Fri.) or check the website (www.assiniboinelodge.com).

Campground and Huts

Lake Magog is the park's main facility area, such as it is. A designated camping area on a low ridge above the lake's west shore provides a source of drinking water, pit toilets, and bear-proof food caches. Open fires are prohibited. Sites are $10 per person per night. No reservations are taken, but even those who visit frequently have told me they've never seen it full. Also at the lake are the **Naiset Huts,** where bunk beds cost $25 per person per night (book through Mount Assiniboine Lodge at 403/678-2883, 8:30am-2:30pm Mon.-Fri., www.assiniboinelodge.com). The cabins

Mount Assiniboine and Lake Magog

contain nothing more than bunk beds with mattresses, so you'll need a stove, cooking utensils, food, a sleeping bag, and your own source of non-gas-powered light.

Information

In addition to the government agency responsible for the park (Ministry of Environment, www.env.gov.bc.ca/bcparks), park information centers in Radium Hot Springs, Lake Louise, and Banff provide information and up-to-date trail conditions.

Getting There

APPROACHING THE PARK ON FOOT

Three trails provide access to **Lake Magog,** the park's largest body of water. The most popular comes in from the northeast, starting at the Sunshine Village winter resort in Banff National Park and leading 29 kilometers (18 miles) via Citadel Pass to the lake. Not only is this trail spectacular, but the high elevation of the trailhead (2,100 meters/6,890 feet) makes for a relatively easy approach. Another approach is from the east, in Spray Valley Provincial Park (Kananaskis Country). The trailhead is at the southern end of Spray Lake; take the Mount Shark staging area turnoff 40 kilometers (25 miles) south of Canmore. By the time the trail has climbed the Bryant Creek drainage to 2,165-meter (7,100-foot) Assiniboine Pass, all elevation gain (450 meters/1,480 feet) has been made. At 27 kilometers (16.8 miles), this is the shortest approach, but its elevation gain is greater than that of the other two trails. The longest and least-used access is from Highway 93 at Simpson River in Kootenay National Park. This trail climbs the Simpson River and Surprise Creek drainages and crosses 2,270-meter (7,450-foot) Ferro Pass to the lake for a total length of 32 kilometers (20 miles).

THE EASY WAY IN

If these long approaches put visiting the park out of your reach, there's one more option: You can fly in by helicopter from the Mount

Shark Heliport, at the southern end of Spray Valley Provincial Park, 40 kilometers (25 miles) southwest of Canmore. Flights depart at 12:30pm Wednesday, Friday, and Sunday and cost $175 per person each way, including an 18-kilogram (40-pound) per-person baggage limit. Although **Alpine Helicopters** (403/678-4802, www.alpinehelicopter.com) operates the flights, all bookings must be made through **Mount Assiniboine Lodge** (call 403/678-2883 8:30am-2:30pm Mon.-Fri., www.assiniboinelodge.com).

If you're planning on hiking into the park, Alpine Helicopters will fly your gear in for $3 per pound (0.45 kilogram). This same company, which also operates from a base in Canmore, charges $300 per person for a 30-minute flightseeing trip over the park. For more information, contact Alpine Helicopters.

SIFFLEUR WILDERNESS AREA

This remote region on the Alberta side of the Canadian Rockies lies south of Highway 11, which crosses west-central Alberta between Rocky Mountain House and Saskatchewan River Crossing, in Banff National Park. It is completely protected from any activities that could have an impact on the area's fragile ecosystems. That includes road and trail development: No bridges have been built over the area's many fast-flowing streams, and the few old trails that do exist are not maintained. Elk, deer, moose, cougars, wolverines, wolves, coyotes, black bears, and grizzly bears roam the area's four main valleys, while the higher alpine elevations harbor mountain goats and bighorn sheep.

The main trail into the 41,200-hectare (101,800-acre) wilderness begins from a parking area two kilometers (1.2 miles) south of the Two O'Clock Creek Campground at Kootenay Plains. The area's northeastern boundary is a seven-kilometer (4.3-mile) hike from here. Even if you're not heading right into the wilderness area, the first section of this trail, which passes through Siffleur Falls Provincial Recreation Area to **Siffleur Falls,** is worth walking. The trail crosses the North Saskatchewan River via a swinging bridge and then at the two-kilometer (1.2-mile) mark crosses the Siffleur River, reaching the falls after four kilometers (2.5 miles); allow 70 minutes one-way. These are the official Siffleur Falls, but others lie farther upstream at the 6.2-kilometer (3.9-mile) and 6.9-kilometer (4.3-mile) marks.

Once inside the wilderness area, the trail climbs steadily alongside the Siffleur River and into the heart of the wilderness. Ambitious hikers can continue through to the Dolomite Creek area of Banff National Park, finishing at the Icefields Parkway, seven kilometers (4.3 miles) south of Bow Summit. Total length of this trail is 68 kilometers (42 miles), a strenuous five-day backcountry expedition. Another access point for the area is opposite Waterfowl Lakes Campground in Banff National Park. From here it is six kilometers (3.7 miles) up Noyes Creek to the wilderness area boundary; the trail peters out after 4.5 kilometers (2.8 miles) and requires some serious scrambling before descending into Siffleur. This trail—as with all others in the wilderness area—is for experienced hikers only.

Campground

Two O'Clock Creek Campground (May-mid-Oct., $20 per night) lies two kilometers (1.2 miles) from the park's main trailhead in Kootenay Plains Provincial Recreation Area. It is a primitive facility with a picnic shelter, firewood, and drinking water; the 24 sites each have a picnic table and fire pit (firewood $4).

WHITE GOAT WILDERNESS AREA

White Goat comprises 44,500 hectares (110,000 acres) of high mountain ranges, wide valleys, hanging glaciers, waterfalls, and high alpine lakes. It lies north and west of Highway 11, abutting the north end of Banff National Park and the south end of Jasper National Park. The area's vegetation zones are easily recognizable: subalpine forests of Engelmann spruce, subalpine fir, and lodgepole pine; alpine tundra higher up. Large mammals here include a sizable population of bighorn sheep, as well as mountain goats, deer, elk, woodland caribou, moose, cougars, wolves, coyotes, black bears, and grizzly bears.

The most popular hike is the **McDonald Creek Trail,** which first follows the Cline River, then McDonald Creek to the creek's source in the heart of the wilderness area. McDonald Creek is approximately 12 kilometers (7.5 miles) from the parking area on Highway 11, but a full day should be allowed for this section because the trail crosses many streams. From where McDonald Creek flows into the Cline River, it is 19 kilometers (11.8 miles) to the McDonald Lakes, but allow another two full days; the total elevation gain for the hike is a challenging 1,222 meters (4,000 feet). Other hiking possibilities include following the Cline River to its source and crossing Sunset Pass into Banff National Park, 17 kilometers (10.6 miles) north of Saskatchewan River Crossing, or heading up Cataract Creek and linking up with the trails in the Brazeau River area of Jasper National Park.

Background

The Landscape 96   Animals 100
Plants 99   History 107

The Landscape

The Rocky Mountains rise from the dense forests of central Mexico and run north through the U.S. states of New Mexico, Colorado, Wyoming, and Montana. Continuing north across the 49th parallel (the U.S.-Canada border), the range forms a natural border between the Canadian provinces of British Columbia and Alberta. Mountainous British Columbia is Canada's westernmost province, extending to the Pacific Ocean, while Alberta, to the east, is mostly prairie. The provincial boundary is the Continental Divide, an imaginary line that runs along the Rockies' highest peaks. Although it is a subjective matter, perhaps most would agree that this particular stretch of the Rocky Mountains—the Canadian Rockies—is the most spectacular segment. North of British Columbia and Alberta, the Rockies descend to their northern terminus in the boreal forests of northern Canada.

The Canadian Rockies are relatively low compared to other well-known mountain ranges of the world; the highest peak, Mount Robson, tops out at 3,954 meters (12,970 feet). Running parallel to the mountains along their eastern edge is a series of long, rolling ridges known as the foothills. To the west is the Rocky Mountain Trench, a long, wide valley that in turn is bordered to the west by various subranges of the Columbia Mountains.

GEOLOGY

The Rocky Mountains began rising 75 million years ago, making them relatively young compared to the world's major mountain ranges. But to fully appreciate the geology of the Rockies, you must look back many hundreds of millions of years, to the Precambrian era. At this time, about 700 million years ago, the Pacific Ocean covered most of the western provinces and states. The ocean advanced, then receded, several times over the next half-billion years. Each time the ocean flooded eastward it deposited layers of silt and sand on its bed—layers that built up with each successive inundation. Starting approximately 550 million years ago, the oceans began to come alive with marine invertebrates and the first crustaceans. As these creatures died and sank to the ocean floor, they added to the layers of sediment. Over time, the ever-increasing sediment load compressed the underlying layers into sandstone, shale, and quartzite.

Birth of the Rockies

Some 200 million years ago, the stability of the ocean floor began wavering along the West Coast of North America, culminating 75 million years ago as two plates of the earth's crust collided. According to plate tectonics theory, the earth's crust is broken into several massive chunks (plates) that are always moving and occasionally bump into each other. This isn't something that happens overnight; a plate may move only a few centimeters over thousands of years. In the case of the Rockies, the Pacific Plate butted into the North American Plate and was forced beneath it. The land at this subduction zone was crumpled and thrust upward, creating the Rocky Mountains. Layers of sediment laid down on the ocean floor over the course of hundreds of millions of years were folded, twisted, and squeezed; great slabs of rock broke away, and in places older strata were pushed on top of younger. By the beginning of the Tertiary period, around 65 million years ago, the present form of mountain contours was established

a glacier-fed stream high above the tree line

and the geological framework of the mountains was in place.

The Ice Ages

No one knows why, but around one million years ago the world's climate cooled a few degrees. Ice caps formed in Arctic regions and slowly moved south over North America and Eurasia. These advances, followed by retreats, occurred four times.

The final major glaciation began moving south 35,000 years ago. A sheet of ice up to 2,000 meters (6,560 feet) deep covered all but the highest peaks of the Rocky Mountains. The ice scoured the terrain, destroying all vegetation as it crept slowly forward. In the mountains, these rivers of ice carved hollows, known as **cirques,** into the slopes of the higher peaks. They rounded off lower peaks and reamed out valleys from their pre-glacier V shape to the trademark, postglacial U shape. The retreat of this ice sheet, beginning around 12,000 years ago, also radically altered the landscape. Rock and debris that

had been picked up by the ice on its march forward melted out during the retreat, creating high ridges known as lateral and terminal **moraines.** Many of these moraines blocked natural drainages, resulting in the formation of lakes. Meltwater drained into rivers and streams, incising deep channels into the sedimentary rock of the plains. Today, the only remnants of this ice age are the scattered ice fields along the Continental Divide, including the 325-square-kilometer (125-square-mile) Columbia Icefield.

Waterways

Water in its various forms has had a profound effect on the appearance of the Canadian Rockies. In addition to the scouring action of the glaciers, flowing water in rivers and streams has, over the millennia, deeply etched the landscape. The process continues today.

The flow of water is directly related to **divides,** or high points of land that dictate the direction of water flow. The dominant divide in the Canadian Rockies, and indeed North America, is the Continental Divide. The natural boundary created by this divide forms the Alberta-British Columbia border, while other, less obvious divides form borders of many parks of the Canadian Rockies. The five national parks are classic examples of this scenario. The divides forming the boundaries of Banff National Park encompass the entire upper watershed of the **Bow River.** The Bow flows southward through the park, then heads east out of the mountains and into the Saskatchewan River system, whose waters continue east to Hudson Bay and the Atlantic Ocean. The Bow River is fed by many lakes famed for their beauty, including **Bow, Louise,** and **Moraine.** To the south, the rivers of Kananaskis Country and Waterton Lakes National Park also drain into the Saskatchewan River system.

The boundary between Jasper and Banff National Parks is an important north-south divide. The **Columbia Icefield,** a remnant of the last ice age, lies on either side of this divide. Runoff from the south side of the ice field

Chinook Winds

On many days in the dead of winter, a distinctive arch of clouds forms in the sky over the southwestern corner of Alberta as a wind peculiar to the Canadian Rockies swoops down over the mountains. The warm wind, known as a *chinook* (snow eater), can raise temperatures by up to 20°C (36°F) in an hour and up to 40°C (72°F) in a 24-hour period. The wind's effect on the snowpack is legendary. One story tells of a backcountry skier who spent the better part of a day traversing to the summit of a snow-clad peak on the front range of the Canadian Rockies. As he rested and contemplated skiing down, he realized that the slope had become completely bare!

Chinooks originate over the Pacific Ocean when warm, moist air is pushed eastward by prevailing westerlies. The air pressure of these winds is less than at lower elevations, and, therefore, as the air moves down the front ranges of the Canadian Rockies, it is subjected to increased pressure. This increasing of the air pressure warms the winds, which then fan out across the foothills and prairies. The "chinook arch" is formed as the clear air clashes with the warmer cloud-laden winds. The phenomenon is most common in southern Alberta but occurs to a lesser degree as far north as the Peace River Valley.

flows south into the Saskatchewan River system, while runoff from the north side forms the upper headwaters of the **Athabasca River** system. The Athabasca flows north through Jasper National Park and into the Mackenzie River system, which continues north to the Arctic Ocean. All water draining off the western slopes of the Continental Divide ends up in the Pacific Ocean via two major river systems: the **Columbia** and the **Fraser.** The mighty Columbia makes a wide northern loop before heading south into the U.S. state of Washington and draining into the Pacific Ocean. Along the way it picks up the waters of the **Kootenay River,** which begins high in Kootenay National Park and makes a lazy loop south through Montana and Idaho before joining the Columbia at Castlegar, British Columbia, and the **Kicking Horse River,** which flows down from the divides that form the borders of Yoho National Park. The **Fraser River,** the longest river entirely within British Columbia, begins in the high reaches of Mount Robson Provincial Park.

CLIMATE

More than any other factor, prevailing moisture-laden westerlies blowing across British Columbia from the Pacific Ocean dictate the climate of the Canadian Rockies. The cold heights of the mountain peaks wring the winds dry, making for clear, sunny skies in southern Alberta. In winter, the dry winds blasting down the eastern slopes of the Rockies can raise temperatures on the prairies by up to 40°C (72°F) in 24 hours. Called **chinooks,** these desiccating blows are a phenomenon unique to Alberta.

Elevation and, to a lesser degree, latitude are two other factors affecting the climate within the mountain ecosystem. Elevations vary from 800 meters (2,600 feet) above sea level at Radium Hot Springs to 1,500 meters (4,920 feet) at Lake Louise to 3,954 meters (12,970 feet) at the summit of Mount Robson. As a general rule, temperatures fall 5°C (9°F) for every 1,000 meters (3,280 feet) of elevation gained. Another interesting phenomenon occurring in the Canadian Rockies is the **temperature inversion,** in which a layer of warm air sits on top of a cold air mass. During these inversions, high- and low-country roles are reversed; prairie residents can be shivering and bundling up, while their mountain fellows are sunning themselves in short sleeves.

The Seasons

Summer in the mountains is short, but the days are long. With up to 17 hours of daylight around the summer solstice of June 21, this is an ideal time for travel and camping out. The months on either side of summer are ideal for touring, especially September, when rainfall is minimal. Winter is cold, but the skiing and snowboarding are fantastic.

January is usually the coldest month, when Banff's average temperature is -10°C (14°F). In winter, extended spells of -30°C (-22°F) are not uncommon anywhere in the mountains, and temperatures occasionally drop below -40°C (-40°F). The coldest temperature recorded was -52°C (-62°F), in Lake Louise on January 25, 1950. Severe cold weather is often accompanied by sunshine; the cold is a dry cold, unlike the damp cold experienced in coastal regions. Cold temperatures and snow can be expected through mid-March.

Although March, April, and May are, more or less, the official months of spring, snow often falls in May, many lakes may remain frozen until June, and snow cover on higher mountain hiking trails remains until early July. During this period of the year, the mountains are often affected by low-pressure weather patterns from the southeast, creating continuous days of rain, especially in the south.

Things warm up in summer. July is the hottest month, with Banff's average daytime temperature topping out above 23°C (73°F). On hot days, the temperature can hit 30°C (86°F) along lower-elevation valleys. Again, because of the dryness of the air, these temperatures are more bearable here than in coastal regions experiencing the same temperatures.

By late September, the mountain air begins to have a distinct chill. October brings the highest temperature variations of the year; the thermometer can hit 30°C (86°F) but also dip as low as -20°C (-4°F). Mild weather can continue until early December, but generally the first snow falls in October, and by mid-November winter has set in.

Plants

Botanists divide the Canadian Rockies into three distinct vegetation zones (also called **biomes**): montane, subalpine, and alpine. The boundaries of these zones are determined by several factors, the most important being altitude. Latitude and exposure are also factors, but less so. Typically, within any 1,500 meters (4,920 feet) of elevation change, you'll pass through each of the three zones. Conifers (evergreens) predominate in the montane and subalpine, whereas above the tree line, in the alpine, only low-growing hardy species survive.

MONTANE

The foothills, along with most major valleys below an elevation of about 1,500 meters (4,920 feet), are primarily cloaked in montane forest. **Aspen, balsam poplar,** and **white spruce** thrive here. **Lodgepole pine** is the first species to emerge after fire. Its hard seed cones are sealed by a resin that is melted only at high temperatures. When fire races through the forest, the resin melts and the cones release their seeds. The lodgepole is named for its straight, slender trunk, which was used as a center pole for tepees. On dry, south-facing slopes, **Douglas fir** is the climax species. Where sunlight penetrates the forest, such as along riverbanks, flowers like **lady's slipper, Indian paintbrush,** and **saxifrage** are common. Large tracts of **fescue grassland** are common at lower elevations. The montane forest holds the greatest diversity of life of any vegetation zone and is prime winter habitat for larger mammals. But this is the habitat where most development occurs and therefore is often much changed from its natural state.

SUBALPINE

Subalpine forests occur where temperatures are lower and precipitation higher than in the montane. In the Canadian Rockies, this is generally 1,500-2,200 meters (4,920-7,220 feet) above sea level. The upper limit of the subalpine zone is the tree line. Approximately half the flora of the mountains falls within this zone. The climax species are **Engelmann spruce** and **subalpine fir** (recognized by its spire-like crown), although extensive forests of **lodgepole pine** occur in areas that have been scorched by fire in the last 100 years. Before lodgepole pines take root in fire-ravished areas, fireweed blankets the scorched earth. At higher elevations, stands of **larch** are seen. Larches are deciduous conifers—unlike those of other evergreens, their needles turn a golden-orange color each fall, producing a magnificent display for photographers.

ALPINE

The alpine zone extends from the tree line to mountain summits. The upper limit of tree growth in the Canadian Rockies varies between 1,800 and 2,400 meters (5,900 and 7,900 feet) above sea level, dropping progressively to the north until it meets the treeless tundra of the Arctic. Vegetation at these high altitudes occurs only where soil has been deposited. Large areas of alpine meadows burst with color for a short period each summer as **lupines, mountain avens, alpine forget-me-nots, avalanche lilies, moss campion,** and a variety of **heathers** bloom.

Animals

One of the biggest attractions of the Canadian Rockies is the abundance of wildlife, especially large mammals such as elk, moose, bighorn sheep, and bears, which are all widespread and easily viewed throughout the mountains.

THE DEER FAMILY
Mule Deer and White-Tailed Deer

Mule deer and white-tailed deer are similar in size and appearance. Their color varies with the season but is generally light brown in summer, turning dirty gray in winter. While both species are considerably smaller than elk, the mule deer is a little stockier than the white-tailed deer. The mule deer has a white rump, a white tail with a dark tip, and large mule-like ears. It inhabits open forests along valley floors. The white-tailed deer's tail is dark on top, but when the animal runs, it holds its tail erect, revealing an all-white underside. Whitetails frequent thickets along the rivers and lakes of the foothills. They are most common on the British Columbia side of the Continental Divide.

Elk

The elk, or **wapiti,** is the most widespread and common of the larger mammals living in the Canadian Rockies. It has a tan body with a dark-brown neck, dark-brown legs, and a white rump. This second-largest member of the deer family weighs 250-450 kilograms (550-1,000 pounds) and stands 1.5 meters (five feet) at the shoulder. Beginning each spring, bulls grow an impressive set of antlers, covered in what is known as velvet. The velvet contains nutrients that stimulate antler growth. By fall, the antlers have reached their full size and the velvet is shed. Rutting season takes place between August and October; listen for the shrill bugles of the bulls serenading the females. During the rut, randy males will challenge anything with their antlers and can be dangerous. The bulls shed their antlers each spring, but don't relax too much because, also in spring, females protecting their young can be equally dangerous. Large herds of elk live in and around the town of Banff, often nonchalantly wandering along streets and feeding on tasty plants in residential gardens.

Moose

The giant of the deer family is the moose, an awkward-looking mammal that appears to have been designed by a cartoonist. It has the largest antlers of any animal in the world, stands up to 1.8 meters (six feet) at the shoulder, and weighs up to 500 kilograms (1,100 pounds). Its body is dark brown, and it has a prominent nose, long spindly legs, small eyes, big ears, and an odd flap of skin called a bell dangling beneath its chin. Apart from all that, it's good-looking. Each spring, the bull begins to grow palm-shaped antlers that by August will be fully grown. Moose are solitary animals preferring marshy areas and weedy lakes, but they are known to wander to higher elevations searching out open spaces in summer. They forage in and around ponds on willows, aspens, birches, grasses, and all aquatic vegetation. They are not particularly common in the Canadian Rockies, numbering around 400. Although they may appear docile, moose will attack humans if they feel threatened.

Caribou

Caribou are also occasionally spotted from the Icefields Parkway south of Sunwapta Falls. Indigenous people named the animal *caribou* (hoof scraper) for the way in which they feed in winter, scraping away snow with their hooves. Caribou are smaller than elk and have a dark brown coat with creamy patches on the neck and rump. Both sexes grow antlers, but those of the females are shorter and have fewer points. On average, males weigh 180 kilograms (400 pounds), females 115 kilograms (250 pounds). Like the elk, they breed in fall, with the males gathering a harem.

BEARS

The two species of bears present in the mountains—black bears and grizzlies—can be differentiated by size and shape. Grizzlies are larger than black bears and have a flatter, dish-shaped face and a distinctive hump of muscle behind their neck. Color is not a reliable way to tell them apart. Black bears are not always black. They can be brown or cinnamon, causing them to be confused with the brown-colored grizzly.

Black Bears

If you spot a bear feeding beside the road, chances are it's a black bear. These mammals are widespread throughout all forested areas of the Canadian Rockies. Their weight varies considerably, but males average 150 kilograms (330 pounds) and females 100 kilograms (220 pounds). Their diet is omnivorous, consisting primarily of grasses and berries but supplemented by small mammals. They are not true hibernators, but in winter they can sleep for up to a month at a time before changing position. During this time, their heartbeat drops to 10 beats per minute, their body temperature drops, and they lose up to 30 percent of their body weight. Females reach reproductive maturity after five years; cubs, usually two, are born in late winter, while the mother is still asleep.

Grizzly Bears

Grizzlies, second largest of eight recognized species of bears worldwide (only polar bears are larger), have disappeared from most of North America but are widespread throughout the Canadian Rockies, numbering around 300 in the region. Grizzlies are only occasionally seen by casual observers; most sightings occur in alpine and subalpine zones, although sightings at lower elevations are not unusual, especially when snow falls early or late. The bears' color ranges from light brown to almost black, with dark tan being the most common. On average, males weigh 200-350 kilograms (440-770 pounds). The bears eat small and medium-size mammals, and berries in fall. Like black bears, they sleep through most of the winter. When they emerge in early spring, the bears scavenge carcasses of animals that succumbed to the winter, until the new spring vegetation becomes sufficiently plentiful. Females first give birth at four years old, and then every three years, with cubs remaining with their mother for 2-3 years.

Wildlife and You

BACKGROUND
ANIMALS

An abundance of wildlife is one of the biggest draws of the Canadian Rockies. To help preserve this precious resource, obey fishing and hunting regulations and use common sense.

Do not feed the animals. Many animals may seem tame, but feeding them endangers yourself, the animal, and other visitors, as animals become aggressive when looking for handouts (even the smallest critters, such as squirrels).

Store food safely. When camping, keep food in your vehicle or out of reach of animals. Just leaving it in a cooler isn't good enough.

Keep your distance. Although it's tempting to get close to wildlife for a better look or a photograph, it disturbs the animal and, in many cases, can be dangerous.

Drive carefully. The most common cause of premature death for larger mammals is being hit by vehicles.

WILD DOGS AND CATS

Coyotes

The coyote is often mistaken for a wolf when in fact it is much smaller, weighing up to only 15 kilograms (33 pounds). It has a pointed nose and a long, bushy tail. Its coloring is a mottled mix of brown and gray, with lighter-colored legs and belly. The coyote is a skillful and crafty hunter, preying mainly on rodents. Coyotes have the remarkable ability to hear the movement of small mammals under the snow, allowing them to hunt these animals without actually seeing them. They are often seen patrolling the edges of highways and crossing open meadows in low-lying valleys.

Wolves

Wolves that inhabit the Canadian Rockies are larger than coyotes and larger than the wolves of eastern Canada. They weigh up to 60 kilograms (132 pounds), stand up to one meter (3.2 feet) high at the shoulder, and resemble large huskies or German shepherds. Their color ranges from snow white to brown or black; those in the Canadian Rockies are, most often, shades of gray. They usually form packs of up to eight members, traveling, hunting, and resting together, and adhering to a hierarchical social order. As individuals, they are complex and intriguing, capable of expressing happiness, humor, and loneliness.

Once the target of a relentless campaign to exterminate the species, the wolf has made an incredible comeback in the Canadian Rockies; today about 120 wolves roam the region, including one pack often seen in winter along the Bow Valley Parkway between Banff and Lake Louise.

Cougars

Rarely encountered by casual hikers, cougars (known in other parts of North America as mountain lions, pumas, or catamounts) measure up to 1.5 meters (five feet) long. The average male weighs 75 kilograms (165 pounds) and the female 40-55 kilograms (90-120 pounds). Cougars are versatile hunters whose acute vision takes in a peripheral span in excess of 200 degrees. They typically kill a large mammal such as an elk or deer every 12-14 days, eating part of it and caching the rest. Their diet also includes chipmunks, ground squirrels, snowshoe hares, and occasionally porcupines. Their athletic prowess puts Olympians to shame. They can spring forward more than 8 meters (26 feet) from a standstill, leap 4 meters (13 feet) into the air, and safely jump from a height of 20 meters (65 feet).

The cougar is a solitary animal with distinct territorial boundaries. This limits its population density, which in turn means that its overall numbers are low. They are most common in the foothills along the eastern slopes of the Canadian Rockies.

Lynx

The elusive lynx is identifiable by its pointy black ear tufts and an oversized tabby cat appearance. The animal has broad, padded paws that distribute its weight, allowing it to float on the surface of snow. It weighs up to 10 kilograms (22 pounds) but appears much larger because of its coat of long, thick fur. The lynx, uncommon but widespread throughout the region, is a solitary creature that prefers the cover of subalpine forests, feeding mostly at night on snowshoe hares and other small mammals.

OTHER LARGE MAMMALS

Mountain Goats

The remarkable rock-climbing ability of these nimble-footed creatures allows them to live on rocky ledges or near-vertical slopes, safe from predators. They also frequent the alpine meadows and open forests of the Canadian Rockies, where they congregate around natural salt licks. The goats stand one meter (3.2 feet) at the shoulder and weigh 65-130 kilograms (140-290 pounds). Both sexes possess a peculiar beard, or rather, goatee. Both sexes have horns. It is possible to determine the sex by the shape of the horns; those of the female grow straight up before curling slightly backward, whereas those of the male curl back in a single arch. The goats shed their thick coats each summer, making them look ragged, but by fall they've regrown a fine, new white woolen coat.

Bighorn Sheep

Bighorn sheep are some of the most distinctive mammals of the Canadian Rockies. Easily recognized by their impressive horns, they are often seen grazing on grassy mountain slopes or at salt licks beside the road. The color of their coat varies with the season; in summer, it's a brownish-gray with a cream-colored belly and rump, turning lighter in winter. Fully grown males can weigh up to 120 kilograms (270 pounds), while females generally weigh around 80 kilograms (180 pounds). Both sexes possess horns, rather than antlers like members of the deer family. Unlike antlers, horns are not shed each year and can grow to astounding sizes. The horns of rams are larger than those of ewes and curve up to 360 degrees. The spiraled horns of an older ram can measure longer than one meter (3.2 feet) and weigh as much as 15 kilograms (33 pounds). During the fall mating season, a hierarchy is established among the rams for

Male bighorn sheep face off to establish dominance.

the right to breed ewes. As the males face off against each other to establish dominance, their horns act as both a weapon and a buffer against the head butting of other rams. The skull structure of the bighorn, rams in particular, has become adapted to these head-butting clashes, keeping the animals from being knocked unconscious.

Bighorn sheep are particularly tolerant of humans and often approach parked vehicles; although they are not especially dangerous, as with all mammals, you should not approach or feed them.

Bison

Before the arrival of Europeans, millions of bison roamed the North American plains, with some entering the valleys of the Canadian Rockies to escape harsh winters. Several factors contributed to their decline, including the combined presence of explorers, settlers, and indigenous peoples. By the late 1800s they were wiped out, and since then a few attempts at reintroduction have taken place, including in the remote Panther River Valley of Banff National Park in 2017. For more information on this project, go to www. bisonbelong.ca.

SMALL MAMMALS
Beavers

One of the animal kingdom's most industrious mammals is the beaver. Growing to a length of 50 centimeters (20 inches) and tipping the scales at around 20 kilograms (44 pounds), it has a flat, rudderlike tail and webbed back feet that enable it to swim at speeds up to 10 kph (6 mph). The exploration of western Canada can be directly attributed to the beaver, whose pelt was in high demand in fashion-conscious Europe in the early 1800s. The beaver was never entirely wiped out from the mountains, and today the animals can be found in almost any forested valley with flowing water. Beavers build their dam walls and lodges of twigs, branches, sticks of felled trees, and mud. They eat the bark and smaller twigs

Columbian ground squirrel

of deciduous plants and store branches under water, near the lodge, as a winter food supply.

Squirrels

Several species of squirrels are common in the Canadian Rockies. The **golden-mantled ground squirrel,** found in rocky outcrops of subalpine and alpine regions, has black stripes along its sides and looks like an oversized chipmunk. Most common is the **Columbian ground squirrel,** which lives in burrows, often in open grassland. It is recognizable by its reddish legs, face, and underside, and a flecked, grayish back. The bushy-tailed **red squirrel,** the bold chatterbox of the forest, leaves telltale shelled cones at the base of conifers. Another member of the species, the nocturnal **northern flying squirrel,** glides through the montane forests of mountain valleys but is rarely seen.

Hoary Marmots

High in the mountains, above the tree line,

hoary marmots are often seen sunning themselves on boulders in rocky areas or meadows. They are stocky creatures, weighing 4-9 kilograms (9-19 pounds). When danger approaches, these large rodents emit a shrill whistle to warn their colony. Marmots are active only for a few months each summer, spending up to nine months a year in hibernation.

Porcupines

This small, squat animal is easily recognized by its thick coat of quills. It eats roots and leaves but is also known as being destructive around wooden buildings and vehicle tires. Porcupines are common and widespread throughout all forested areas, but they're hard to spy because they feed most often at night.

Other Rodents

Widespread throughout western Canada, **muskrats** make their mountain home in the waterways and wetlands of all low-lying valleys. They are agile swimmers, able to stay submerged for up to 12 minutes. They grow to a length of 35 centimeters (18 inches), but the best form of identification is the tail, which is black, flat, and scaly. Closely related to muskrats are **voles,** which are often mistaken for mice. They inhabit grassed areas of most valley floors.

Shrews

A member of the insectivore family, the **furry shrew** has a sharp-pointed snout and is closely related to the mole. It must eat almost constantly because it is susceptible to starvation within only a few hours of its last meal. Another variety present throughout the region, the **pygmy shrew** is the world's smallest mammal; it weighs just four grams (0.1 ounces).

Pikas

Pikas, like rabbits, are lagomorphs, which are distinguished from rodents by a double set of incisors in the upper jaw. The small, grayish pika is a neighbor to the marmot, living among the rubble and boulders of scree slopes above timberline.

Weasels

The weasel family, comprising 70 species worldwide, is large and diverse, but in general, all members have long, slim bodies and short legs, and all are carnivorous and voracious eaters, consuming up to one-third of their body weight each day. Many species can be found in the Canadian Rockies, including the **wolverine,** largest of the weasels worldwide, weighing up to 20 kilograms (44 pounds). Known to indigenous peoples as *carcajou* (evil one), the wolverine is extremely powerful, cunning, and cautious. This solitary creature inhabits forests of the subalpine and lower alpine regions, feeding on any available meat, from small rodents to the carcasses of larger mammals. Rarely sighted by humans, the wolverine is a true symbol of the wilderness.

The **fisher** has the same habitat as the wolverine but is much smaller, reaching just five kilograms (11 pounds) in weight and growing up to 60 centimeters (24 inches) in length. This nocturnal hunter preys on small birds and rodents, but reports of fishers bringing down small deer have been made. Smaller still is the **marten,** which lives most of its life in the trees of the subalpine forest, preying on birds, squirrels, mice, and voles. Weighing just one kilogram (2.2 pounds) is the **mink,** once highly prized for its fur. At home in or out of water, it feeds on muskrats, mice, voles, and fish. Mink numbers in the Canadian Rockies are low.

As well as being home to the largest member of the weasel family, the region also holds the smallest—the **least weasel** (the world's smallest carnivore), which grows to a length of just 20 centimeters (8 inches) and weighs a maximum of 60 grams (2 ounces). Chiefly nocturnal, it feeds mostly on mice and lives throughout open wooded areas, but it is not particularly common.

REPTILES AND AMPHIBIANS

Two species of snakes, the **wandering garter snake** and the **red-sided garter snake** (North America's northernmost reptile), are found at lower elevations in the Canadian Rockies. **Frogs** are also present; biologists have noted two different species, which are also found at the lower elevations in the Canadian Rockies.

FISH

The lakes and rivers of the Canadian Rockies hold a variety of fish, most of which belong to the trout and salmon family and are classed as cold-water species—that is, they inhabit waters where the temperature ranges 4-18°C (39-64°F). The predominant species, the **rainbow trout,** is not native to the mountains; it was introduced from more northern Canadian watersheds as a sport fish and is now common throughout lower-elevation lakes and rivers. It has an olive-green back and a red stripe running along the center of its body. Only three species of trout are native to the mountains. One of these, the **bull trout,** is Alberta's provincial fish. Throughout the mid-1900s, this truly native Canadian trout was perceived as a predator of more favored introduced species and was mostly removed. Today, what was once the most widespread trout east of the Continental Divide is confined to the headwaters of the Canadian Rockies' river systems and is classed as a threatened species. While the bull trout has adapted to the harsh conditions of its reduced habitat, its continuing struggle for survival can be attributed to many factors, including a scarcity of food and a slow reproductive cycle. Bull trout grow to 70 centimeters (27 inches) in length and weigh up to 10 kilograms (22 pounds).

The **lake trout,** which grows to 20 kilograms (44 pounds), is native to large, deep lakes throughout the mountains. Identified by a silvery-gray body and irregular white splotches along its back, this species grows slowly, taking up to 8 years to reach maturity

and living up to 25 years. Named for a bright red dash of color that runs from below the mouth almost to the gills, the **cutthroat trout** is native to southern Alberta's mountain streams, but it has been introduced to high-elevation lakes and streams on both sides of the Canadian Rockies. The **brown trout,** introduced from Europe in 1924, is found in the Bow and Red Deer Rivers and some slower streams in the eastern zones of Kananaskis Country. Its body is a golden-brown color, and it is the only trout with both black and red spots. The **brook trout** is a colorful fish identified by a dark-green back with pale-colored splotches and purple-sheened sides. It is native to eastern Canada but was introduced to the mountains as early as 1903 and is now widespread throughout lakes and streams on the Alberta side of the Continental Divide. **Golden trout** were introduced to a few mountain lakes around 1960 as a sport fish. They are a smallish fish, similar in color to rainbow trout.

The **mountain whitefish** (commonly but incorrectly called arctic grayling by Albertan anglers) is a light-gray fish native to most lower-elevation lakes and rivers of the Canadian Rockies. Also inhabiting the region's waters are **arctic grayling** and **Dolly Varden** (named for a colorful character in a Charles Dickens story).

BIRDS

Bird-watching is popular in the mountains, thanks to the approximately 300 resident bird species and the millions of migratory birds that pass through each year. All it takes is a pair of binoculars, a good book detailing species, and patience. Dense forests hide many species, making them seem less common than they actually are.

Raptors

A wide variety of raptors are present in the Canadian Rockies—some call the mountains home year-round, while others pass through during annual spring and fall migrations. **Golden eagles** migrate across the Canadian Rockies, heading north in spring to Alaska and crossing back over in fall en route to Midwest wintering grounds. Golden eagles—more than 10,000 of them annually—soar high above the mountains on thermal drafts. **Bald eagles** also soar over the Canadian Rockies during annual migrations; mature birds can be distinguished from below by their white head and tail (immature birds resemble the dark-brown-colored golden eagle). **Ospreys** spend summers in the region, nesting high up in large dead trees, on telephone poles, or on rocky outcrops, but always overlooking water. They feed on fish, hovering up to 50 meters (160 feet) above water, watching for movement, then diving into the water, thrusting their legs forward and collecting prey in their talons.

Distinct from all previously listed species is a group of raptors that hunt at night. Best known as owls, these birds are rarely seen because of their nocturnal habits but are widespread throughout forested areas of the mountains. Most common is the **great horned owl,** identified by its prominent "horns," which are actually tufts of feathers. Also present are the **snowy owl** and, in the north of the region, the **great gray owl,** the largest of the owls, which grows to a height of 70 centimeters (27.6 inches).

Other Birds

Bird-watchers will be enthralled by the diversity of eastern and western bird species in the Canadian Rockies. Widespread are **magpies, sparrows, starlings, grouse, ravens,** and **crows. Blackbirds, finches, thrushes, hummingbirds, woodpeckers, flycatchers,** and 28 species of **warblers** are common in forested areas. **Ptarmigan** are common in open meadows above the tree line. A popular campground visitor, the cheeky **gray jay** is similar in appearance to the curious **Clark's nutcracker.**

History

THE EARLIEST INHABITANTS

Human habitation of the Canadian Rockies began at the end of the last ice age, approximately 11,000 years ago. The descendants of the people who migrated from northeast Asia across a land bridge spanning the Bering Strait had fanned out across North America, and as the receding ice cap began to uncover the land north of the 49th parallel, groups of people moved northward with it, in pursuit of large mammals at the edge of the melting ice mass. The mountain landscape then was far different from what it is today. Forests were nonexistent; the retreating ice had scoured the land, and most of the lower valleys were carpeted in tundra.

The following gives an overview of the people and their cultures. To learn more, plan on visiting Banff's **Buffalo Nations Luxton Museum.**

The Kootenay

The Kootenay (other common spellings include Kootenai, Kootenae, and Kutenai) were the first human beings to enter the Canadian Rockies. Once hunters of buffalo on the great American plains, they were pushed westward by fierce enemies. As the ice cap melted, they moved north, up the western edge of the Rocky Mountains. This migration was by no means fast—perhaps only 40 kilometers (25 miles) in each generation—but about 10,000 years ago the first Kootenay arrived in the Columbia River Valley. They were hunters and gatherers, wintering along the Columbia and Kootenay River Valleys, then moving to higher elevations during the warmer months. Over time they developed new skills, learning to fish the salmon-rich rivers using spears, nets, and simple fish weirs. The Kootenay were a serious people with few enemies. They mixed freely with the Shuswap. They regularly traveled east over the Rockies to hunt—to the wildlife-rich Kootenay Plains or farther south to the Great Plains in search of bison. But as the fearsome Blackfoot extended their territory westward to the foothills of present-day Alberta, the Kootenay made fewer trips onto the plains. By the early 1700s, they had been driven permanently back to the west side of the Continental Divide.

The Shuswap

The Shuswap make up only a small chapter in the human history of the Canadian Rockies, although they traveled into the mountains on and off for many thousands of years. They were a tribe of Salish people who, as the Kootenay did farther east, moved north, then east, with the receding ice cap. By the time the Kootenay had moved into the Kootenay River Valley, the Salish had fanned out across most of southwestern and interior British Columbia, following the salmon upstream as the glacial ice receded. Those who settled along the upper reaches of the Columbia River became known as the Shuswap. They spent summers in the mountains hunting caribou and sheep, put their fishing skills to the test each fall, and then wintered in pit houses along the Columbia River Valley. The descendants of these people live on the Kinbasket Shuswap Reserve, just south of Radium Hot Springs.

The Stoney

The movement of humans into the mountains from the east was much more recent. Around 1650, the mighty Sioux nation began splintering, with many thousands moving north into present-day Canada. Although these immigrants called themselves Nakoda (people), other tribes called them Assiniboine (people who cook with stones) because their traditional cooking method was to heat stones in a fire, place the hot stones in a rawhide or birchbark basket with water, and cook meat and vegetables in the hot water. The white people translated *Assiniboine* as Stone People, or Stoney for short.

Pictographs are artwork left behind by the Rockies' earliest inhabitants.

Slowly, generation after generation, smaller groups of the Stoney moved westward along the Saskatchewan River system, allying themselves with the Cree but keeping their own identity. They pushed through the Blackfoot territory of the plains and reached the Rockies' foothills about 200 years ago. There they split into bands, moving north and south along the foothills and penetrating the wide valleys where hunting was productive. They lived in small family-like groups and developed a lifestyle different from that of the Plains Indians, diversifying their skills and becoming less dependent on buffalo. Moving with the seasons, they gathered berries in fall and became excellent hunters of mountain animals. They traveled over the mountains to trade with the Shuswap but rarely ventured onto the plains, home of the warlike Piegan, Blackfoot, and Blood bands of the Blackfoot Confederacy. The Stoney were a steadfast yet friendly people. Alexander Henry the Younger reported in 1811 that the Stoney, "although the most arrant horse thieves in the world, are at

David Thompson: Canadian Explorer

One of Canada's greatest explorers, David Thompson was a quiet, courageous, and energetic man who drafted the first comprehensive and accurate map of western Canada. He arrived in Canada from England as a 14-year-old apprentice clerk for the Hudson's Bay Company. With an inquisitive nature and a talent for wilderness navigation, he quickly acquired the skills of surveying and mapmaking. Indigenous peoples called him Koo-koo-sint, which translates as "the man who looks at stars."

Between 1786 and 1812, Thompson led four major expeditions into western Canada—the first for the Hudson's Bay Company and the last three for its rival, the North West Company. The longest and most important one was the last, during which he traveled up and crossed the Continental Divide at **Howse Pass**. After descending into the Columbia River Valley, he established Kootenae House on Lake Windermere, using this outpost for a five-year odyssey of exploration of the entire Columbia River system. In the process, he discovered **Athabasca Pass**, which for the next 40 years was the main route across the Canadian Rockies to the Pacific Ocean.

In 1813, Thompson began work on a master map covering the entire territory controlled by the North West Company. The map was four meters (13 feet) long and two meters (seven feet) wide, detailing more than 3.9 million square kilometers (1.5 million square miles). On completion it was hung out of public view in the council hall of a company fort in the east. Years later, after his death in 1857, the map was discovered, and Thompson became recognized as one of the world's greatest land geographers.

the same time the most hospitable to strangers who arrive in their camps."

As the great buffalo herds were decimated, the Stoney were affected less than the Plains Indians, but the effect of white settlers' intrusion on their lifestyle was still apparent. The missionaries of the day found their teachings had more effect on the mountain people than on those of the plains, so they intensified their efforts on the Stoney. Reverend John McDougall gained their trust and in 1873 built a small mission church by the Bow River at Morleyville. When the Stoney were presented with Treaty 7 in 1877, they chose to locate their reserve around the Morleyville church. Abandoning their nomadic lifestyle, they quickly became adept at farming; unlike the Plains Indians, who relied for their survival on government rations, the Stoney were almost self-sufficient on the reserve.

EUROPEAN EXPLORATION AND SETTLEMENT

In 1670, the British government granted the Hudson's Bay Company the right to govern Rupert's Land, roughly defined as all the land that drained into Hudson Bay. A vast area of western Canada, including present-day Manitoba, Saskatchewan, Alberta, Northwest Territories, and Nunavut, fell under that definition. The land was rich in fur-bearing mammals, which both the British and the French sought to exploit for profit. The Hudson's Bay Company first built forts around Hudson Bay and encouraged Indians to bring furs to the posts. But soon, French fur traders based in Montreal began traveling west to secure furs, forcing their British rivals to do the same. On one such trip, Anthony Henday became the first white man to view the Canadian Rockies when, on September 11, 1754, he climbed a ridge above the Red Deer River near present-day Innisfail. Henday returned to the east the following spring, bringing canoes loaded with furs and providing reports of snowcapped peaks.

In 1792, Peter Fidler became the first in a long succession of Europeans to actually enter the mountains. The following year, Alexander Mackenzie became the first man to cross the continent, traveling the Peace and Fraser

River watersheds to reach the Pacific Ocean. Mackenzie's traverse was long and difficult, so subsequent explorers continued to seek an easier route farther south. In 1807, David Thompson set out from Rocky Mountain House, traveling up the North Saskatchewan River to Howse Pass, where he descended to the Columbia River. He established a small trading post near Windermere Lake, but warring Piegan and Kootenay forced him to search out an alternate pass to the north. In 1811, he discovered Athabasca Pass, which was used as the main route west for the next 40 years.

In 1857, with the fur trade in decline, the British government sent Captain John Palliser to investigate the agricultural potential of western Rupert's Land. During his three-year journey, Palliser explored many of the watersheds leading into the mountains, including one trip up the Bow River and over Vermilion Pass into the area now encompassed by Kootenay and Yoho National Parks.

The Dominion of Canada

By the 1860s, some of the eastern provinces were tiring of British rule, and a movement was abuzz to push for Canadian independence. The British government, wary of losing Canada as it had lost the United States, passed legislation establishing the Dominion of Canada. At that time, the North-West Territories, as Rupert's Land had become known, was a foreign land to those in eastern Canada; life out west was primitive with no laws, and no outpost held more than a couple dozen residents. But in an effort to solidify the Dominion, the government bought the North-West Territories back from the Hudson's Bay Company in 1867. In 1871, British Columbia agreed to join the Dominion as well, but only on the condition that the federal government build a railway to link the fledgling province with the rest of the country.

The Coming of the Railway

The idea of a rail line across the continent, replacing canoe and cart routes, was met with scorn by those in the east, who saw it as unnecessary and uneconomical. But the line pushed westward, reaching Winnipeg in 1879 and what was then Fort Calgary in 1883.

Many routes across the Continental Divide were considered by the Canadian Pacific Railway (CPR), but Kicking Horse Pass, surveyed by Major A. B. Rogers in 1881, got the final nod. The line and its construction camps pushed into the mountains, reaching Siding 29 (known today as Banff) early in the fall of 1883 and Laggan (Lake Louise) a couple of months later. They then crossed the divide and reached the Field construction camp in the summer of 1884. The following year, on November 7, 1885, the final spike was laid, opening up the lanes of commerce between British Columbia and the rest of Canada. In 1914, rival company Grand Trunk Pacific Railway completed a second rail line across the Rockies, to the north through what is now Jasper National Park.

PARKS AND TOURISM
The Parks of Today Take Shape

In 1883, three CPR workers stumbled on hot springs at the base of Sulphur Mountain, near where the town of Banff now lies. This was the height of the Victorian era, when the great spa resorts of Europe were attracting hordes of wealthy clients. With the thought of developing a similar-style resort, the government designated a 2,600-hectare (6,425-acre) reserve around the hot springs, surveyed a townsite, and encouraged the CPR to build a world-class hotel there. In 1887, Rocky Mountains Park was officially created, setting aside 67,300 hectares (166,300 acres) as a "public park and pleasure ground for the benefit, advantage, and enjoyment of the people of Canada." The park was later renamed Banff. It was Canada's first national park and only the third national park in the world.

Across the Continental Divide to the west, the railway passed by a small reserve that had been created around the base of Mount Stephen. This was the core of what would become Yoho National Park, officially dedicated in 1901. In anticipation of a flood of visitors to the mountains along the more northerly Grand Trunk Pacific Railway, Jasper Forest Park was established in 1907 (renamed Jasper National Park in 1930). Kootenay National Park was created to protect an eight-kilometer-wide (five-mile-wide) strip of land on either side of the Banff-Windermere Road, which was completed in 1922. Of the five national parks in the Canadian Rockies, Waterton Lakes National Park was the only one created purely for its aesthetic value. It was established after tireless public campaigning by local resident John George "Kootenai" Brown, who also became the park's first superintendent.

The First Tourists Arrive

In the era the parks were created, the Canadian Rockies region was a vast wilderness accessible only by rail. The parks and the landscape they encompassed were seen as economic resources to be exploited rather than as national treasures to be preserved. Logging, hunting, and mining were permitted inside park boundaries; all but Kootenay National Park had mines operating within them for many years (the last mine, in Yoho National Park, closed in 1952). To help finance the rail line, the CPR began encouraging visitors to the mountains by building grand mountain resorts: Mount Stephen House in 1886, the Banff Springs Hotel in 1888, a lodge at Lake Louise in 1890, and Emerald Lake Lodge in 1902. Knowledgeable locals, some of whom had been used as guides and outfitters during railway construction, offered their services to the tourists the railway brought. Tom Wilson, "Wild" Bill Peyto, Jim and Bill Brewster, the Otto Brothers, and Donald "Curly" Phillips are synonymous with this era, and their names grace everything from pubs to mountain peaks.

Early Mountaineering

Recreational mountaineering has been popular in the Canadian Rockies for more than

100 years. Reports of early climbs on peaks around Lake Louise spread, and by the late 1880s the area had drawn the attention of both European and American alpinists. Many climbers were inexperienced and ill equipped, but first ascents were nevertheless made on peaks that today are still considered difficult. In 1893, Walter Wilcox and Samuel Allen, two Yale schoolmates, spent the summer climbing in the Lake Louise area, making two unsuccessful attempts to reach the north peak of Mount Victoria. The following summer they made first ascents of Mount Temple and Mount Aberdeen, extraordinary achievements considering their lack of experience and proper equipment. Accidents were sure to happen, and they did. During the summer of 1896, P. S. Abbot slipped and plunged to his death attempting to climb Mount Lefroy. In doing so, he became North America's first mountaineering fatality. Following this incident, Swiss mountain guides were employed by the CPR to satisfy the climbing needs of wealthy patrons of the railway and make the sport safer. During the period of their employment, successful climbs were made of Mount Victoria, Mount Lefroy, and Mount Balfour.

In 1906, Arthur O. Wheeler organized the Alpine Club of Canada, which was instrumental in the construction of many trails and backcountry huts still in use today. In 1913, Swiss guide Conrad Kain led a group of the club's members on the successful first ascent of Mount Robson, the highest peak in the Canadian Rockies. By 1915, most of the other major peaks in the range had been climbed as well.

Changing Times

One major change that occurred early on was the shift from railroad-based to automobile-based tourism. Until 1913, motorized vehicles were banned from the mountain parks, allowing the CPR a monopoly on tourists. Wealthy visitors to the mountains came in on the train and generally stayed in the CPR's own hotels for weeks on end and often for the entire summer. The burgeoning popularity of the automobile changed all this; the motor-vehicle ban was lifted, and road building went ahead full steam. Many of the trails that had been built for horseback travel were widened to accommodate autos, and new roads were built: from Banff to Lake Louise in 1920, to Radium Hot Springs in 1922, and to Golden in 1930. The Icefields Parkway was finally completed in 1940. Visitor numbers increased, and facilities expanded to keep pace. Dozens of bungalow camps were built specially for those arriving by automobile. Many were built by the CPR, far from their rail line, including in Kootenay National Park and at Radium Hot Springs. Lodges were also built deep in the backcountry, including at Mount Assiniboine and Lake O'Hara.

Another major change is in the way the complex human-wildlife relationship in the parks has been managed. Should the relationship be managed to provide the visiting public the best viewing experience, or rather to provide the wildlife with the most wild and natural environment possible? Today the trend favors the wildlife, but early in the history of the Canadian Rockies' parks, the operating strategy clearly favored the visitor. The Victorian concept of wildlife was that it was

either good or evil. Although an early park directive instructed park superintendents to leave nature alone, it also told them to "endeavor to exterminate all those animals which prey upon others." A dusty century-old philosophy, perhaps, but as recently as the 1960s a predator-control program led to the slaughter of nearly every wolf in the park. Seventy years ago, you could view a polar bear on display behind the Banff Park Museum. In the 1970s, hotels were taking guests to local dumps to watch bears feeding on garbage. Creating a balance between growth and its impact on wildlife is today's most critical issue in the Canadian Rockies. Many high-traffic areas are fenced, with passes built over and under the highway for animal movement. Development in the national park towns of Banff and Jasper is strictly regulated, unlike areas outside the parks, such as Canmore and the Columbia River Valley, where development continues unabated.

Amazingly enough, throughout unsavory sagas of the 20th century and ever-increasing human usage, the Canadian Rockies have remained a prime area for wildlife viewing and will hopefully continue to be so for a long time to come.

Lake O'Hara Lodge

Essentials

Getting There 114

Getting Around. 119

Recreation. 121

Accommodations
   and Camping 128

Travel Tips 132

Health and Safety. 134

Information and Services 135

Getting There

For international travelers, Vancouver and Calgary are the main gateways to the Canadian Rockies. From these two cities, as well as points across Canada, scheduled train and bus services pass through the region year-round.

AIR

The closest city to the Canadian Rockies is **Calgary,** Alberta, 128 kilometers (80 miles) east of Banff. **Vancouver,** British Columbia's largest city, is a major gateway to the mountains for international travelers. It lies on Canada's West Coast, 830 kilometers (515 miles) west of Banff. **Edmonton,** 360 kilometers (224 miles) east of Jasper, also has an international airport. Even though Vancouver is a lot farther from the Canadian Rockies than Calgary, it is a popular starting point, as the trip across British Columbia by rail, bus, or car is spectacular.

Air Canada

Canada's national airline, **Air Canada** (604/688-5515 or 888/247-2262, www.air-canada.com) is one of the world's largest airlines. It offers direct flights to Calgary and Vancouver from all major Canadian cities, as well as from Portland, Los Angeles, San Francisco, Las Vegas, Denver, Phoenix, Houston, Chicago, and New York.

From Europe, Air Canada flies directly from London and Frankfurt to Vancouver and Calgary, and from other major European cities via Toronto. From the South Pacific, Air Canada operates flights from Sydney and in alliance with Air New Zealand from Auckland and other South Pacific islands to Vancouver. Asian cities served by direct Air Canada flights to Vancouver include Beijing,

Nagoya, Osaka, Seoul, Shanghai, Taipei, and Tokyo. Air Canada's flights originating in the South American cities of Buenos Aires, São Paulo, Lima, and Bogotá are routed through Toronto, where you'll need to change planes for either Calgary or Vancouver.

WestJet

Canada's other major carrier is **WestJet** (604/606-5525 or 800/538-5696, www.westjet.com), which has daily flights to its Calgary hub, as well as to Vancouver and Edmonton from across Canada as far east as St. John's, Newfoundland.

From the United States

Air Canada offers the most flights into Calgary and Vancouver from the United States, but one or both of the cities are also served by the following U.S. carriers: **Alaska Airlines** (800/252-7522, www.alaskaair.com) from Anchorage and Los Angeles; **American Airlines** (800/433-7300, www.aa.com) from Chicago and Dallas; **Delta** (800/221-1212, www.delta.com), with summer-only flights from Atlanta and Salt Lake City; and finally **United Airlines** (800/241-6522, www.united.com) from Chicago, Denver, Houston, San Francisco, and Seattle.

From Europe

In addition to Air Canada's flights from London to Calgary and Vancouver, **British Airlines** (800/247-9297, www.britishairlines.com) also flies this route daily. Air Canada flights between Vancouver and Continental Europe are routed through Toronto. **Lufthansa** (800/563-5954, www.lufthansa.com) has a daily flight between Frankfurt and Vancouver.

Air Taxes

The Canadian government collects a variety of "departure taxes" on all flights originating from Canada. These taxes are generally not in the advertised fare, but they will all be included in the ticket purchase price. First up is the **Air Travellers Security Charge,** $5-10 each way for flights within North America and $25 round-trip for international flights. **NAV Canada** also dips its hand in your pocket, collecting $10-25 per flight for maintaining the country's navigational systems. All major Canadian airports charge an **Airport Improvement Fee** to all departing passengers, with Vancouver and Calgary charging $20 and $30, respectively, per passenger. You'll also need to pay this fee from your original departure point, and if connecting through Toronto, another $4 is collected. And, of course, the above taxes are taxable, with the Canadian government collecting the 5 percent goods and services tax. While there is no bright side to paying these extras, it is made easy for consumers, with airlines lumping all the charges together and into the ticket price.

From Australia and New Zealand

Qantas (604/279-6611, www.qantas.com.au) flies to Vancouver from Sydney; flights originating in Melbourne and Brisbane are routed through Los Angeles. **Air New Zealand** (800/663-5494, www.airnewzealand.com) operates in alliance with Air Canada to either Calgary or Vancouver, with a variety of interesting options, including stops in South Pacific destinations like Nandi (Fiji). **Air Pacific** (800/227-4446, www.airpacific.com) offers flights from points throughout the Pacific to Honolulu and then on to Vancouver.

From Asia

Vancouver is the closest West Coast gateway to Asia, being more than 1,200 kilometers (746 miles) closer to Tokyo than Los Angeles. This and Vancouver's large Asian population mean that it is well served by carriers from across the Pacific. In addition to Air Canada's multiple Asian destinations, Vancouver is served by **Air China** (800/685-0921, www.airchina.com) from Beijing; **ANA** (888/422-7533, www.ana.co.jp) from Osaka and Tokyo in affiliation with Air Canada; **Cathay Pacific** (604/606-8888, www.cathaypacific.com) twice daily from Hong Kong; **Japan Airlines** (800/525-3663, www.jal.co.jp) from Tokyo; **Korean Air** (800/438-5000, www.koreanair.com) from Seoul; **Philippine Airlines** (800/435-9725, www.philippineairlines.com) from Manila; and **Singapore Airlines** (800/663-3046, www.singaporeair.com) from Singapore via Seoul. For the short hop between Vancouver and Calgary on Air Canada, expect to pay around $150 extra each way.

RAIL

The original transcontinental line passed through Banff, crossing the Continental Divide at Kicking Horse Pass and continuing to Vancouver via Rogers Pass. But this form of transportation, which opened up the Canadian Rockies to tourists, began to fade with the advent of efficient air services, and the last scheduled services on this line ended in 1991. Government-run VIA Rail provides coast-to-coast rail service using a more northerly route that passes through Jasper National Park. At Jasper, the westbound transcontinental line divides, with one set of tracks continuing west to Prince Rupert via Prince George and the other heading southwest to Vancouver. Another, more luxurious option is the privately run Rocky Mountaineer, with summer service to Banff and Jasper from Vancouver.

VIA Rail

Government-run **VIA Rail** (416/366-8411 or 888/842-7245, www.viarail.ca) provides passenger-train service right across Canada. The *Canadian* is a service between Toronto and Vancouver via Winnipeg, Saskatoon, Edmonton, Jasper, and Kamloops. Service is provided in two classes of travel: Economy features lots of leg room, reading lights, pillows

Cutting Flight Costs

Ticket structuring for air travel has traditionally been so complex that finding the best deal required some time and patience (or a good travel agent), but the process has become much easier in recent years. Air Canada leads the way, with streamlined ticketing options that are easy to understand.

The first step when planning your trip to the Canadian Rockies is to check online at the websites of airlines that fly from your home city to Vancouver or Calgary and search out the best price they have for the time of year you wish to travel. **Air Canada** (www.aircanada.com) has a streamlined fare structure that makes it easy to find the fare that serves your needs and budget. While the Internet has changed the way many people shop for tickets, having a travel agent whom you are comfortable dealing with—who takes the time to call around, does some research to get you the best fare, and helps you take advantage of any available special offers or promotional deals—is an invaluable asset in starting your travels off on the right foot.

Within Canada, **Travel Cuts** (866/246-9762, www.travelcuts.com) and **Flight Centre** (888/967-5302, www.flightcentre.ca), both with offices in all major cities, consistently offer the lowest airfares available, with the latter guaranteeing the lowest. Flight Centre offers a similar guarantee from its U.S. offices (866/967-5351, www.flightcenter.com), as well as those in the United Kingdom (tel. 0870/499-0040, www.flightcentre.co.uk), Australia (tel. 13/31-33, www.flightcentre.com.au), and New Zealand (tel. 0800/24-35-44, www.flightcentre.co.nz). In London, **Trailfinders** (194 Kensington High St., Kensington, tel. 020/7938-3939, www.trailfinders.com) always has good deals to Canada and other North American destinations. Reservations can be made directly through airline or travel agency websites, or use the services of an Internet-only company such as **Travelocity** (www.travelocity.com) or **Expedia** (www.expedia.com).

When you have found the best fare, open a **frequent flyer** membership affiliated with the airline—**Air Canada** (www.aeroplan.com) has a very popular reward program that makes rewards easily obtainable.

and blankets, and a Skyline Car complete with food and bar service, while Sleeper Plus and Prestige Sleeper are more luxurious, featuring sleeping rooms, daytime seating, all meals, a lounge and dining car, and shower kits for all passengers. At Jasper, the westbound transcontinental line divides, with one set of tracks continuing slightly north to Prince Rupert. Along this route, the train makes three trips per week. It is a daytime-only service, with passengers transferred to Prince George accommodations for an overnight stay. It offers Economy and Touring Class.

If you're traveling anywhere in western Canada from the eastern provinces, the least expensive way to travel is on a **Canrailpass,** which allows unlimited trips anywhere on the VIA Rail system for 60 days. During high season (June 1-Oct. 15) the pass is $849 per person.

On regular fares, discounts of 25-40 percent apply to travel in all classes October-June. Those over 60 and under 18, as well as students under 25, receive an additional 10 percent discount that can be combined with other seasonal fares. Check for advance-purchase restrictions on all discount tickets.

Rocky Mountaineer

Rocky Mountaineer Vacations (604/606-7245 or 877/460-3200, www.rockymountaineer.com) runs a luxurious rail trip between Vancouver and Banff or Jasper, through the spectacular interior mountain ranges of British Columbia. Travel is during daylight hours only so you don't miss anything. Trains depart in either direction in the morning (every second or third day), overnighting at Kamloops. One-way travel in RedLeaf Service, which includes light meals, nonalcoholic drinks, and Kamloops accommodations, costs $1,399 per person d from Vancouver to either Banff or Jasper and $1,549 from Vancouver to Calgary. SilverLeaf is a step up in quality, with a glass-domed car allowing a wide range of viewing opportunities. Prices in SilverLeaf are $1,899 per person d from Vancouver to either Banff or Jasper and $2,059 from Vancouver to Calgary. GoldLeaf Service is the ultimate in luxury. Passengers ride in a two-story glass-domed car, eat in a separate dining area, and stay in Kamloops's most luxurious accommodations. GoldLeaf costs $2,499 per person d from Vancouver to Banff or Jasper and $2,549 to Calgary. Outside of high season (mid-Apr.-May and the first two weeks of Oct.), all fares are reduced a few hundred dollars. Trains terminate in Vancouver off Terminal Avenue at 1755 Cottrell Street (behind Pacific Central Station).

BUS
Greyhound

Greyhound (403/762-1092 or 800/661-8747, www.greyhound.ca) serves areas throughout Canada and the United States. Travel by Greyhound is simple—just roll up at the depot and buy a ticket. No reservations are necessary. Greyhound bus depots are always close to downtown and generally link up with local public transportation. Always check for any promotional fares that might be available at the time of your travel. Regular-fare tickets are valid for one year and allow unlimited stopovers between paid destinations.

From Calgary: Greyhound runs up to five times daily from its depot (877 Greyhound Way SW, 403/260-0877) to Canmore and Banff, with most services continuing through Lake Louise to Golden and beyond.

From Edmonton: Buses run year-round between Edmonton's depot (10324 103rd St., 780/420-2424) and Jasper along a route through western Canada that extends as far west as Prince Rupert and Vancouver.

From Vancouver: The main Greyhound routes from Vancouver include the Trans-Canada Highway to Golden, Field, and Banff; a northern route along Highway 5 through Jasper to Edmonton and beyond;

and a southern route on Highway 3 through Cranbrook to Radium Hot Springs and on to Banff. The fare between Vancouver and Banff is around $195 one-way. The bus depot in Vancouver is at 1150 Station Street (604/683-8133).

From the United States: If you're traveling from the United States, get yourself to Great Falls, Montana, from where regular services continue north to the Coutts/Sweetgrass port of entry. There you change to a Canadian Greyhound bus for Calgary, where you can make connections to Banff.

When calling for ticket information, ask about any special deals. Other discounts apply to regular-fare tickets bought 7, 14, and 21 days in advance; to travelers 65 and over; and to two people traveling together.

From Calgary International Airport

This airport, 128 kilometers (80 miles) east of Banff, is the main gateway to the Canadian Rockies. In addition to car rental desks, shuttle bus companies are represented opposite the baggage carousels. Companies that offer service out to the Canadian Rockies are **Brewster** (403/762-6767 or 800/661-1152, www.brewster.ca) and **Banff Airporter** (403/762-3396 or 888/449-2901, www.banffairporter.com). Brewster is the only one of these two services that continues beyond Lake Louise to Jasper. Reserve a seat by booking over the phone or online in advance. Expect to pay $62 each way to Banff and around $76 to Lake Louise. Brewster charges $120 for the Calgary-Jasper run. **Sundog Tours** (780/852-4056 or 888/786-3641, www.sundogtours.com, adult $135, child $95) operates a winter-only shuttle linking Jasper and Banff.

Backpacker Bus

For young travelers on a budget, the **Moose Travel Network** (604/297-0255 or 888/244-6673, www.moosenetwork.com) is an excellent way to travel to and around the Canadian Rockies and beyond. It runs along a number of different routes, including a seven-day loop originating in Vancouver and traveling to Jasper and Banff via Whistler ($698 per person), a three-day Banff-Jasper-Banff trip ($329), and a two-day Banff-Vancouver shuttle ($249). On any of these trips, you can get on and off wherever you please (and jump aboard the next bus as it passes through) or bond with the crowd and stay on the fixed itinerary. Nights are spent at hostels en route. This cost isn't included in the tour, but your reservation is (so you don't need to worry about trying to find an empty bed at each stop). Food is also extra, but often all travelers pitch in a token amount to purchase dinner at a grocery store along the way. Buses run 3-7 times a week through an April-to-October season.

CAR

Driving to the Canadian Rockies is possible from anywhere in North America but is most convenient if you live in western Canada or the Pacific Northwest. Driving saves money on transportation costs and allows you to bring along camping equipment and sporting gear such as mountain bikes and canoes.

Driver's licenses from all countries are valid in Canada for up to three months. You should also obtain a one-year **International Driving Permit** before leaving home (U.S.-licensed drivers do not require an IDP to drive in Canada) if your license is in a language other than English. Inexpensive and available from most motoring organizations, an IDP allows you to drive in Canada (in conjunction with your regular license), without taking a test, for up to three months. You should also carry vehicle registration papers or rental contracts. Proof of insurance must also be carried, and you must wear seat belts. All highway signs in Canada give distances in **kilometers** and speeds in **kilometers per hour** (kph). The speed limit on most major highways is 100 kph (62 mph).

Insurance

If entering Canada from the United States in your own vehicle, check that your insurance covers travel in Canada and be sure to carry proof of insurance from your insurer. To save any hassles, request that your insurer issue you a Canadian Non-resident Inter-provincial Motor Vehicle Liability Insurance Card.

When renting a vehicle in Canada, you have the option of purchasing a Loss Damage Waiver, along with other types of insurance, such as for your personal effects. Before leaving home, find out if you're already covered.

The Icefields Parkway is one of the world's most scenic driving routes.

Many people are—through gold credit cards, higher levels of motoring association membership, or home insurance (in the case of personal effects)—and additional coverage may be unnecessary.

Routes in Canada

The Trans-Canada Highway (Highway 1) stretches from one end of Canada to the other and is the world's longest national highway (7,821 km/4,860 mi from end to end). It passes through the Canadian Rockies towns of Canmore, Banff, and Golden. The first major city east of the mountains is Calgary, 128 kilometers (80 miles) from Banff along the Trans-Canada. The northern route across western Canada is the Yellowhead Highway, which passes through the town of Jasper, in Jasper National Park, 364 kilometers (226 miles) east of Edmonton. From Vancouver, on the west coast of British Columbia and the major air gateway from Asia, it's 836 kilometers (519 miles) west to Banff along the Trans-Canada Highway and 781 kilometers (486 miles) northwest to Jasper along Highway 5. The Trans-Canada and Yellowhead Highways are linked within the Canadian Rockies by the Icefields Parkway, which runs parallel to the Continental Divide between Lake Louise and Jasper, a distance of 230 kilometers (143 miles).

Routes from the United States

Reaching the Canadian Rockies from the United States is possible via a number of routes. From Seattle, the shortest approach is to follow I-5 north to Vancouver and jump on the Trans-Canada Highway. If you're traveling north from the Rocky Mountain states, U.S. Highway 93 will provide a warm-up for the mountain scenery north of the border. This route crosses into Canada north of Kalispell, Montana, merging with U.S. Highway 95 from Coeur d'Alene, Idaho, at Cranbrook, then continuing up the west side of the Canadian Rockies to Radium Hot Springs, where you can cut through Kootenay National Park to Banff. Much quicker is I-15, which begins in Los Angeles and loops through Las Vegas and Salt Lake City on its way north to Montana. I-15 enters Canada at the 24-hour Coutts/Sweetgrass border crossing south of Lethbridge, Alberta. From Lethbridge, it's a three-hour drive to Banff, or you can choose to head west to Waterton Lakes National Park. Total distance from Los Angeles to Banff via I-15 is 2,600 kilometers (1,617 miles). From the Midwest and eastern states, there are innumerable options, including I-94 through Minneapolis or crossing into Canada east of the Great Lakes and driving the entire way within Canada.

Getting Around

BUS

Getting around the Canadian Rockies is easiest with your own vehicle because public transportation is limited. **Brewster** (403/762-6767 or 800/661-1152, www.brewster.ca) is primarily a tour company but also runs a scheduled bus service linking Calgary International Airport, Canmore, Banff, and Lake Louise with a summer-only service between Lake Louise and Jasper. **Greyhound** (403/762-1092 or 800/661-8747, www.greyhound.ca) serves the Trans-Canada Highway, providing a link between Canmore, Banff, Lake Louise, and Golden three times daily. Once daily, buses run through Kootenay National Park, between Banff and Radium Hot Springs. You can also take **Moose Travel Network** buses (604/297-0255 or 888/244-6673, www.moosenetwork.com) between Banff and Jasper.

CAR
Driving in Canada

U.S. and international driver's licenses are

valid in Canada. All highway signs give distances in kilometers and speeds in kilometers per hour. Unless otherwise posted, the maximum speed limit on the highways is 100 kph (62 mph).

Use of safety belts is mandatory, and motorcyclists must wear helmets. Infants and toddlers weighing up to nine kilograms (20 pounds) must be strapped into an appropriate children's car seat. Use of a child car seat for larger children weighing 9-18 kilograms (20-40 pounds) is required of British Columbia residents and recommended to nonresidents. Before venturing north of the 49th parallel, U.S. residents should ask their vehicle insurance company for a Canadian Non-resident Inter-provincial Motor Vehicle Liability Insurance Card. You may also be asked to prove vehicle ownership, so carry your vehicle registration form.

If you're a member in good standing of an automobile association, take your membership card—the Canadian AA provides members of related associations full services, including free maps, itineraries, excellent tour books, road- and weather-condition information, accommodations reservations, travel agency services, and emergency road services. For more information, contact the **Alberta Motor Association** (780/430-6800, www.ama.ab.ca) or the **British Columbia Automobile Association** (604/268-5600, www.bcaa.com).

Note: Drinking and driving (with a blood-alcohol level of 0.05 percent or higher) in Canada can get you imprisoned on a first offense and will cost you your license for up to 12 months.

Car Rental

All major car rental agencies have outlets at Calgary and Vancouver International Airports. Car rentals are also available in Banff, Canmore, and Jasper, but it is strongly recommended to rent a vehicle *before* arriving in the Canadian Rockies for two reasons: cost and mileage charges (the now-standard unlimited mileage with major car rentals

doesn't apply in Banff, Canmore, or Jasper). Generally, vehicles can be booked through parent companies in the United States. Rates start at $80 per day for a small economy car, $95 for a midsize car, and $105 for a full-size car, although you can expect to pay more if renting from an airport.

Major rental companies with outlets in Calgary, Edmonton, and Vancouver are **Avis** (800/974-0808, www.avis.ca), **Budget** (800/268-8900, www.budget.com), **Discount** (800/263-2355, www.discountcar.com), **Dollar** (800/800-4000, www.dollar.com), **Enterprise** (800/325-8007, www.enterprise.com), **Hertz** (800/263-0600, www.hertz.ca), **National** (800/227-7368, www.nationalcar.com), and **Rent-A-Wreck** (800/327-0116, www.rentawreck.ca).

RV Rental

Camper vans, recreational vehicles, and travel trailers are a great way to get around the Canadian Rockies without having to worry about accommodations each night. The downside is cost. The smallest vans, capable of sleeping two people, start at $200 per day with 100 free kilometers (62 miles) per day. Standard extra charges include insurance, a preparation fee (usually around $60 per rental), a linen/cutlery charge (around $80 per person per trip), and taxes. Major agencies, with rental outlets in both Calgary and Vancouver, include **Cruise Canada** (403/291-4963, 800/671-8042, or 800/327-7778, www.cruisecanada.com), **Canadream** (403/291-1000 or 888/480-9726, www.canadream.com), and **Go West** (604/528-3900 or 800/661-8813, www.go-west.com). In most cases, a drop-off fee of $500 applies to drop-offs made in Vancouver from rentals originating in Calgary, or vice versa. At the end of the summer season (early September), look for some great online bargains.

Gas Stations

All towns in the Canadian Rockies have gas stations, including Banff, Lake Louise, Canmore, Jasper, Golden, Radium Hot

Springs, and Bragg Creek. There are also gas stations off the main highways, including along the Icefields Parkway and in Kananaskis Country, but expect to pay significantly more for a fill. Outside of summer, don't rely on these more remote stations to be open. Gas station hours vary greatly, but at least one in Banff and one in Jasper opens at 6am, and most are closed by 10pm. To avoid summer lines at Banff and Jasper gas stations, plan on filling up earlier in the morning—waiting vehicles often spill onto surrounding streets during the middle of the day. Also note that all gas purchases in the Canadian Rockies are pre-pay, meaning you must pay at the pump prior to filling up or, in the case of those with non-Canadian credit cards, go inside and leave your credit card with the clerk.

Gasoline is sold in liters (3.78 liters equals one U.S. gallon) and is generally $1.10-1.30 per liter for regular unleaded, rising to $1.60 along the Icefields Parkway. Gas is generally less expensive in Alberta (Banff and Jasper), as British Columbia (Golden and Radium Hot Springs) has additional taxes.

TOURS

For those with limited time, an organized tour is the best way to see the Canadian Rockies. **Brewster Travel Canada** (403/760-6934 or 800/760-6934, www.brewster.ca) offers day tours and overnight tours throughout the mountains, as well as car rental and accommodation packages. **Rocky Mountaineer** (604/606-7245 or 877/460-3200, www.rockymountaineer.com) offers a wide variety of longer tours in conjunction with rail travel between Vancouver and Banff or Jasper. At the opposite end of the price spectrum, by joining a **Moose Travel Network** (604/777-9905 or 888/244-6673, www.moosenetwork.com) tour, you get to see the Canadian Rockies with like-minded budget travelers.

Recreation

The Canadian Rockies are a four-season playground, their great outdoors offering something for everyone. Hiking grabs first place in the popularity stakes; many thousands of kilometers of trails crisscross the entire region. But you can also enjoy canoeing and kayaking, mountain climbing, golfing, horseback riding, photography, skiing and snowboarding, scuba diving, and everything in between.

HIKING

The Canadian Rockies are a hiker's paradise. Hiking is free, and the mountains offer some of the world's most spectacular scenery. With exceptions made for the most popular overnight hikes, all trails detailed in this book are day hikes. Anyone of moderate fitness could complete them in the time allotted. Strong hikers will need less time, and if you stop for lunch, it will take you a little longer.

Remember, all distances and times are one-way (unless otherwise noted), so allow yourself time at the destination and time to return to the trailhead. Basic trail descriptions are available through local information centers, but anyone planning on focusing their trip around hiking should pick up a copy of the *Canadian Rockies Trail Guide,* authored by Brian Patton and Bart Robinson; check www.canadianrockiestrailguide.com for more information.

Banff National Park holds the greatest variety of trails. Here you can find anything from short interpretive trails with little elevation gain to strenuous slogs up high alpine passes. Trailheads for some of the best hikes are accessible on foot from the town of Banff. Those farther north begin at higher elevations, from which access to the tree line is less arduous.

Scrambling

The Canadian Rockies hold many peaks that can be reached without ropes or climbing skills, provided you have a good level of fitness and, more important, common sense. Obviously, this type of activity has more inherent dangers than hiking, but these can be minimized by planning ahead. Check weather forecasts; take food, water, and warm clothing; and be aware of the terrain. Routes to the top of the most popular peaks are flagged with tape or marked with rock cairns showing the way, but you should always check with information centers or locals before attempting any ascent. The Bow Valley offers a good selection of well-traveled scrambles. These include Mount Rundle and Cascade Mountain.

Backpacking

Most hikers are just out for the day or a few hours, but staying overnight in the backcountry offers many rewards. Some effort is involved in a backcountry trip—you'll need a backpack, lightweight stove, and tent, among other things—but you'll be traveling through country inaccessible to the casual day hiker, well away from the crowds and far from any road. **Mount Assiniboine Provincial Park** is a popular spot far from civilization. There's a lodge for hikers not equipped to camp out. Banff, Jasper, and Yoho National Parks also have backcountry lodges. Another option for backcountry accommodations is offered by the **Alpine Club of Canada** (403/678-3200, www.alpineclubofcanada.ca). The club maintains a series of huts, each generally a full-day hike from the nearest road, throughout the Canadian Rockies.

Heli-Hiking

Heli-hiking is an easy way to appreciate high alpine areas without having to gain the elevation on foot. The day starts with a helicopter ride into the alpine, where short, guided hikes are offered and a picnic lunch is served. For details, contact **Alpine Helicopters** (Canmore, 403/678-4802, www.alpinehelicopter.com). Expect to pay from $550 per person for 30 minutes of flight time, a guided hike, and a mountaintop lunch. Primarily known for its heli-skiing operations, **Canadian Mountain Holidays** (403/762-7100 or 800/661-0252, www.cmhhike.com) has a summer program of heli-hiking trips, with overnights spent in luxurious backcountry lodges; expect to pay about $750 per person per night, all-inclusive.

Hiking is a great way for children to experience the region.

Safe Hiking

When venturing out on the trails of the Canadian Rockies, using a little common sense will help keep you from getting into trouble. First, don't underestimate the forces of nature; weather can change dramatically anywhere in the mountains at any time. That clear, sunny sky that looked so inviting during breakfast can turn into a driving snowstorm within hours. Go prepared for all climatic conditions (always carry food, a sweater, a waterproof jacket, and matches) and take plenty of water—open slopes can get very hot on sunny days.

At the beginning of hiking trail descriptions throughout this book, I have included some very important information that you should read before heading out. Length is of course important (most people walk between 3-4 km/1.9-2.5 miles per hour on flat ground), but so is Elevation Gain, which can slow down even the fittest of hikers. I've combined these two elements to give one of three difficulty Ratings: Easy, Moderate, and Difficult. It is very important that you assess your own level of fitness combined with the three elements discussed above to decide if a trail is suited to you—a three-kilometer (2.1-mile) hike with 400 meters (1,200 feet) of elevation gain is much harder than an eight-kilometer (5.3-mile) trail with no elevation gain.

All national park visitors centers post daily trail reports and weather forecasts. Check trail conditions before heading out; lingering snow, wildlife closures, or a washed-out trail could ruin your best-laid plans. Also, hikers must register at park information centers for all overnight hikes in national parks.

Topographic maps aren't required for the hikes detailed in this book, but they provide an interesting way to identify natural features. For extended hiking in the backcountry, topo maps are vital. For most hikes, the maps produced by **Gem Trek Publishing** (www.gemtrek.com) are sufficient. You can purchase them from park information centers, bookstores, gas stations, and other outlets throughout the region.

CLIMBING AND MOUNTAINEERING

The Canadian Rockies are a mecca for those experienced in climbing and mountaineering, but for those who aren't, instruction is available. Experienced climbers should also gather as much information as possible before attempting any unfamiliar routes; quiz locals, hang out at climbing stores, and contact park information centers.

For the inexperienced, the Canadian Rockies are the perfect place to learn to climb. Climbers and mountaineers can't live on past accomplishments alone, so to finance their lifestyle, some turn to teaching others the skills of their sport. Canmore is home to many qualified mountain guides who operate both in and out of Banff National Park. One of these—and one of North America's most respected climbing schools—is **Yamnuska** (403/678-4164, www.yamnuska.com). Learn basic climbing skills over an Outdoor Rock Intro weekend ($395 per person), with the option to make a full climb (an extra $285). The school also offers guided climbs of peaks throughout the Canadian Rockies, wilderness first-aid classes, and ice-climbing instruction.

ROAD CYCLING AND MOUNTAIN BIKING

The Canadian Rockies are perfect for both road biking and mountain biking. On-road cyclists will appreciate the wide shoulders on all main highways, while those on mountain bikes will enjoy the many designated trails. One of the most popular paved routes is the **Legacy Trail** between Banff and Canmore, which links up with the Bow Valley Parkway to Lake Louise. The most challenging and scenic on-road route is the 290-kilometer (180-mile) **Icefields Parkway** between Lake Louise and Jasper (*Outside* magazine rates it as one of North America's 10 best). Most cyclists allow 4-5 days, but it's easy to spend a lot longer on the parkway. With 11 campgrounds, four hostels, and four lodges along the way, you'll have plenty of accommodation options. An extension of the Icefields Parkway is the **Bow Valley Parkway,** the original route between Banff and Lake Louise, which can easily be cycled in one day.

Backroads (510/527-1555 or 800/462-2848, www.backroads.com) offers biking trips through the Canadian Rockies, as well as trips that include hiking and touring. These trips are designed to suit all levels of fitness and all budgets. On the biking trips, around six hours are spent cycling each day. The per-week cost, inclusive of luxury accommodations, is US$3,298, which includes all meals.

Mountain biking is allowed on designated trails throughout the national parks. Park information centers hand out brochures detailing these trails and giving them ratings. Peter Oprsal's *Bow Valley Mountain Bike Trail Guide* covers all the major trails in the Bow Valley; pick up a copy from local bookstores. Bikes can be rented throughout the national parks. Road and town bikes rent for $8-15 per hour and $40-55 per day. Most bike shops rent front- and full-suspension bikes; expect to pay up to $25 per hour and $100 per day for these.

biking along the Bow Valley Parkway

ride (usually covering around 3 km/1.9 mi), $70-80 for a two-hour ride, and $110-140 for a ride that includes a meal.

HORSEBACK RIDING

Horses were used for transportation in the mountains by the earliest explorers. Even after the completion of the railway, horses remained the most practical way to get deep into the backcountry because crossing unbridged rivers and carrying large amounts of supplies were impossible on foot. The names of early outfitters—Tom Wilson, Jim and Bill Brewster, Bill Peyto, Jimmy Simpson, and Curly Phillips were the best known—crop up again and again through the mountains. Another legacy of their trade is that many of the main hiking trails began as horse trails.

The tradition of travel by horseback continues today in the Canadian Rockies; some companies have been operating since before the parks were established. For trail riding, expect to pay around $45-60 for a one-hour

Pack Trips and Guest Ranches

Overnight pack trips consist of up to six hours of riding per day, with nights spent at a remote mountain lodge or a tent camp, usually in a scenic location where you can hike, fish, or ride farther. Rates range $180-275 per person per day, which includes the riding, accommodations, and food. Trip operators include **Brewster Adventures** (403/762-5454, www.brewsteradventures.com) and **Banff Trail Riders** (403/762-4551 or 800/661-8352, www.horseback.com).

GOLFING

The Canadian Rockies hold special appeal for golfers because some of the world's most scenic courses lie in their midst. All of the best courses are public, located in national parks or on provincial land, so anyone can play at any time. The scenery alone stands the courses of the Canadian Rockies apart from others, but there are many other reasons that the region is a golf destination in itself. Stanley Thompson, generally regarded as one of the preeminent golf course architects of the early 1900s, designed three courses in the Canadian Rockies, typified by holes aligned with distant mountains, elevated tee boxes, and fairways following natural contours of the land. (As most of Thompson's work was in Canada, he is still little known in the United States.)

The golfing season is fairly short, May-early October, depending on snow cover. But with the long days of summer, there's plenty of time for golfing. Greens fees range from $18 at the historic nine-hole Nordegg Golf Course to $240 for 18 holes at the Banff course. At the resort courses, greens fees usually include the use of practice facilities and a cart (complete with global positioning system at Silvertip). The sport's popularity in the mountains is such that tee times need to booked well in advance—up to a month for preferred times at some courses.

The jewel in the golfing crown is the **Fairmont Banff Springs Golf Course,** a 27-hole layout that graces the grounds of the Fairmont Banff Springs and is rated one of the world's most scenic courses.

ON THE WATER
Paddlesports

Canoeing and stand-up paddleboarding are great ways to explore the waterways of the mountains that are otherwise inaccessible—places such as **Vermilion Lakes** in Banff National Park, where beavers, elk, and a great variety of birds can be appreciated from water level. Canoes and paddleboards can be rented on the **Bow River** (in the town of Banff) and canoes are available for rent at **Lake Louise** and **Moraine Lake** in Banff National Park. Expect to pay around $35-70 per hour.

White-Water Rafting

The rafting season is relatively short, but the thrill of careening down a river laced with rapids is not easily forgotten. Qualified guides operate on many rivers flowing out of the mountains. The **Kicking Horse River,** which flows through Yoho National Park to Golden, is run by companies based in Golden, Lake Louise, and Banff. This is the most popular river for rafting trips. For a more sedate river trip, try the **Bow River** in Banff National Park. All companies offer half- and full-day trips, including transportation, wet suits, and often light snacks.

Scuba Diving

Being landlocked, the Canadian Rockies are not renowned for scuba diving. A few interesting opportunities do exist, however, and rentals are available in Lethbridge, Calgary, and Edmonton. The old townsite of **Minnewanka Landing,** in Banff National Park, has been flooded, and although an easy dive, the site is interesting. For a list of dive shops and sites, contact the **Alberta Underwater Council** (780/427-9125 or 888/307-8566, www.albertaunderwatercouncil.com).

scuba diving in Lake Minnewanka

FISHING

The Canadian Rockies are an angler's delight. Fish are abundant in many lakes and rivers (the exceptions to good fishing are the lakes and rivers fed by glacial runoff, such as Lake Louise), and outfitters provide guiding services throughout the mountains. Many lakes are stocked annually with a variety of trout—most often rainbows—and although stocking was discontinued in the national parks in 1988, populations have been maintained. In Banff National Park, **Lake Minnewanka** is home to the mountains' largest fish—lake trout—as well a variety of other trout and whitefish. This lake is one of the most popular accessible fishing centers, with boats and tackle for rent and guides offering their services.

Fishing is popular throughout the Canadian Rockies.

Fish Species

Rainbow trout are the fighting fish of the Canadian Rockies. Although not native, through stocking they are found in lakes and streams throughout the mountains. The Bow River is considered one of the world's great trout rivers, but most of the action happens downstream of Calgary. Wet flies and small spinners are preferred methods of catching these fish. The largest fish found in the region is the **lake trout,** which grows to 18 kilograms (40 pounds). It feeds near the surface after winter breakup and then moves to deeper, colder water in summer. Long lines and heavy lures are needed to hook these giants. **Brown trout,** introduced from Europe, are found in the Upper Bow River (downstream from Banff) and slow-flowing streams in the foothills of Kananaskis Country. They are most often caught on dry flies, but they are finicky feeders and therefore difficult to hook. **Brook trout** are widespread throughout lower-elevation lakes and streams. **Cutthroat trout** inhabit the cold and clear waters of the highest lakes, which generally require a hike to access. Fishing for cutthroat requires using the lightest of tackle because the water is generally very clear; fly casting is most productive on the still water of lakes, while spinning is the preferred river-fishing method.

Arctic grayling, easily identified by their large dorsal fins, are common in cool, clear streams throughout the far north, but they are not native to the Canadian Rockies. **Dolly Varden** can be caught in many high-elevation lakes on the British Columbia side of the mountains. **Whitefish** are a commonly caught fish in lower-elevation lakes and rivers (many anglers in Alberta call whitefish "arctic grayling," but they are in fact two distinct species—and grayling aren't native to the mountains). Hydroelectric dams are popular with anglers chasing whitefish.

Note: The **bull trout** is an endangered species and is a catch-and-release fish. Possession of bull trout—a dark-colored fish with light spots—is illegal. The defining difference between the bull trout and the brook trout, with which it is often confused, is that the bull trout has *no black spots on its dorsal fin;* due to its status, correct identification of this species is especially important.

Regulations and Licenses

Three different licenses are in effect in the Canadian Rockies—one license covers all the national parks, another Albertan waters, and a third the freshwater of British Columbia.

National parks: Licenses are available from park offices and some sport shops; $10 for a one-day license, $35 for an annual license. The brochure *Fishing Regulations Summary,* available from all park information centers, details limits and closures.

Alberta: Alberta has an automated licensing system, with licenses sold online and through sporting stores, hardware stores, and gas stations. To purchase a license, the vendor needs you to supply a Wildlife Identification Number (WIN) card. These numbers are sold online and by all license vendors and cost $8 (valid for five years). Once you have your card, it is swiped through a vending machine to purchase a license. An annual license for Canadian residents older than age 16 is $28 (no license required for those 16 years or younger or Albertans older than 64); for nonresidents older than age 16, it is $71, or pay $28 for a one-day license or $48 for five days. The *Alberta Guide to Sportfishing Regulations,* which outlines all the open seasons and bag limits, is available from outlets selling licenses and online at www.mywildalberta.com. In addition to having the entire regulations online, this site also holds statistics for the provincial stocking program (which lakes, when, and how many fish) and details of Alberta's barbless hook rules.

British Columbia: In British Columbia, the cost of a license varies according to your age and place of residence. British Columbia residents pay $38 for a freshwater adult license, good for one year. All other Canadians pay $22 for a one-day license, $38 for an eight-day license, or $65 for a one-year license. Nonresidents of Canada pay $28, $58, and $92, respectively. For more information, visit www.fishing.gov.bc.ca, which offers the same online purchase process as neighboring Alberta.

WINTER RECREATION
Downhill Skiing and Snowboarding

Of the world-class winter resorts perched among the high peaks of the Canadian Rockies, the largest—and Canada's second largest (only Whistler/Blackcomb is larger)—is **Lake Louise,** overlooking the lake of the same name in Banff National Park. The

Wintertime brings a whole new world of wonders.

resort boasts 1,700 hectares (4,200 acres) of skiing and boarding on four distinct faces, with wide-open bowls and runs for all abilities. Banff's other two resorts are **Sunshine Village,** sitting on the Continental Divide and accessible only by gondola, and **Ski Norquay,** a resort with heart-pounding runs overlooking the town of Banff.

Winter is low season in the mountains, so many accommodations reduce their rates drastically. Lift-and-lodging package deals at many resorts start around $100 per person per night. Sunshine Village has on-slope lodging, while the other resorts are served by shuttle buses from the nearest towns. Most resorts open in early December and close in May.

Heli-Skiing

Helicopters are banned in the national parks of the Canadian Rockies, but two surrounding heli-ski operators provide transfers from Banff and Jasper. One such company is **R.K. Heli-Ski** (250/342-3889 or 800/661-6060, www.rkheliski.com), which is based on the west side of the mountains at Panorama but provides daily transfers from Banff and Lake Louise for a day's heli-skiing or boarding high in the Purcell Mountains. The cost is $850-1,100 per person.

The town of Banff is headquarters for the world's largest heli-skiing operation, **Canadian Mountain Holidays** (403/762-7100 or 800/661-0252, www.canadianmountainholidays.com), although the skiing and boarding terrain is accessed from 12 upscale lodges scattered throughout eastern British Columbia. Seven-day packages begin at around $6,800 per person, rising to more than $9,000 in the high season.

Other Winter Activities

Many hiking trails provide ideal routes for **cross-country skiing,** and some are groomed for that purpose. Anywhere you can cross-country ski you can **snowshoe,** a traditional form of winter transportation that is making a comeback. **Sleigh rides** are another option offered in Banff, Lake Louise, and Jasper.

Winter travel brings its own set of potential hazards, such as hypothermia, avalanches, frostbite, and sunburn. Necessary precautions should be taken. All park information centers can provide information on hazards and advise on current weather conditions.

Accommodations and Camping

Following is a summary of the types of accommodations you can expect to find throughout the Canadian Rockies. Nearly all accommodations now have toll-free numbers and websites, through which you can find out more information about each property and make bookings.

Accommodation Taxes

Except for campgrounds and bed-and-breakfasts with fewer than four guest rooms, accommodations collect tax on behalf of various levels of government. In British Columbia, an 8 percent provincial hotel room tax is administered, while in Alberta, a 4 percent Tourism Levy is added. Banff also has a 2 percent Tourism Improvement Fee. These taxes are in addition to the Canada-wide 5 percent goods and services tax. As a general rule, quoted rates don't include any of these taxes.

HOTELS AND MOTELS

Hotels and motels throughout the Canadian Rockies range from substandard road motels to sublime resorts such as the famous Fairmont Banff Springs. Bookings throughout the mountains, but especially in Banff and Lake Louise, should be made as far in advance as possible. Finding inexpensive lodging in the mountain national parks is difficult

Getting the Best Lodging Deal

Rates quoted in this book are for a standard double room throughout the high season, which generally extends late June–mid-September. Almost all accommodations are less expensive outside of these busy months. As a general rule of thumb, the more expensive the property, the steeper the discount. For example (and at different ends of the spectrum), the cost of a dorm bed at the Banff Alpine Centre drops $5 per night on September 15, while in downtown Banff, already reasonably priced Brewster's Mountain Lodge cuts its rates from $345 to under $200 in winter, with graduated discounts in spring and fall. Plan on traveling a few weeks on either side of the peak season, then use hotel websites to check when individual properties are offering discounts. Most accommodations post seasonal specials on their websites well in advance.

While you have no influence over seasonal pricing fluctuations, *how* you reserve a room *can* make a difference in how much you pay. Book through a central reservations agency or travel agent, or pay for accommodations as part of a tour package, and you'll pay the full published price.

In some years, getting a room in July and August without advance reservations is almost impossible. Leaving reservations until the last minute is a risky proposition if you're not prepared to be flexible. As a general rule, hotels raise their rates as demand dictates, while lodges don't, so you'll know with the latter what you'll be paying with advance reservations, or booking the day of your arrival.

Most hotels offer auto association members an automatic 10 percent discount, and whereas senior discounts apply only to those 60 or 65 and older on public transportation and at attractions, most hotels offer discounts to those over 50. Some chains, such as Best Western, also allow senior travelers a late checkout. Corporate rates are a lot more flexible than in years past; some hotels require nothing more than the flash of a business card for a 10-20 percent discount. Finally, when it comes to frequent flyer programs, you really do need to be a frequent flyer to achieve free flights, but the various loyalty programs offered by hotel chains often provide benefits simply for signing up.

ESSENTIALS ACCOMMODATIONS AND CAMPING

in summer. By late afternoon, the only rooms left will be in the more expensive categories, and by nightfall all of these will go.

Hotel rooms in Banff begin at $300 in peak season. Accommodation prices are slashed by as much as 50 percent outside summer. Always ask for the best rate available and check local tourist literature for discount coupons. All rates quoted in this handbook are for the cheapest category of rooms during the most expensive time period (summer).

Park-at-your-door, single-story road motels are mostly a thing of the past in the mountains. In most cases rooms are fine, but check before paying, just to make sure. Most have a few rooms with kitchenettes, but these fill fast. Expect to pay around $100 for a double room.

Information and Reservations

For a list of all hotels, motels, lodges, and bed-and-breakfasts in Alberta, pick up a copy of *Alberta Accommodation Guide*, available online, or order a free copy through **Travel Alberta** (780/427-4321 or 800/252-3782, www.travelalberta.com). The same association produces the *Alberta Campground Guide* (also online). **Tourism British Columbia** (250/387-1642 or 800/435-5622, www.hellobc.com) produces the free *British Columbia Approved Accommodation* brochure, which lists all accommodations and campgrounds in the province.

BED-AND-BREAKFASTS

The bed-and-breakfast phenomenon is well entrenched in Canada. This type of accommodation is a good option if you don't mind sacrificing some privacy to meet locals and to mingle with like-minded travelers. Bed-and-breakfasts are usually private residences, with up to four guest rooms, although bylaws are different throughout the region. Amenities can vary greatly—the "bed-and-breakfast" may be a single spare room in an otherwise regular family home or a full-time business in a beautifully restored heritage home. This uncertainty as to what to expect upon arrival can be off-putting for many people, especially with the possibility of sharing a bathroom with other guests—which is both a common and accepted practice in European bed-and-breakfasts. If having a bathroom to yourself is important to you, clarify with the bed-and-breakfast operator when reserving. Also, as bed-and-breakfasts also function as private residences, book in advance—don't just turn up. Finally, check payment methods when booking; not all establishments take credit or debit cards.

The best way to find out about individual lodging is from local tourist information centers or from listings in the *Alberta Accommodation Guide* or *British Columbia Approved Accommodation* brochure.

Bed-and-Breakfast Associations and Agencies

The **British Columbia Bed and Breakfast Innkeepers Guild** (www.bcsbestbnbs.com) represents bed-and-breakfasts across the region. The association produces an informative brochure with simple descriptions and a color photo of each property, but it doesn't take bookings.

Canada-West Accommodations (604/990-6730 or 800/561-3223, www.b-b.com) does take bookings, along with providing recommendations based on your likes and dislikes.

OTHER LODGING OPTIONS
Seasonal Accommodations

As roads through the mountains were improved in the 1920s, the number of tourists arriving by automobile increased greatly. To cater to this new breed of traveler, many bungalow camps were constructed along the highways. Some remain today (mostly in Jasper National Park), offering a high standard of accommodation away from the hustle and bustle of the towns. Generally, they consist of freestanding, self-contained units and are open for the summer only.

Backcountry Huts and Lodges

Throughout the backcountry of the Canadian Rockies is an extensive system of 18 rustic huts managed by the **Alpine Club of Canada** (403/678-3200, www.alpineclubofcanada.ca). Due to their locations around favorite climbing areas, they are most often used by mountaineers as an overnight stop before assaulting some of the park's highest peaks, but they are available to anyone who wishes to take advantage of their remote location. Often of historical significance, each of the huts has a stove, lantern, kitchen utensils, and foam mattresses. Rates range $18-32 per person per night.

Banff National Park has two backcountry lodges: **Shadow Lake Lodge,** northwest of Banff, and **Skoki Lodge,** east of Lake Louise. The lodges require some degree of effort to reach—either on foot or on horseback in summer, or on cross-country skis or snowshoes in winter. **Mount Assiniboine Lodge** is farther from the road system but can be reached by helicopter. Rates at these lodges begin at $225 per person, including three meals. None have television, but all have running water and a congenial atmosphere.

BACKPACKER ACCOMMODATIONS

Throughout the Canadian Rockies, traditional hostels operated by Hostelling International are still the most common form of accommodation for budget travelers, but other options do exist. Banff has privately run backpacker lodges, as well as a YWCA with dormitory accommodations for men and women. Generally, you need to supply your own sleeping bag or linens, but most places supply extra bedding at a minimal cost.

Hostelling International

Hostelling International operates five hostels in Banff National Park. The organization also has a hostel on the edge of downtown Calgary. Whenever you can, make reservations in advance, especially in summer. Bookings can be made online at www.hihostels.ca.

All of the hostels are equipped with a kitchen and lounge room, and some have laundries and private rooms. Those in Banff and Lake Louise are world-class, with hundreds of beds as well as libraries and cafés. The rustic hostels along the Icefields Parkway are evenly spaced, perfect for a bike trip along one of the world's great mountain highways. A sheet or sleeping bag is required at more remote locations, although these can usually be rented. Rates for members are $25-59 per night, nonmembers $28-64. Staying in hostels is an especially good bargain for skiers and snowboarders; packages including accommodation and a day pass at a local resort start at $120.

You don't *have* to be a member to stay in an affiliated hostel of Hostelling International, but membership pays for itself after only a few nights of discounted lodging. Aside from lower rates, benefits of membership vary from country to country but often include discounted air, rail, and bus travel; discounts on car rental; and discounts on some attractions and commercial activities. For Canadians, the membership charge is $35 annually, or $175 for a lifetime membership. For more information, contact **HI-Canada** (613/237-7884, www.hihostels.ca). Joining the Hostelling International affiliate of your home country entitles you to reciprocal rights in Canada, as well as around the world. In the United States, the contact information is **Hostelling International USA** (301/495-1240, www.hiusa.org); annual membership is adult US$28 and senior 55 and over US$18, or become a lifetime member for US$250. International chapters include **YHA England and Wales** (tel. 0870/770-8868, www.yha.org.uk); **YHA Australia** (422 Kent St., Sydney, tel. 02/9261-1111, www.yha.com.au), also based in all capital cities; and **YHA New Zealand** (tel. 03/379-9970, www.yha.org.nz). Otherwise, click through the links on the Hostelling International website (www.hihostels.com) to your country of choice.

CAMPING

Camping is the way to stay cheaply in the Canadian Rockies. The five national parks

Hostels in the Canadian Rockies are rustic, yet comfortable.

have excellent campgrounds, which have a combined total of 6,000 sites plus large areas set aside for overflow camping. Many of the campgrounds consist of nothing more than picnic tables, drinking water, pit toilets, and firewood ($9 per site per night), but at least one campground in each park has hot showers and full hookups.

Sites at the most popular national park campgrounds can be reserved through the **Parks Canada Campground Reservation Service** (877/737-3783, www.pccamping.ca) for a nonrefundable $12 reservation fee. If you're traveling in the height of summer and require electrical hookups, this booking system is highly recommended. The remaining campsites in the national parks operate on a first-come, first-served basis and often fill by midday in July and August.

Backcountry camping in all national parks is $10 per person per night, or purchase an annual pass ($70), valid for unlimited backcountry travel and camping for 12 months from its purchase date. Before heading out, you must register at the respective park information center (regardless of whether you have an annual pass) and pick up a Backcountry Permit (for those without an annual pass, the cost is the nightly camping fee multiplied by the number of nights you'll be in the backcountry). Many popular backcountry campgrounds have quotas, with reservations taken up to three months in advance. The reservation fee is $12 per party per trip. Most campgrounds in the backcountry have pit toilets, and some have bear bins for secure food storage. Fires are discouraged, so bring a stove.

Travel Tips

WHAT TO PACK

You'll find little use for a suit and tie in the Canadian Rockies. Instead, pack for the outdoors. At the top of your must-bring list should be walking or **hiking boots.** Even in summer, you should be geared up for a variety of weather conditions, especially at the change of seasons. Do this by preparing to **dress in layers,** including at least one pair of fleece pants and a heavy long-sleeved top. For dining out, **casual dress** is accepted at all but the most upscale restaurants.

Electrical appliances from the United States work in Canada, but those from other parts of the world will require a current **converter** (transformer) to bring the voltage down. Many travel-size shavers, hair dryers, and irons have built-in converters.

EMPLOYMENT AND STUDY

Banff is especially popular with young workers from across Canada and beyond.

Aside from Help Wanted ads in local papers, a good place to start looking for work is the **Job Resource Centre** (314 Marten St., Banff, 403/760-3311, www.jobresourcecentre.com).

International visitors wishing to work or study in Canada must obtain authorization *before* entering the country. Authorization to work will only be granted if no qualified Canadians are available for the work in question. Applications for work and study are available from all Canadian embassies and must be submitted with a nonrefundable processing fee. The Canadian government has a reciprocal agreement with Australia for a limited number of **holiday work visas** to be issued each year. Australian citizens ages 30 and under are eligible; contact your nearest Canadian embassy or consulate. For general information on immigrating to Canada, contact **Citizenship and Immigration Canada** (604/666-2171, www.cic.gc.ca).

VISITORS WITH DISABILITIES

A lack of mobility should not deter you from traveling to the Canadian Rockies, but you should definitely do some research before leaving home. **Flying Wheels Travel** (507/451-5005, www.flyingwheelstravel.com) caters solely to the needs of travelers with disabilities. The **Society for Accessible Travel and Hospitality** (212/447-7284, www.sath.org) supplies information on tour operators, vehicle rentals, specific destinations, and companion services. For frequent travelers, the annual membership fee (adult US$49, senior US$29) is well worthwhile. *Emerging Horizons* (www.emerginghorizons.com) is a U.S. online quarterly magazine dedicated to travelers with special needs.

Access to Travel (800/465-7735, www.accesstotravel.gc.ca) is an initiative of the Canadian government that includes information on travel within and between Canadian cities. The website also has a lot of general travel information for those with disabilities. The **Canadian National Institute for the Blind** (800/563-2642, www.cnib.ca) offers a wide range of services from offices in Edmonton (780/488-4871) and Vancouver (604/431-2020). Finally, **Spinal Cord Injury Alberta** (780/424-6312, www.sci-ab.ca) is another good source of information on local resources.

TRAVELING WITH CHILDREN

The natural wonders of the Canadian Rockies are a marvelous place to bring children on a vacation, and luckily for you, many of the best things to do—walking, watching wildlife, and more—don't cost a cent.

Admission and tour prices for children are included throughout this guide. As a general rule, these reduced prices are for children ages 6-16 years. For two adults and two or more children, always ask about family tickets. Children under six nearly always get in free. Most hotels and motels will happily accommodate children, but always try to reserve your room in advance and let the reservations desk know the ages of your kids. Often, children stay free in major hotels, and in the case of some major chains, such as Holiday Inn, eat free also. Generally, bed-and-breakfasts aren't suitable for children and in some cases don't accept kids at all. Ask ahead.

As a general rule when it comes to traveling with children, let them help you plan the trip, looking at websites and reading up on the Canadian Rockies together. To make your vacation more enjoyable if you'll be spending a lot of time on the road, rent a minivan (all major rental agencies have a supply). Don't forget to bring along favorite toys and games from home—whatever you think will keep your kids entertained when the joys of sightseeing wear off.

The websites of **Travel Alberta** (www.travelalberta.com) and **Tourism British Columbia** (www.hellobc.com) have sections devoted to children's activities within the two provinces. Another useful online tool is the website **Travel with Your Kids** (www.travelwithyourkids.com). The website **Family Fun Canada** (www.familyfun-canada.com) is a Calgary-based operation with lots of tips and stories about travel to the Canadian Rockies.

Health and Safety

Compared to other parts of the world, Canada is a relatively safe place to visit. That said, wherever you are traveling, carry a medical kit that includes bandages, insect repellent, sunscreen, antiseptic, antibiotics, and water-purification tablets. Good first-aid kits are available through most outdoor shops.

It's a good idea to get health insurance or some form of coverage before heading to Canada if you're going to be there for a while, but check that your plan covers foreign services. Hospital charges vary from place to place but can start at around $1,000 a day, and some facilities impose a surcharge for nonresidents. Some Canadian companies offer coverage specifically aimed at visitors.

If you're on medication, take adequate supplies with you and get a prescription from your doctor to cover the time you will be away. You may not be able to get a prescription filled at Canadian pharmacies without visiting a Canadian doctor, so don't wait till you've almost run out. If you wear glasses or contact lenses, ask your optometrist for a spare prescription in case you break or lose your lenses, and stock up on your usual cleaning supplies.

Believe it or not, AIDS and other venereal and needle-communicated diseases are as much of a concern in the Canadian Rockies as anywhere in the world today. Take exactly the same precautions you would at home—use condoms, and don't share needles.

Giardia

Giardiasis, also known as beaver fever, is a real concern for those who drink water from backcountry water sources. It's caused by an intestinal parasite, *Giardia lamblia,* that lives in lakes, rivers, and streams. Once the parasite is ingested, its effects, although not instantaneous, can be dramatic; severe diarrhea, cramps, and nausea are the most common. Preventive measures should always be taken. **Pristine** (www.advancechemicals.ca) is a Canadian company that has developed water bottles with built-in filters; the alternative is boiling water for at least 10 minutes or treating with iodine.

Winter Travel

Travel through the Canadian Rockies during winter months should not be undertaken lightly. Before setting out in a vehicle, check antifreeze levels, and always carry a spare tire and blankets or sleeping bags. **Frostbite** is a potential hazard, especially when cold temperatures are combined with high winds (a combination known as **windchill**). Most often it leaves a numbing, bruised sensation, and the skin turns white. Exposed areas of skin, especially the nose and ears, are most susceptible.

Hypothermia occurs when the body fails to produce heat as fast as it loses it. It can strike at any time of year but is more common during cooler months. Cold weather, combined with hunger, fatigue, and dampness, creates a recipe for disaster. Symptoms are not always apparent to the victim. The early signs are numbness, shivering, slurring of words, and dizziness, and, in extreme cases, violent behavior, unconsciousness, and even death. The best way to dress for the cold is in layers, including a waterproof outer layer. Most important, wear headgear. The best treatment for hypothermia is to get the patient out of the cold, replace wet clothing with dry, slowly give hot liquids and sugary foods, and place the victim in a sleeping bag. Warming too quickly can lead to heart attacks.

Information and Services

All prices quoted in this guide are in Canadian dollars and cents unless otherwise noted.

Canadian currency is based on dollars and cents, with 100 cents equal to one dollar. Coins come in denominations of 1, 5, 10, and 25 cents, and one and two dollars. The 11-sided, gold-colored, one-dollar coin is known as a "loonie" for the bird featured on it. The unique two-dollar coin is silver with a gold-colored insert. The most common notes are $5, $10, $20, and $50. A $100 bill does exist but is uncommon.

Visa and MasterCard credit and debit cards are also readily accepted in the Canadian Rockies; American Express charge cards are less widely accepted. By using these cards, you eliminate the necessity of thinking about the exchange rate—the transaction and rate of exchange on the day of the transaction will automatically be reflected in the bill from your credit-card company. On the downside, you'll always get a better exchange rate when dealing directly with a bank.

It's also handy to carry small amounts of Canadian cash. Banks offer the best exchange rates, but other foreign-currency exchange outlets are available.

Currency Exchange

At the time of writing, exchange rates (into CDN$) for major currencies are:

- US$1 = $1.24
- AUS$1 = $0.97
- €1 = $1.50
- HK$10 = $1.62
- NZ$1 = $0.87
- GBP£1 = $1.69
- ¥100 = $1.13

On the Internet, check current exchange rates at www.xe.com/currencyconverter.

All major currencies can be exchanged at banks in Banff or at airports in the gateway cities of Calgary, Edmonton, and Vancouver. Many Canadian businesses will accept U.S. currency, but you will get a better exchange rate from the banks.

Costs

The cost of living in the Canadian Rockies is generally higher than in other parts of Canada, especially when it comes to accommodations. Provincially, the cost of living is lower in Alberta than in British Columbia but higher than in the United States. By planning ahead, having a tent or joining Hostelling International, and being prepared to cook your own meals, it is possible to get by on $80 per person per day.

Tipping charges are not usually added to your bill. You are expected to add a tip of 15 percent to the total amount for waiters and waitresses, barbers and hairdressers, taxi drivers, and other such service providers. Bellhops, doormen, and porters generally receive $1 per item of baggage.

Taxes

Canada imposes a 5 percent **goods and services tax (GST)** on most consumer purchases. The British Columbia government imposes its own 7 percent tax (PST) onto everything except groceries. Alberta has no provincial tax. So when you are looking at the price of anything, remember that the final cost you pay will include an additional 5-12 percent in taxes.

MAPS AND TOURIST INFORMATION

Maps

The best maps of the Canadian Rockies are produced by **Gem Trek Publishing.** They

Heading Farther Afield

If your travels take you beyond the Canadian Rockies, you may find the following resources helpful for pretrip planning:

- **Travel Alberta:** 780/427-4321 or 800/252-3782, www.travelalberta.com

- **Tourism British Columbia:** 250/387-1642 or 800/435-5622, www.hellobc.com

- **Yukon Department of Tourism and Culture:** 867/667-5036 or 800/661-0494, www.travelyukon.com

- **State of Alaska Tourism:** www.travelalaska.com

- **NWT Tourism:** 867/873-7200 or 800/661-0788, www.spectacularnwt.com

- **Tourism Saskatchewan:** 306/787-9600 or 877/237-2273, www.sasktourism.com

- **Travel Manitoba:** 204/945-3777 or 800/665-0040, www.travelmanitoba.com

cover all of the Canadian Rockies, using computer-generated 3-D imagery to clearly define changes in elevation and GPS to plot hiking trails. The backs of maps are filled with trail information as well as tidbits of history.

Maps are available at bookstores, gas stations, and gift shops throughout the Canadian Rockies. In Banff, head to **The Viewpoint** (201 Banff Ave., 403/762-0405, 10am-8pm daily) for the full range of Gem Trek maps. In Calgary, **Map Town** (400 5th Ave. SW, 403/266-2241) is a specialist map shop worth stopping at as you pass through. In Vancouver, pick up maps at these specialty bookstores: **International Travel Maps & Books** (530 W. Broadway, 604/879-3621), **The Travel Bug** (3065 W. Broadway, 604/737-1122), or **Wanderlust** (1929 W. 4th Ave., Kitsilano, 604/739-2182).

Park Information

Each of the five national parks in the Canadian Rockies has at least one **park information center.** These are the places to head for interpretive displays, all park-related information, trail reports, weather forecasts, and wilderness passes. The national parks are managed by **Parks Canada** (www.pc.gc.ca). On the Alberta side of the Canadian Rockies, all other parks are managed by **Alberta Parks**

(www.albertaparks.ca). British Columbia's provincial parks are managed by **BC Parks** (www.bcparks.ca).

Tourism Information

The government tourist offices of Alberta and British Columbia: **Travel Alberta** (780/427-4321 or 800/252-3782, www.travelalberta.com) and **Tourism British Columbia** (250/387-1642 or 800/435-5622, www.hellobc.com), can provide useful literature and maps, which can be ordered by phone or through their respective websites.

In Calgary, you'll find an information booth on the Arrivals level of the airport. The **Vancouver Visitor Centre** (604/683-2000) is at 200 Burrard Street, although information on the Canadian Rockies is limited. For general tourism information, towns such as Banff have information centers that provide advice on local attractions, accommodations, and restaurants.

COMMUNICATIONS

Postal Services

Canada Post (www.canadapost.ca) issues postage stamps that must be used on all mail posted in Canada. First-class letters and postcards sent within Canada are $1, to the United States $1.20, to other international destinations $2.50. Prices increase along with the weight of the mailing. You can buy stamps at post offices, automatic vending machines, some hotel lobbies, the airports, many retail outlets, and some newsstands.

Phones and Cell Reception

Alberta and British Columbia have three and four area codes respectively. The **area code** for southern Alberta, including Banff is **403**. The area code for northern Alberta, including Jasper National Park, is **780**. The area code **587** covers all of the province. The area code for all of British Columbia except Vancouver and environs is **250**. The area code for Vancouver is **604**. The area codes **778** and **236** overlay the entire province. Unless otherwise noted, all numbers must be dialed with this prefix, including local calls made from within Alberta. The country code for Canada is 1, the same as the United States.

Cell phone reception is good in populated areas, but you will lose reception quickly beyond town boundaries. For example, there is no reception along the Icefields Parkway between Lake Louise and Jasper, and on the Trans-Canada Highway between Lake Louise and Golden. Even busy thoroughfares such as the Trans-Canada Highway between Banff and Lake Louise have spotty coverage.

Internet Access

Most Internet providers allow you to access your email away from your home computer, or open an email account with Outlook (www.live.com) or Gmail (www.gmail.com). Although there are restrictions to the size and number of emails you can store, these services are handy and, best of all, free.

Public Internet access is available throughout the Canadian Rockies. Most lodgings have wireless Internet access from guest rooms (the exceptions are lodges in remote locations), and it's usually free (the exceptions are larger hotels like the Fairmont chain). Except for wilderness hostels, backpacker lodges also provide free Internet access. You'll also find Internet cafés with computers in towns such as Banff, as well as free wireless Internet in cafes and public areas throughout the region.

WEIGHTS AND MEASURES
The Metric System

Canada officially adopted the metric system back in 1975, though you still hear grocers talking in ounces and pounds, golfers talking in yards, and sailors talking in nautical miles. Metric is the primary unit used in this guide, but we've added imperial conversions for readers from the United States, Liberia, and Myanmar, the only three countries that have not adopted the metric system.

Time Zones

Alberta is in the **mountain time zone,** one hour later than Pacific standard time, two hours earlier than Eastern standard time. The mountain time zone extends west into southern British Columbia, which includes Yoho and Kootenay National Parks as well as the towns of Golden and Radium Hot Springs. The rest of British Columbia, including Mount Robson Provincial Park, is in the **Pacific time zone.**

Daylight saving time is in effect from the second Sunday of March to the first Sunday in November. This corresponds with the United States (except Arizona) and all other Canadian provinces (except Saskatchewan).

Resources

Suggested Reading

NATURAL HISTORY

The Atlas of Breeding Birds of Alberta. Edmonton: Federation of Alberta Naturalists, 1992. Comprehensive study of all birds that breed in Alberta with easy-to-read distribution maps, details on nesting and other behavioral patterns, and color plates.

Dettling, Peter. *The Will of the Land.* Victoria: Rocky Mountain Books, 2010. Filled with stunning images, this book includes thoughtful dialogue on the often controversial relationship between man and wolf.

Dolson, Sylvia. *Bearology.* Whistler: Get Bear Smart Society, 2009. An easy-to-read book filled with bear facts and trivia.

Gadd, Ben. *Canadian Rockies Geology Road Tours.* Canmore: Corax Press, 2009. The best reference for those interested in the geology of the Canadian Rockies. Includes information on almost 300 roadside stops.

Gadd, Ben. *Handbook of the Canadian Rockies.* Canmore: Corax Press, 2009. At over 800 pages and one kilogram (2.2 pounds), this is the classic field guide to the Canadian Rockies. It is in full color, and although bulky for backpackers, it's a must-read for anyone interested in the natural history of the region.

Hallworth, Beryl, and C. C. Chinnappa. *Plants of Kananaskis Country.* Calgary: University of Calgary Press, 1997. An incredibly detailed book, encompassing more than 400 species of flora, complete with detailed black-and-white illustrations. It could be used in the field anywhere in the Canadian Rockies.

Hare, F. K., and M. K. Thomas. *Climate Canada.* Toronto: John Wiley & Sons, 1974. One of the most extensive works on Canada's climate ever written. Includes a chapter on how the climate is changing.

Herrero, Stephen. *Bear Attacks: Their Causes and Avoidances.* New York: The Lyons Press, 2018. Through a series of gruesome stories, this book catalogs the stormy relationship between people and bruins, provides hints on avoiding attacks, and tells what to do in case you're attacked.

Kerr, Michael. *The Canadian Rockies Guide to Wildlife Watching.* Calgary: Fifth House, 2000. A handy reference for wildlife enthusiasts. Complete with color illustrations and tips to find the best viewing spots.

Leckie, Dale. *Rocks, Ridges, and Rivers.* Calgary: self-published, 2017. Explores the geology of Banff, Yoho, and Jasper National Parks through detailed descriptions of the best-known natural attractions, including Lake Louise and Mount Edith Cavell.

Marty, Sid. *The Black Grizzly of Whiskey Creek.* Toronto: McClelland & Stewart, 2008. True story of a grizzly bear that went on a terrifying rampage near the town of Banff.

Musiani, Marco. *A New Era for Wolves and People.* Calgary: University of Calgary Press, 2009. A detailed analysis of the relationship between wolves and people in both North America and Europe. All contributors are wolf experts; includes stunning images.

Patterson, W. S. *The Physics of Glaciers.* London: Butterworth-Heinemann, 1999. A highly technical look at all aspects of glaciation, why glaciers form, how they flow, and their effect on the environment. The first edition was published in 1969 by Pergamon Press (Toronto).

Rezendes, Paul. *Tracking and the Art of Seeing.* Charlottesville, VA: Camden House Publishing, 1992. This is one of the best of many books dedicated to tracking North American mammals. It begins with a short essay on the relationship of humans with nature.

Scotter, George. *Wildflowers of the Rocky Mountains.* Vancouver: Whitecap Books, 2007. Simplified descriptions, color-coded chapters, and the delicate photography of Halle Flygare combine to create the region's best wildflower field guide.

Sharp, Robert P. *Living Ice: Understanding Glaciers and Glaciation.* Cambridge, England: Cambridge University Press, 1988. A detailed but highly readable book on the formation, types, and results of glaciers.

Sheldon, Ian. *Animal Tracks of the Rockies.* Edmonton: Lone Pine Publishing, 1997. A pocket-sized book that illustrates the tracks of almost all animal species present in the Canadian Rockies.

Slinger, Joey. *Down & Dirty Birding.* Toronto: Key Porter Books, 1996. A hilarious but practical look at the art of bird-watching, with sections of text such as "How to steer clear of people who think bird-watching is better than sex."

Whitaker, John. *National Audubon Society Field Guide to Mammals.* New York: Alfred A. Knopf, 1996. One of a series of field guides produced by the National Audubon Society, this one details mammals through color plates and detailed descriptions of characteristics, habitat, and range.

Wilkinson, Kathleen. *Wildflowers of Alberta.* Edmonton: University of Alberta Press, 1999. Color plates of all flowers found in the mountain national parks and beyond. The detailed color plates and line drawings are indispensable for identification.

HUMAN HISTORY

Barnes, Christine. *Great Lodges of the Canadian Rockies.* Seattle: Sasquatch Books, 1999. This book delves into the history of the many famous mountain lodges—such as the Fairmont properties—and lesser known but equally interesting historic accommodations like Num-ti-jah and Skoki.

Engler, Bruno. *Bruno Engler Photography.* Victoria: Rocky Mountain Books, 2002. Swiss-born Engler spent 60 years exploring and photographing the Canadian Rockies. This impressive hardcover book showcases more than 150 of his most timeless black-and-white images.

Hart, E. J. (Ted). *Ain't it Hell.* Banff: Summerthought Publishing, 2008. "Wild" Bill Peyto was one of the most interesting and colorful characters in the history of the Canadian Rockies. This book tells his story through fictional diary entries.

Hart, E. J. (Ted). *Banff: A History of the Park and Town.* Banff: Summerthought Publishing, 2015. The complete history of Banff in one hardcover book. Hart is arguably the most knowledgeable person alive when it comes to the history of the park, making this limited edition an obvious choice for those looking to learn about local history.

Hart, E. J. (Ted). *Cave and Basin*. Banff: Summerthought Publishing, 2017. The region's preeminent historian tells the story of the discovery of Banff's Cave and Basin and its importance to the creation of Canada's national park system.

Hart, E. J. (Ted). *Jimmy Simpson: Legend of the Rockies*. Victoria: Rocky Mountain Books, 2009. Details the life of one of the most colorful of the pioneer outfitters in the Canadian Rockies.

Hempstead, Andrew. *Exploring the History of Banff*. Banff: Summerthought Publishing, 2012. A guidebook to 88 historic sites and heritage properties in and around the town of Banff.

Lavallee, Omer. *Van Horne's Road*. Montreal: Railfare Enterprises, 1974. William Van Horne was instrumental in the construction of Canada's first transcontinental railway. This is the story of his dream and the boomtowns that sprang up along the route. Lavallee devotes an entire chapter to telling the story of the railway's push over the Canadian Rockies.

Marty, Sid. *Switchbacks: True Stories from the Canadian Rockies*. Toronto: McClelland & Stewart, 1999. This book tells of Marty's experiences in the mountains and of the people he came in contact with in his role as a park warden. Along the way, he describes how his experiences with both nature and fellow humans have shaped his views on conservation today.

McMillan, Alan D. *Native Peoples and Cultures of Canada*. Vancouver: Douglas & McIntyre, 1995. A comprehensive look at the archaeology, anthropology, and ethnography of the native peoples of Canada. The last chapters delve into the problems facing these people today.

Robinson, Bart. *Banff Springs: The Story of a Hotel*. Banff: Summerthought Publishing, 2018. This detailed history of one of the world's best-known hotels includes up-to-date changes, rare black-and-white photographs, and interviews with longtime employees.

Schäffer, Mary T. S. *A Hunter of Peace*. Banff: Whyte Museum of the Canadian Rockies, 2014. This book was first published in 1911 by G. P. Putnam & Sons, New York, under the name *Old Indian Trails of the Canadian Rockies*. Tales of Schäffer's adventures recount the exploration of the Rockies during the turn of the 20th century. Many of the author's photographs appear throughout.

Scott, Chic. *Pushing the Limits*. Victoria: Rocky Mountain Books, 2000. A chronological history of mountaineering in Canada, with special emphasis on many largely unknown climbers and their feats, as well as the story of Swiss guides in Canada and a short section on ice climbing.

Twigger, Robert. *Voyageur: Across the Rocky Mountains in a Birchbark Canoe*. London: Weidenfeld, 2006. This is the rollicking tale of author Twigger's adventures building a canoe and crossing the Canadian Rockies on a diet of porridge, fish, and whiskey—exactly as Alexander Mackenzie had 200 years previously.

RECREATION

Corbett, Bill. *The 11,000ers*. Calgary: Rocky Mountain Books, 2004. A reference to all 54 mountain peaks in the Canadian Rockies that are higher than 11,000 feet. The author discusses the human history of each, as well as access and popular routes.

Gadd, Ben. *The Canadian Hiker's and Back-packer's Handbook.* Vancouver: Whitecap Books, 2008. Whether you're interested in learning the basics or a seasoned traveler, this is the best book for reading up on your backcountry and hiking skills.

Kane, Alan. *Scrambles in the Canadian Rockies.* Calgary: Rocky Mountain Books, 2015. Routes detailed in this regularly revised guide lead to summits without the use of ropes or mountaineering equipment.

Martin, John, and Jon Jones. *Sport Climbs in the Canadian Rockies.* Calgary: Rocky Mountain Books, 2011. Details 2,000 routes through the Bow Valley and Banff National Park. Includes maps and photographs.

Mitchell, Barry. *Alberta's Trout Highway.* Red Deer: Nomad Creek Books, 2001. "Alberta's Trout Highway" is the Forestry Trunk Road (Highway 40), which runs the length of the Canadian Rockies. Entertaining and useful descriptions of Mitchell's favorite fishing holes are accompanied by maps and plenty of background information.

Patton, Brian, and Bart Robinson. *Canadian Rockies Trail Guide.* Banff: Summerthought Publishing, 2011, revised 2017. First published in 1971 and now in its ninth edition, this book covers 230 hiking trails and 3,400 kilometers (2,100 miles) in the mountain national parks as well as in surrounding provincial parks. At least one full page is devoted to each trail, making it the most comprehensive hiking book available.

Patton, Brian, and Bart Robinson. *50 Walks and Hikes in Banff National Park.* Banff: Summerthought Publishing, 2008. The authors of the *Canadian Rockies Trail Guide* detail their favorite short walks and day trips in this full-color guidebook.

Potter, Mike. *Fire Lookouts in the Canadian Rockies.* Calgary: Luminous Compositions, 1998. This book specializes in hikes to fire lookouts. Trail descriptions are detailed, and each is accompanied by the history of the lookout.

Scott, Chic. *Ski Trails of the Canadian Rockies.* Calgary: Rocky Mountain Books, 2013. After reading this book, it quickly becomes apparent that there is a lot more to wintertime than the downhill alpine resorts.You'll find yourself spoiled for options with this book covering both groomed and backcountry trails.

GUIDEBOOKS AND MAPS

Gem Trek Publishing. Victoria, BC. This company produces maps for all regions of the Canadian Rockies. Relief shading clearly and concisely shows elevation, and all hiking trails have been plotted using a global positioning system. On the back of most maps are descriptions of attractions and hikes, along with general, practical, and educational information. Highly recommended. Website: www.gemtrek.com.

Hempstead, Andrew. *Moon British Columbia.* Berkeley, CA: Avalon Travel. Regularly updated guides that comprehensively cover Canada's westernmost province.

MapArt. Driving maps for all of Canada, including provinces and cities. Maps are published as old-fashioned foldout versions, as well as laminated and in atlas form. Website: www.mapart.com.

The Milepost. Bellevue, WA: Vernon Publications. This annual publication is a must-have for those traveling through western Canada and Alaska. The maps and logged highway descriptions are incredibly detailed. Most northern bookstores stock *The Milepost,* or call 800/726-4707 or go to www.milepost.com.

Patton, Brian. *Parkways of the Canadian Rockies*. Banff: Summerthought Publishing, 2008. A comprehensive map and driving guide to all major highways. Includes color photography and details of many short hikes.

PERIODICALS

The Canadian Alpine Journal. Canmore, AB. The annual magazine of the Alpine Club of Canada, with mountaineering articles from its members and climbers from around the world. Website: www.alpineclubofcanada.ca.

Canadian Geographic. Ottawa: Royal Canadian Geographical Society. Bimonthly publication pertaining to Canada's natural and human histories and resources. Website: www.canadiangeographic.ca.

Explore. Toronto. Bimonthly publication of adventure travel throughout Canada. Website: www.explore-mag.com.

Nature Canada. Ottawa. Quarterly magazine of the Canadian Nature Federation. Website: www.cnf.ca.

Western Living. Vancouver, BC. Lifestyle magazine for western Canada. Includes travel, history, homes, and cooking. Website: www.westernliving.ca.

REFERENCE

Daffern, Tony. *Avalanche Safety for Skiers & Climbers.* Calgary: Rocky Mountain Books, 1992. Covers all aspects of avalanches, including their causes, practical information on how to avoid them, and a section on rescue techniques and first aid.

Guide to Manuscripts: The Fonds and Collections of the Archives, Whyte Museum of the Canadian Rockies. Banff: Whyte Museum of the Canadian Rockies, 1988. This book makes finding items in the museum easy by providing alphabetical lists of all parts of the collection.

Karamitsanis, Aphrodite. *Place Names of Alberta.* Calgary: University of Alberta Press, 1991. Volume 1 alphabetically lists all geographic features of the mountains and foothills, with explanations of each name's origin. Volume 2 does the same for southern Alberta.

Internet Resources

TRAVEL PLANNING

Canadian Tourism Commission
www.canada.travel
Official tourism website for all of Canada.

Tourism British Columbia
www.hellobc.com
Learn more about the province, plan your travels, and order tourism literature.

Travel Alberta
www.travelalberta.com
Similar to the British Columbia tourism website, but includes information on Banff and Jasper National Parks.

Thecanadianrockies.com
www.thecanadianrockies.com
Extensive travel planning website for all of the Canadian Rockies; includes a blog that addresses local tourism issues.

PARKS

Alberta Parks
www.albertaparks.ca
BC Parks
www.env.gov.bc.ca
These departments oversee management of the provincial parks in Alberta and British Columbia. The websites detail facilities, fees, and seasonal openings of each park.

Parks Canada
www.pc.gc.ca
Official website of the agency that manages Canada's national parks and national historic sites. The website has information on each park and historic site, including fees, camping, and wildlife.

Parks Canada Campground Reservation Service
www.pccamping.ca
Online reservation service for national park campgrounds.

GOVERNMENT

Citizenship and Immigration Canada
www.cic.gc.ca
Check this government website for anything related to entry into Canada.

Environment Canada
www.weather.gc.ca
Seven-day forecasts from across Canada, including dozens of locations throughout the Canadian Rockies. Includes weather archives such as seasonal trends and snowfall history.

Government of Canada
www.gc.ca
The official website of the Canadian government.

ACCOMMODATIONS

Banff Lodging Co.
www.bestofbanff.com
Operates nine hotels within the town of Banff.

Canadian Rocky Mountain Resorts
www.crmr.com
Small chain of upscale Canadian Rockies resorts.

Fairmont Hotels and Resorts
www.fairmont.com
Lodging chain that owns famous mountain resorts such as the Banff Springs and Chateau Lake Louise.

Hostelling International-Canada
www.hihostels.ca
Canadian arm of the worldwide organization.

Mountain Park Lodges
www.mpljasper.com
Six locally owned Jasper hotels and lodges.

CONSERVATION

Biosphere Institute of the Bow Valley
www.biosphereinstitute.org
Canmore-based organization mandated to gather and circulate information on management of the Bow River watershed. Online references include studies, publications, and human-use guidelines for the region.

Bow Valley Wildsmart
www.wildsmart.ca
This nonprofit organization has put together a wealth of information on how to stay safe in the Bow Valley watershed, including reported wildlife sightings.

Canadian Parks and Wilderness Society
www.cpaws.org
Nonprofit organization that is instrumental in highlighting conservation issues throughout Canada. The link to the Calgary chapter provides local information and a schedule of guided walks.

Yellowstone to Yukon Conservation Initiative
www.y2y.net
Network of 800 groups working on conservation issues in the Canadian Rockies and beyond.

TRANSPORTATION AND TOURS

Air Canada
www.aircanada.ca
Canada's national airline.

Brewster
www.brewster.ca
Banff-based operator offering day trips, airport shuttles, and package tours.

Rocky Mountaineer
www.rockymountaineer.com
Luxurious rail service from Vancouver to Banff and Jasper.

VIA Rail
www.viarail.ca
Passenger rail service across Canada.

PUBLISHERS

Gem Trek
www.gemtrek.com
You can pick up basic park maps free from local information centers, but this company produces much more detailed maps covering all the most popular regions of the Canadian Rockies.

Lone Pine
www.lonepinepublishing.com
Respected for its field guides, this company has books on almost every natural history subject pertinent to the Canadian Rockies.

Rocky Mountain Books
www.rmbooks.com
Check out this publisher's catalog, and you'll surely be impressed by the list of local history and outdoor recreation guides.

Summerthought Publishing
www.summerthought.com
The world's only publisher devoted solely to publishing books about the Canadian Rockies. If you plan on doing lots of hiking, you'll want a copy of their authoritative *Canadian Rockies Trail Guide.*

Index

AB

accommodations: 128–131
air travel: 114–115, 116
Alymer Lookout: 41
animals: 20–22, 100–107
auto travel: 118–121
backpacking: 122
Backswamp Viewpoint: 34
Banff Centre: 31–32
Banff Gondola: 30
Banff Mountain Book Festival: 52
Banff Mountain Film Festival: 52
Banff National Park, maps of: 2–3, 16–19, 26, 27
Banff Park Museum: 25, 28
Banff Summer Arts Festival: 51
Banff, town of: 25–67; map 26
Banff Upper Hot Springs: 29
Banff Visitor Centre: 37
Banff World Media Festival: 51
bicycling: 37, 38, 123–124, see also mountain
  biking
Big Beehive: 74
birds/bird-watching: 22, 32, 106–107
boating: 34, 44, see also kayaking/canoeing;
  rafting
Bourgeau Lake: 41
Bow Falls: 31
Bow Glacier Falls: 87–88
Bow Lake: 84
Bow Peak: 84
Bow River: 44
Bow River/Hoodoos: 37
Bow River Loop: 72
Bow Summit: 84
Bow Valley Parkway: 34–37; map 35
Brewster, Jim and Bill: 46
Buffalo Nations Luxton Museum: 28
bus travel: 117–118, 119

C

camping: 63–64, 82, 90–91, 92–93, 94, 131–132
Canada Day (Banff): 51
Canada Day (Lake Louise): 76
car travel: 118–121
Cascade Amphitheatre: 40
Cascade Falls: 33
Cascade Gardens: 28
Cascade Ponds: 33
Castle Lookout: 42

Castle Mountain: 36
Cave and Basin National Historic Site: 29
caves/caverns: 89
cell phones: 137
Chephren Lake: 88
children, traveling with: 133
Cirque Lake: 88
C Level Cirque: 40
climate: 98–99
climbing: 32, 39–40, 70–71, 84, 122, 123
communications: 136–137
Consolation Lakes: 76
Continental Divide: 85 86
Cory Pass: 41
costs: 135
cross-country skiing: 38, 47–48, 77, 128
Crowfoot Glacier: 84
currency: 135

DEF

disabilities, travelers with: 133
Eiffel Lake: 75–76
Eiffel Peak: 76
elk: 21
emergencies: 66
employment: 132
expenses: 135
Fairmont Banff Springs: 30–31, 57, 61–62
Fairmont Chateau Lake Louise: 70, 79, 81
fauna: 20–22, 100–107
Fenland: 37
Fireside: 34
fish/fishing: 34, 44, 88, 106, 126–127
flora: 15, 99–100

GH

geology: 96–98
Glacier Lake: 89
golf: 44–45, 124–125
gratuities: 135
health and safety: 134
Hector Lake Viewpoint: 83
Helen Lake: 87
heli-hiking: 122
Herbert Lake: 83
hiking: 34, 37–42, 72–76, 87–89, 91–92, 93–94,
  121–123
history: 22–24, 107–112
Hole-in-the-Wall: 34

horseback riding: 43, 76, 124
hospital: 66
Howse Peak: 85

IJKL

Icefields Parkway: 83–91
indoor recreation: 49
Ink Pots: 36
Internet access: 137
Johnson Lake: 34
Johnston Canyon: 34–36
kayaking/canoeing: 44, 125
Kicking Horse River: 43
Lake Agnes: 73–74
Lake Agnes Teahouse: 76
Lake Annette: 75
Lake Louise: 47, 68–83; maps 69, 70
Lake Louise Resort: 76–77
Lake Louise sightseeing gondola: 71–72
Lake Magog: 91, 93
Lake Minnewanka: 33–34
Larch Valley: 75
Louise Creek Trail: 72
Louise Lakeshore: 72–73
Lower Bankhead: 33
Lower Waterfowl Lake: 86

M

mail: 136–137
maps and tourist information: 135–136
McDonald Creek Trail: 94
Melissa's Road Race: 52
metric system: 137
Mistaya Canyon: 86
Mistaya Lake: 85
mobile phones: 137
money: 135
Moraine Lake: 71
mountain biking: 42–43, 123–124
Mount Assiniboine Provincial Park: 91–93
Mount Balfour: 84
Mount Chephren: 86
Mount Forbes: 86
Mount Hector: 83
Mount Murchison: 86
Mount Norquay: 47
Mount Norquay Road: 32
Mount Outram: 86
Mount Patterson: 85
Mount Rundle: 39–40
Mount Temple: 75, 83
Mount Victoria: 70
Mount Wilson: 86
Muleshoe: 34

NOP

Nigel Pass: 89
Norquay: 32, 46
North Saskatchewan River: 86
packing tips: 132
Paradise Valley: 74–75, 76
Park Distillery: 49
Parker's Ridge: 89
Park Interpretive Program: 51
passports: 9
Peyto, Bill: 24
Peyto Glacier: 85
Peyto Lake: 84–85, 88
phones: 137
Plain of the Six Glaciers: 73
planning tips: 8–10
plants: 15, 99–100
postal services: 136–137

QRS

rafting: 43–44, 125
rail travel: 115–117
rental cars: 120
resources: 138–144
Rockbound Lake: 42
Rock Isle Lake: 39
RV rental: 120
Saddleback: 74
safety: 134
Sally Borden Fitness & Recreation Facility: 48
Santa Claus, visit by: 52
scenic drives: 32, 34–37, 83–86
scuba diving/snorkeling: 125
Sentinel Pass: 75
Shadow Lake: 41
Siffleur Falls: 93–94
Siffleur Wilderness Area: 93–94
Silver City: 36
skiing/snowboarding: 32, 46–47, 76–77, 127–128
Skoki Valley: 76
Slush Cup: 51
Snow Days: 52
spas: 48–49
Spray River: 38
Stoney Squaw: 40
study opportunities: 132
Sulphur Mountain: 30
Sulphur Mountain Boardwalk: 30
Sundance Canyon: 38
Sunshine Meadows: 39, 47
Sunshine Village: 46–47
Sunwapta Pass: 86

T
taxes: 115, 135
telephones: 137
Thompson, David: 109
time zones: 137
tipping: 135
tours: 45, 121
train travel: 115–117
Tramline: 72
transportation: 114–121
Tunnel Mountain: 37
Two Jack Lake: 34

UVWXYZ
Upper Bankhead: 33
Upper Waterfowl Lake: 86

Vermilion Lakes: 32
visas: 9
Walter Phillips Gallery: 32
Wapta Icefield: 85
waterfalls: 31, 33, 34, 36, 75, 86, 87, 93–94
water sports: 34, 43–44, 48, *see also specific
    activity*
weather: 98–99
Weeping Wall: 86
White Goat Wilderness Area: 94
Whyte Museum of the Canadian Rockies: 28
wildlife/wildlife-watching: 20–22, 30, 32, 34, 86,
    93, 94, 100–107
Willow Stream Spa: 48
winter sports: 45–48, 76–78, 86, 128, *see also
    specific activity*
World Cup Downhill: 52

List of Maps

Front Map
Banff National Park and Vicinity: 2–3

Banff National Park
Banff National Park: 16–17
Banff National Park (continued): 18–19
Town of Banff: 26
Vicinity of Banff: 27
Bow Valley Parkway: 35
Lake Louise and Vicinity: 69
Lake Louise: 70